20TH CENTURY FIRST EDITION FICTION: A PRICE AND IDENTIFICATION GUIDE

THE COMPLETE GUIDE FOR COLLECTORS OF USED BOOKS

BY
THOMAS LEE

BOOK EMPORIUM PRESS
ROCKVILLE, MARYLAND

ISBN 0-9653429-1-3

Published by The Book Emporium Press, 17045 Briardale Road, Rockville, Maryland
Printed in the United States of America

THE COMPLETE GUIDE FOR COLLECTORS OF USED BOOKS

Table of Contents

Introduction

Collecting first edition books can be an extremely challenging and rewarding experience. Although volumes of books-on-books have been written, I have yet to find a single book or even a reasonably small set of books that answered most of the basic questions commonly asked by new collectors of modern first editions. Book dealers are very knowledgeable about these kind of things (it's their business and they have extensive reference libraries) but they don't always have the time to share this knowledge with beginning collectors. This guide provides answers to most of the questions that a beginning collector would ask. Beyond answering the obvious question of how much a book is worth, this guide contains an accumulation of much of the knowledge I have gained through years of running a used book business. It addresses the hows of assembling a collection of books that can satisfy both your needs and your budget. The guide explains how to identify what is a true first edition (the words "FIRST EDITION" aren't always the best indicator), which dust jackets go with which first edition, how grading (estimating condition) is done, and what first editions in various grades are worth. Terms commonly used in book collecting are explained and the meaning of each is discussed. Although the narrative on collecting is intended for beginning collectors, all collectors of fiction will find the pricing section an invaluable reference for the price estimates and for identification of first editions. The guide contains information on 878 books by 69 of today's most popular authors.

Grading

Many factors influence the value of a used book. Foremost among these is the condition of the book and its dust jacket. A quick look through the pricing section of this price guide shows how a book's value drops as its condition worsens. The guide contains prices for six different grades for most of the listed books. Although the top condition for any book is "as new", this price guide does not contain prices for these books, because this high grade is seldom, if ever, actually seen. In today's collecting world so many collectors find faults with books even as they are put on the shelves at retail stores, that "as new" has become synonymous with "perfect" and no book is ever truly perfect. The highest condition used in the guide is F/F. This describes a book (the first letter) and its dust jacket (the second letter) which are both in fine (F) condition. A book in fine condition is one that looks and feels almost new. The book typically has been carefully read once. The pages are clean and free of bumps, the binding is tight and straight, and the covers show no significant edge wear or scuffing. The dust jacket has no tears or scuffing and the suggested sales price has not been clipped (p.c.). In actual practice, a F/F book can have some minor imperfections but must not exhibit any major defects (described below). For the purpose of pricing in this guide, conditions below F/F are listed with the dust jacket grade being one grade lower than that of the book. Although not all books pick up wear in the same manner, the general pattern is such that the dust jacket normally does wear faster than the book itself. For books where the condition doesn't fit this pattern, some extrapolation between guide prices becomes necessary.

Condition

The authoritative list of descriptive terms for grading used books was first published by Antiquarian Bookman in 1975. Terms, as described in this reference, are as follows:

"As New is to be used only when the book is in the same immaculate condition in which it was first published. There can be no defects, no missing pages, no library stamps, etc., and the dust jacket must be perfect, without any tears.

Fine approaches the condition of As New, but without being crisp. For the use of the term Fine there must also be no defects, etc. and if the jacket has a small tear, or other defect, or looks worn, this should be noted.

Very Good can describe a used book that does show some small signs of wear - but no tears - on either binding or paper. Any defects must be noted.

Good describes the average used and worn book that has all pages or leaves present. Any defects must be noted.

Fair is a worn book that has complete text pages but may lack endpapers, half title, etc. Binding, jacket, etc., may also be worn. All defects must be noted.

Poor describes a book that is sufficiently worn that its only merit is as a reading copy because it does have the complete text, which must be legible

Ex-library copies must always be designated as such no matter what the condition of the book.

Book Club editions must always be noted as such no matter what the condition of the book."

The collecting community uses gradations on these "condition terms" with the addition of the following grades:

NF+

Near Fine (NF)

NF-

VG+

VG-

Translating these terms into what, for example, a book described as "VG+/VG in dj" looks like can be difficult for the beginning collector. Consider that each book begins its life in As New condition. This book has clean, unbumped pages, a tight spine that cracks when opened, and an unscuffed, unwrinkled dust jacket. After the book has been read once and handled carefully, its condition drops to F/F. Although the spine not longer cracks when this book is opened, it is still very tight with no slope. The dust jacket may show very minor wrinkling (normally at the top and bottom of the spine) but no tears. As the book is reread, with the pages being turned repeatedly and with the book being slid on to and off bookshelves, minor wear starts to show on the page edges and on the bottom of the book boards. Along the way, the book may even have been dropped resulting in a bumped corner on one of the book boards. This book is working its way toward becoming a Very Good book by the definition above. Unfortunately, events unrelated to wear will accelerate the worsening of the condition of a book. A listing of these events is shown in the next section. The effect that each of these defects has on the overall grade of a book tends to be subjective. For example, an inscription on the front free end page will immediately lower an otherwise F/F book down to no better than NF/F. That same inscription on a VG/VG- book would have virtually no impact. The description accompanying each of the major defects tells how each defect affects the grading of a book.

Major Defects

Defects (as distinguished from wear) which lower the grade of a book or a dust jacket include:

Water Staining is one of the worst fates that can befall a

book. Any significant amount staining to the pages of the book will automatically drop the grade to no better than Good (regardless of wear) and, in all probably, below that. Even very light staining to the boards (which results in running of the color dye onto the back of the dust jacket) generally results in a book that is no better than Good. Books with evidence of contact with water are best avoided completely.

Bookplates, also called private library labels, when used are

commonly located on the front free end page. A bookplate will reduce an otherwise F/F book to no better than NF/F but at lower grades will have less of an impact on the grade. For example, a bookplate on a book that is otherwise NF/F will move the book's grade approximately one-third of the way to VG/F. The book would probably be graded as NF-/F. On lower graded books, the effect is so small that the grade would not change, but the value would be reduced slightly. When describing a book, bookplates must always be mentioned since there are collectors who will not buy a book if it has a bookplate.

A removed bookplate, where evidence of its former placement remains, is treated the same as an intact bookplate.

Inscriptions can be as simple as a former owner's name

neatly penned on the front free end page to a long rambling narrative covering several pages. Short inscriptions affect a book's grade about the same as a bookplate does. Longer or more obtuse ones will have a greater impact. Again, when describing a book, inscriptions must always be mentioned since there are collectors who will not buy a book if it has any writing on it.

Creases in Book Pages will always reduce the

grade of a book. The severity of the creasing determines the amount of downgrading. For a single creased page, the effect is the same as having a bookplate. For ceases which cause a disruption in the smooth flow of the top or bottom page edges, Very Good would be the highest grade the book could achieve.

Ripped Pages, if the AB guide is to be followed literally, will

immediately reduce a book grade to below Very Good. In actual practice, the impact is less severe. An otherwise F/F book with a small, unrepaired (for repaired, see Tape below) tear in one of the book pages is often described as "1/2 inch tear to bottom of pg 216 otherwise F/F" and will be valued at NF/F. For more pronounced tears, the grade drops to a greater degree.

Removed Pages, even removed free end pages, result in a

grade of no higher than Fair, which in book terms, is a very undesirable

Tearing Along Book Hinge, although not as bad
as removed pages, will always result in a grade below Good. This condition normally accompanies a very worn book and is therefore seldom seen in books with little wear.

Cracked Spine occurs when a book is folded opened to the
point where the plane of the spine cracks from the top of the spine to the bottom. The pages do not come loose from the spine. For book otherwise at F/F, a spine crack would reduce the grade to NF.

Slanting of Book Spine (or Slope) occurs
when a book is stored in a position other than perfectly flat or straight up and down. The slanting is most noticeable when the book is viewed from the top or the bottom. On books with spine slanting, the spine will not form a right angle with the front and rear book boards. This condition, which is irreversible, is slightly worst than having a bookplate.

Looseness of Book Spine occurs naturally as a
book wears. For book grades below F/F, some looseness is to be expected. When the condition becomes excessive, a slight adjustment in grade is called for.

Wrinkled Book Spine is noticeable as a waviness in
the otherwise naturally flat spine surface. The effect is the same as for a bookplate.

Remainder Marks are used by the publisher for
identifying books that are not intended to be sold through retail stores at the full suggested retail price. Most often these books are publisher's overstock that is sold by the publisher directly to a wholesale outlet. These marks, which are located on either the tops or the bottoms of the pages, take many forms. Random House uses a red hand stamped likeness of the two-story house used as their logo. Simon and Schuster uses a blue hand stamped "Simon and Schuster" man. Doubleday uses a spray that leaves the page tops or bottoms with a speckled appearance (which is actually quite attractive). Other publishers used either a line or a dot drawn using a red or black magic marker. A remainder mark is quite undesirable to some in the collecting world while other collectors are unaffected by one. In general, a remainder mark would move a book down one grade.

Corner or Edge Bumps generally affect the boards
that serve to protect the pages. When only the board corners are involved and when the bumps are not severe, this condition is considered a normal part of wear. For more serious dents or where the

book is otherwise in fine condition, a reduction of grade will occur.

Browning of Book Pages Due to Age is

usually an indication that inferior paper was used to produce the book. The word "foxing" is used by the collector community to describe pages that are turning brown. It seems that collectors are tolerant of factors that result from graceful aging. For old books where this condition is considered normal, there often is no reduction in a book's grade because of foxing.

Browning Due to Inlaid Paper is generally

an irregular browning that follow the shape of a piece of paper left in the book over an extended period. The browning is caused by acid in the inlaid paper. This condition is more common for books kept in hot, humid conditions. A variation on this is browning of end papers and free end papers caused by the glue used to hold the end papers down. This type of browning is never described as foxing. The impact on a book's grade is minimal.

Tape or Tape Remnants (Ghosts) on a

book or a dust jacket will lower theitem's grade. If the tape has been used carefully to repair a tear, the downgrading caused by the tape (down grading because of tears will still take place) will be minimal. If tape has been used for other reasons (to hold the dust jacket on, for example) the downgrading will be at least one full grade and more if the original grade of the book was high.

Price Clipping of Dust Jacket occurs when the

portion of the dust jacket that contains the suggested retail price is cut off. A dust jacket that has been price clipped (p.c.) will generally be missing a triangular piece on the top of the front flap. Price clipping, which is fairly common, has no effect on the grade of the book itself. The effect that price clipping has on a dust jacket varies enormously. It lowers the grade of common dust jackets in about the same way that a bookplate reduces a book grade. However, for dust jackets where the price is the only indicator of a first issue (see Centennial by Michener), price clipping reduces the value of an otherwise first issue dust jacket to the value of a practically valueless later issue dust jacket.

Creases in Dust Jacket would reduce a dust jacket's

grade by an amount proportional to the severity of the creasing.

Chipping of Dust Jacket is a general term

referring to small pieces of the edge of the dust jacket that are missing. Chipping and small tears influence a dust jacket's grade more than overall wear does. A Fine dj will have no chipping. Very little chipping is allowed for a NF dj. A VG+ dj will typically have wrinkling on the top and bottom 1/8 inch of the spine but not a significant amount of paper

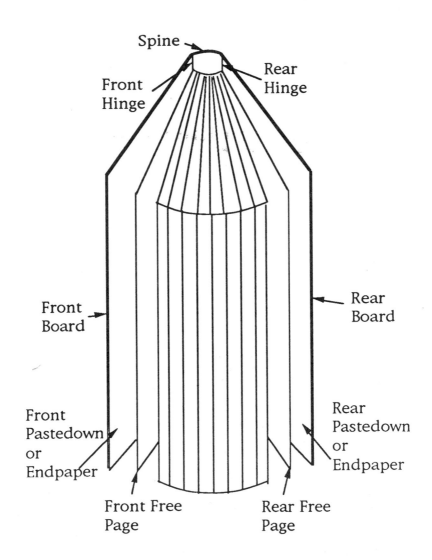

Figure 1. Terms Used to Describe a Hardcover Book

lost to chipping. A VG dj will exhibit obvious chipping, even to the extend of the top 1/16 inch of the spine paper being gone. At VG-, the missing area may be as great as 1/8 inch across the top or bottom of the spine. A VG- dj may also have larger pieces (dime sized) missing.

Surface chipping (which is really wear) occurs to areas along folds. Some surface chipping begins to be obvious on a VG+ dj.

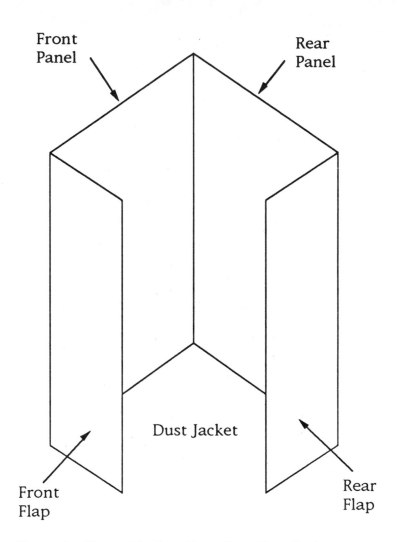

Figure 2. Terms Used to Describe a Dust Jacket

Tears in Dust Jacket are not as bad as tears in the

pages of a book. At grades below Near Fine, some small tears are almost expected. For example, tears on the order of 1/8 inch in a VG+ dj would not reduce the grade of the dust jacket at all. On the other hand, a long tear across an entire panel would reduce an otherwise NF dj to VG-.

Trimming of Dust Jacket is equivalent to missing

pages in a book. A trimmed dust jacket would have a grade no higher than Good. Trimming refers to removing a small amount of paper from one or more edges of the dust jacket. This is considered tampering with the book and makes the dj highly undesirable.

Identifying First Editions

Before discussing terms like "first edition", "first printing", "first issue", "first state" or "first impression", just a word about special editions. The first release of a book to the general buying public is the first edition of that book. This is not usually the first time the book has appeared in print. Advanced Reading Copies are often specially printed for advertising purposes. These are generally large paperback (called wrapps) books with publicity information printed on the cover. In addition, presentation copies (for the author's private use) are sometimes printed and various other special limited editions are common. This guide does not attempt to address this very specialized aspect of book collecting. Prices shown in this guide are for true first editions. Recognizing when a book is a true first edition is not as simple as the beginning collector may think. The words "First Edition" or "First Printing" on the copyright page, although reassuring, are often not the best indicator of a book's pedigree.

Collector's of first edition books strictly speaking are interested in only a subset of a book's first edition. A book may (and usually is) reprinted often without the edition changing. An edition change occurs only when major alterations are made to the book or to its text. Collectors are interested in the first printing (also called first impression) of a book's first edition. For some books, minor changes (to correct errors) are made in the middle of a print run. This will result in a further subdivision of the first edition. The first copies to be printed - those before the correction - are called the "first issue" or the "first state" (interchangeable terms) and are the most desirable. Knowing when a particular book is the first state of a first printing of a first edition is tricky business. The characteristics that are unique to a first edition and that are used to identify a first edition are referred to as first edition points.

The first step in determining whether a book is a first edition is to eliminate the possibility that it is a Book of the Month Club volume. Three telltale signs of a BOMC book are 1) smaller physical size than other copies of the same book (which is difficult to assess if you don't have that "other copy" to compare with), 2) a dust jacket with no suggested retail price or with words to the effect of "Book Club Edition" (although some first edition dust jackets have no price - The Hunt for Red October being the most notable), and 3) an identification mark on bottom of rear cover board near spine in the form of either a small indentation (blind stamp) or a colored dot. The indentation mark referred to here is approximately 1/8 inch across (sometimes square, sometimes a leaf or other publisher-related symbol) and should not be confused with the indented company logos that are often in the same location but are much larger. Book of the Month Club books (all valued in the $2 to $3 range) are of no interest to collectors of first editions. Publishers known as mainly reprint houses include Grosset & Dunlap, Tower, Triangle, Sun Dial, and Garden City Publishing.

If a volume is not a BOMC edition and if the words "First Edition", "First Printing", "First Trade Edition", etc. appear somewhere on the copyright page, then the book almost certainly is a true first edition. (A term to be careful of is "First Edition Thus". This refers to the first printing of a book that retains the name of an earlier work but that is essentially a different book because major changes have been made. These are not true first editions.)

Unfortunately, not all first editions contain words that explicitly describe them as such. Knowing when the words should be there and when they should not is a big part of first edition collecting. For example, first editions of Leon Uris' popular novel about Ireland, _Trinity_, have six lines of text at the bottom of the page on the reverse of the title page (copyright page) as shown in below. Later printings have only five lines of text and no reference to the fact that the book is a later printing.

ISBN: 0-385-03458-X
Library of Congress Catalog Card Number: 75-14844
Copyright© 1976 by Leon Uris
All Rights Reserved
Printed in the United States of America
First Edition

(a) First Edition

ISBN: 0-385-03458-X
Library of Congress Catalog Card Number: 75-14844
Copyright© 1976 by Leon Uris
All Rights Reserved
Printed in the United States of America

(a) Later Editions

Figure 3. _Trinity_

First editions that have no reference to printing or edition number are much more difficult to identify. On these books, later editions contains words such as "Second Printing", "Second Impression", etc. John D. MacDonald's earlier hardcover novels illustrate this type of book. The bottom portions of the copyright pages of a first printing and of a second printing of his _The Dreadful Lemon Sky_ are shown in Figure 4.

(a) First Printing

(b) Later Printing

Figure 4. *The Dreadful Lemon Sky*

First editions from Viking Publishing are almost certainly the most difficult to identify. A general rule of thumb for Viking is that if a line such as "First Published by Viking Publishing in 1963" appears and no reference is made to a later printing, then the book has a chance of being a first edition. Publishers known to <u>occasionally</u> omit the words "First Edition" and list later printings include Putnam's, Lippincott, Coward-McCann, Covice, and Jonathan Cape (U.K.). Because none of these publishers is consistent in its method of marking first editions, this guide contains information used for identifying first editions for many books listed.

Terms such as "Second Printing Before Publication" identify books printed before the first edition printing run is released for sale by retail outlets. Publishers set a publication date that is the date on which retail sales are supposed to begin. This date is often several weeks ahead of when printing of the first edition run is completed. The time between printing and release is needed for shipping and distribution of the first edition books. Reprinting before the publication date is done when early orders exceed estimates and demand at the wholesale level is such that another printing run is warranted. There are also times when a literary guild or book club purchases an entire print run and a "Second Printing Before Publication" will be done for that purpose. In any event, these printings are later printings and have little collector value.

Book Bindings

Occasionally first editions can be recognized by a binding that is different from the one on later editions. Figure 5 shows the four most common binding styles and the terms associated with each. This guide contains first edition binding information for many books listed. Included in this binding information is a description of top stain color, i.e., the color of the top edges of the book pages. This information can be of great help in eliminating non-first editions when a collector is searching through large quantities of shelved books. For example, the true first edition of Herman Wouk's *Caine Mutiny* has no top stain while most later printings have a yellow stain. Tilting a shelved copy of a book out will expose the top edges and a yellow top stain will immediately eliminate a book from consideration by a serious collector.

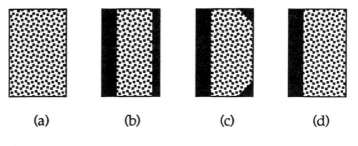

(a)   (b)   (c)   (d)

Figure 5. Binding Styles

(a) Full bound with complete cloth cover; (b) Half-bound with cloth back and edges and paper sides; (c) Half-bound with cloth back and corners and paper sides; (d) Quarter-bound with cloth back and paper sides.

Another designation that will sometimes appear in the description of a book is the fold pattern. The meanings of these designations is illustrated in Figure 6. These designations are presented as information only since this guide does not use these terms.

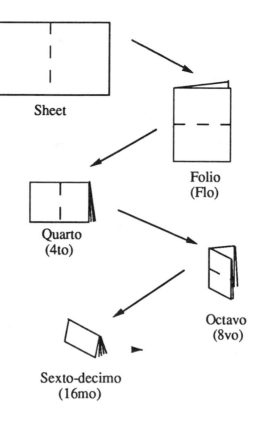

Sheet

Folio
(Flo)

Quarto
(4to)

Octavo
(8vo)

Sexto-decimo
(16mo)

Figure 6. Paper Folds

Dust Jackets

Dust jackets (or dust wrappers) are a relatively new addition to books. Prior to the middle 1920's, dust jackets were almost nonexistent. Since the late 1920's, most first edition fiction books have been issued with a dust jacket. When a dust jacket is missing, the value of a book is severely diminished. In some cases, the dust jacket is 90% of the value of the book/dj combination. "Marrying" a dust jacket and a book is the process by which a book that was without a dust jacket is given one from another book. This process is perfectly acceptable as long as the correct dust jacket is found. Some dust jacket are identified as being associated with the first edition of a book and for a book like this, only another first issue dust jacket could be used. The _Grapes of Wrath_ is an example of such a book. Its dust jacket contains a "slug" (or triangular portion) which states "First Edition". Many other books are issued with dust jackets that are unchanged for many editions after the first editions. Where a first edition dust jacket exists, its relative value is reflected in the column of the price guide under "w/o dj". This column may contain a percentage as low as 10%, meaning that if the dust jacket is missing, the book is worth only 10% of the value listed in the guide.

Locating First Editions

Successfully collecting first-edition fiction, like collecting anything of value, requires knowledge, perseverance, and more than a little bit of luck. Perseverance and luck are the responsibility of the collector. This Price Guide with provide the average serious collector with all the knowledge they will need for the books and authors covered by the Guide. But where are the books? The simple answer is that they are everywhere. A good place to start looking is a used book store in your area. Don't be afraid to look for bargains. It's important to realize that the store owner probably does NOT know as much as you do about the particular books and authors that you have chosen to become an expert in. As long as you have done your homework and prepared yourself, you will know as much, if not more, than the store owner. Remember that that owner is dealing in fiction, non-fiction, history, sci-fi, children's books, cookbooks, etc. (the list goes on and on) and usually specializes in only a few of those fields. Often dealers will buy entire book collections just to get a few books in the collection. When this happens, the dealer usually wants to sell off the rest of the collection as fast as possible. If the "rest of the collection" contains books you are interested in, there should be bargains to be had. By way of illustrating that there are desirable books to be had cheaply, there is a network of semi-dealers, called "scouts", who buy used books from one store and sell to another. Dealers welcome these scouts as much for the insight they provide as for the books they have to sell.

Used book stores are a good beginning but very few stores turn over their stock often enough to be a steady supply of books for the serious collector. Yard sales can yield some good books. Estate sales are also a good source of quality books. But an excellent good opportunity to buy good books quite cheaply is the so-called used book sale. Being at the right sale at the right time can be the best chance that the average collector will have to find book bargains. Why do I say the right sale? Last year I purchased a book that claimed to be a listing of 4,000 book sales throughout the United States for the upcoming year. The listings were nothing but the times and locations for public library sales - very, very little of collectible value. In fact, although the listings book gave the impression that quality sales take place all the time, there are relatively few good book sales. Each year the Washington, D.C. area has two book sales that are generally considered to be among the best in the country. These are the Goodwill Industries Sale in the fall and the Stone Ridge Sale in the spring. Each sale has hundred's of thousands of very high quality books. More importantly, each sale allows absolutely no dealer previews or advanced sales. Both of these sales are run by organizations that sell books that have been donated to them with the profits going to worthy not-for-profit causes; both have lines that form hours before the doors open on the first day; both have extensive media coverage (from a human interest point of view); and both are extremely well run. If you're serious about collecting books and you live in the area, you wouldn't think about not being at each of these sales. Although each sale runs for five days, the real event is over in about an hour. By the time an hour has passed, most of the hidden gold nuggets have long since been identified and picked up.

April 26th, the first day of this year's Stone Ridge Sale had been circled on my calendar for a year. I arrived at the sale at 6:15AM - almost two hours before the doors opened - with Larry Pignone (my book collecting mentor and one of the original The Book Emporium gang) and we were handed slips of paper telling us we were numbers 65 and 66. The numbers allowed us to leave the line and return later and still have our place in line. We were also given a map showing the layout of the gymnasium floor and the locations of the different types of books. With a couple of lawn chairs, a copy of The Washington Post, and 20 ounces of 7-11 coffee we were set for the wait. By 7:00AM the line had gone around the corner and the Channel 4 News truck had showed up. I heard the newscaster say that there were 300 people in line at 7:15AM. At 7:55AM Larry brought the lawn chairs back to the car and we were ready to go. The doors opened promptly at 8:00AM and the line filed quickly - but orderly - into an entire gym filled with table after table of books. The line fanned out as the collectors rushed to the tables of interest to them. Three areas were of interest to me. Hardback Mysteries, Hardback Fiction, and First Editions - in that order. Although I was 65th in line, I was the second person to arrive at the Mystery table. Person #64 was interested in Military History. Numbers 62 and 63 were after Cookbooks.

The challenge at this point was to scan as many book spines as possible, identifying books of interest, and claiming the ones I wanted before someone else did. I carried two large shopping bags with me - enough to hold at least 30 books - and my hope was to fill them both. The first books I picked up were three by Elmore Leonard - LaBrava, Glitz, and Cat Chaser. All were firsts and all looked to be F/F (although I'd sit down later before I checked out and look more carefully for defects that might cause me to change my mind). At $3 each for books that will sell in the $20-$35 range, the day was starting off okay. A few more nice but unspectacular books got added to my bag before I spotted Patricia Cornwell's All That Remains on the other side of the table. I reached to pick it up and an elderly gentleman on the other side of the table offered that there was another book by her over there and he handed me Body of Evidence. Both were firsts and both were F/F although Body of Evidence was price-clipped. While I was looking at these books, I heard someone nearby say they had found a first of Hunt for Red October. Wow! That's a tough one to identify because the copyright page doesn't state that it's a first edition and the dust jacket has no price on it so it's easy to mistake for a book club edition. At that point I almost expected to find a copy of Cornwell's Post Mortem - no such luck! By 10:00AM my shopping bags were practically full and the tables were pretty well picked over. Included in the bags were two more very nice books - Sara Paretsky's Bitter Medicine and Martha Grimes' The Old Fox Deceiv'd, both of which I'm sure were passed over by dozens of collectors before I recognized them. By 10:30AM the Stone Ridge Building Fund was $147 richer for having had me visit their book show. I went home and circled April 25th on next year's calendar.

Pricing and References

Prices shown is this price guide are all based on a listing of over 5,000 advertised books, their condition, and their sale price which the author assembled over the past eighteen months. Entries were obtained from various dealer catalogs, from advertisements in Bookman Weekly, and from personal observations at book shows. An example of the form of the listings is shown below.

Carrie	1974	$300	1st ed NF in dj w/ several nicks	Second Story	6/1/94 Cat
Carrie	1974	$425	1st ed VG-NF in dj	Masters	10/18/93 AB
Carrie	1974	$500	1st ed Signed minor corner bumping o/w F in dj	Kleier	10/18/93AB
Carrie	1974	$650	1st ed Signed F-/FDS	Pepperland	7/18/94AB
Carrie	1974	$675	1st ed dj has sm hole on fr bottom else F/F	N.E. Antiq	10/18/93AB
The Shining	1977	$175	1st ed NF in dj w/ 1" fr tear & 1/4" fr tear	Second Story	6/1/94Cat
The Shining	1977	$200	1st ed remainder spray F/F	Kleier	10/18/93AB
The Shining	1977	$250	1st ed pc o/w VG+/F	Book Heaven	5/23/94AB
The Shining	1977	$250	1st ed VG/VG	Book Heaven	7/4/94AB
The Shining	1977	$275	1st ed F/F-	Pepperland	7/18/94AB
The Shining	1977	$450	1st ed F/F	N.E. Antiq	10/18/93AB
The Stand	1978	$60	1st ed inclipped G/G	Title Wave	5/9/94AB
The Stand	1978	$200	1st ed F/F	Kleier	10/18/93AB
The Stand	1978	$275	1st ed VF/VF	Pepperland	7/18/84AB
The Stand	1978	$300	1st ed F/VG	Laius	10/18/93AB
The Stand	1978	$350	1st ed sm tear on top of spine else F/F	N.E. Antiq	10/18/93AB
The Stand	1978	$675	1st ed Ltd ed in black box VF #461/1,250	Pepperland	7/18/94AB

Most of the information about first edition points was obtained by studing actual first edition books and dust jackets. Additional information about first edition points was obtained from the following references:

Ahearn, Allen and Pat, Author Price Guides, Box 5365, Rockville, Maryland

Beahm, George, The Stephen King Companion, Andrews and McMeel, Kansas City & New York 1989.

Bradley, Van Allen, The Book Collector's Handbook of Values: 1982-83 Edition,

Bruccoli, Matthew J. and Clark, C.E. Frazer, Jr., First Printings of American Authors, Gale Research, Inc., Detroit (1977-1979) 5 volumes.

Bruccoli, Matthew J., John O'Hara, A Checklist, Random House, New York 1972.

Goldstone, Adrian H. and Payne, John R., John Steinbeck - A Bibliographical Catalogue of the Adrian H. Goldstone Collection, The University of Texas at Austin, 1974.

Lepper, Gary M., A Bibliographical Introduction to Seventy-Five Modern Authors, Serendipity Books, Berkeley (1976)

Modern First Editions, The Clique Limited, York, England (1993)

Sarner, Harvey, A Checklist of The Works Of Herman Wouk, Brunswick Press, P.O. Box 2244, Cathedral City, CA, 1995.

Shine, Walter and Jean, A MacDonald Potpourri, The University of Florida Libraries, 1988.

AB Bookman's Weekly (Periodical), Clifton, NJ.

Douglas Adams

Hitchhiker's Guide to the Galaxy 1980 First book in the five book _Hitchhiker's_ Trilogy.

"Harmony Books / New York" on title page. No date on title page. Copyright page - 26th (of 28) line "10 9 8 7 6 5 4 3 2 1". Twenty-seventh line - "First American edition published 1980 by Harmony Books". DJ price - $6.95.
Quarter bound - violet cloth with blue sides and no top stain. Bright blue pastedowns.

		F/F	F/NF	NF/VG+	VG+/VG	VG/VG-	Good	w/o dj
1st ed		$50	$45	$35	$30	$25	$15	80%

The Restaurant at the End of the Universe 1981 Second book in the five book _Hitchhiker's_ Trilogy.

"Harmony Books / New York" on title page. No date on title page. Copyright page - 20th and 21st (of 21) lines - "10 9 8 7 6 5 4 3 2 1/First Edition". DJ price - $7.95.
Quarter bound - blue cloth with black sides and no top stain. Yellow pastedowns.

		F/F	F/NF	NF/VG+	VG+/VG	VG/VG-	Good	w/o dj
1st ed		$30	$25	$20	$12	$8	$5	80%

Life, The Universe and Everything 1982 Third book in the five book _Hitchhiker's_ Trilogy.

"Harmony Books / New York" on title page. No date on title page. Copyright page - 20th and 21st (of 21) lines - "10 9 8 7 6 5 4 3 2 1/First Edition". DJ price - $9.95.
Full bound - black cloth with no top stain and violet pastedowns.

		F/F	F/NF	NF/VG+	VG+/VG	VG/VG-	Good	w/o dj
1st ed		$15	$12	$10	$7	$5	$4	80%

So Long, and Thanks for All the Fish 1985 Fourth book in the five book _Hitchhiker's_ Trilogy.

"Harmony Books / New York" on title page. No date on title page. Copyright page - 23rd and 24th (of 24) lines - "10 9 8 7 6 5 4 3 2 1/First Edition". DJ price - $12.95.
Full bound - black cloth with no top stain and violet pastedowns.

		F/F	F/NF	NF/VG+	VG+/VG	VG/VG-	Good	w/o dj
1st ed		$15	$12	$10	$7	$5	$4	80%

Mostly Harmless 1992 Fifth book in the five book _Hitchhiker's_ Trilogy.

"Harmony Books/New York" on title page. No date on title page. Copyright page - 22nd and 23rd (of 23) lines - "10 9 8 7 6 5 4 3 2 1/First Edition". DJ price - $20.00.
Quarter bound - black cloth with lime green sides and no top stain. White pastedowns.

		F/F	F/NF	NF/VG+	VG+/VG	VG/VG-	Good	w/o dj
1st ed		$15	$12	$10	$7	$5	$4	80%

Eric Ambler

Background To Danger 1937

	F/F	F/NF	NF/VG+	VG+/VG	VG/VG-	Good	w/o dj

1st ed		$500	$450	$325	$250	$200	$125	25%

Cause For Alarm   1939

"NEW YORK ALFRED A. KNOPF 1939" on title page. Copyright page - 8th (of 8) line "FIRST AMERICAN EDITION". Full bound - light green with red ink. Red top stain and white pastedowns.

		F/F	F/NF	NF/VG+	VG+/VG	VG/VG-	Good	w/o dj
1st ed		$450	$400	$250	$175	$125	$60	25%

A Coffin For Dimitrios   1939

		F/F	F/NF	NF/VG+	VG+/VG	VG/VG-	Good	w/o dj
1st ed		$425	$375	$225	$150	$100	$50	25%

Journey Into Fear   1940

		F/F	F/NF	NF/VG+	VG+/VG	VG/VG-	Good	w/o dj
1st ed		$400	$350	$200	$150	$100	$50	25%

Judgement on Deltchev   1952

"ALFRED A KNOPF/New York: 1951" on title page. Copyright page - 7th (of 7) "FIRST EDITION". DJ price - $3.00. Full bound - brown cloth with green top stain and white pastedowns.

		F/F	F/NF	NF/VG+	VG+/VG	VG/VG-	Good	w/o dj
1st ed		$60	$50	$40	$30	$25	$10	60%

The Schirmer Inheritance   1953

"ALFRED A KNOPF/New York: 1953" on title page. Copyright page - 9th (of 9) "FIRST AMERICAN EDITION". DJ price - $3.00. Full bound - yellow cloth with pale yellow designs and black top stain. White pastedowns.

		F/F	F/NF	NF/VG+	VG+/VG	VG/VG-	Good	w/o dj
1st ed		$50	$45	$35	$25	$20	$7	70%

State of Siege   1956

"ALFRED A KNOPF/New York: 1956" on title page. Copyright page - 10th (of 12) "FIRST AMERICAN EDITION". DJ price - $3.50. Quarter bound - black cloth with blue sides and yellow top stain. White pastedowns.

		F/F	F/NF	NF/VG+	VG+/VG	VG/VG-	Good	w/o dj
1st ed		$45	$40	$35	$25	$20	$7	70%

Passage of Arms   1962

"1962/Alfred A Knopf NEW YORK" on title page. Copyright page - 10th (of 10) "FIRST AMERICAN EDITION". DJ price - $3.95. Full bound - light burnt-orange cloth with gray-green top stain. White pastedowns.

		F/F	F/NF	NF/VG+	VG+/VG	VG/VG-	Good	w/o dj
1st ed		$40	$35	$30	$20	$15	$7	70%

The Light of Day 1963

"1963/*Alfred A Knopf* NEW YORK" on title page. Copyright page - 11th (of 11) "FIRST AMERICAN EDITION". DJ price - $3.95. Full bound - green cloth with red top stain. Map on pastedowns.

		F/F	F/NF	NF/VG+	VG+/VG	VG/VG-	Good	w/o dj
1st ed		$40	$35	$30	$20	$15	$7	70%

A Kind of Anger 1964

"*New York* Atheneum/1964" on title page. Copyright page - 8th (of 8) "First Edition". DJ price - $4.95. Full bound - red cloth on top and blue cloth on bottom with steel-gray top stain. Olive green pastedowns.

		F/F	F/NF	NF/VG+	VG+/VG	VG/VG-	Good	w/o dj
1st ed		$35	$30	$25	$18	$15	$7	70%

Dirty Story 1967

(1st U.K. ed) "THE BODLEY HEAD/LONDON SYDNEY/TORONTO" on title page. Copyright page - 7th (of 7) "*First published 1967*". Full bound - brown cloth with no top stain and white pastedowns.

		F/F	F/NF	NF/VG+	VG+/VG	VG/VG-	Good	w/o dj
1st ed		$30	$25	$20	$15	$12	$7	70%

The Intercom Conspiracy 1969

"New York Atheneum/1969" on title page. Copyright page - 7th (of 7) "*First Edition*". DJ price $5.95. Yellow cloth (top one third), orange cloth (bottom two thirds) with red top stain and red pastedowns.

		F/F	F/NF	NF/VG+	VG+/VG	VG/VG-	Good	w/o dj
1st ed		$25	$20	$15	$12	$10	$6	80%

The Levanter 1972

"New York Atheneum/1972" on title page. Copyright page - 7th (of 7) "*First Edition*". DJ price $6.95. White cloth (top one third), green cloth (bottom two thirds) with light olive top stain and olive pastedowns.

		F/F	F/NF	NF/VG+	VG+/VG	VG/VG-	Good	w/o dj
1st ed		$20	$18	$15	$12	$10	$6	80%

Jeffrey Archer

Not a Penny More, Not a Penny Less 1976

"DOUBLEDAY & COMPANY, INC/GARDEN CITY, NEW YORK/1976" on title page. Copyright page - last (19th) line -"*First Edition*". DJ price - $6.95
Quarter bound - black cloth with olive green paper and no top stain. White pastedowns.

	F/F	F/NF	NF/VG+	VG+/VG	VG/VG-	Good	w/o dj
1st ed	$50	$45	$35	$30	$25	$15	70%

Shall We Tell the President? 1977

"THE VIKING PRESS NEW YORK" on title page. No date on title page. Copyright page - 3rd (of 20) lines - "First published in 1977 by The Viking Press." DJ price - $8.95 Quarter bound - blue cloth with gray paper and no top stain. White pastedowns.

	F/F	F/NF	NF/VG+	VG+/VG	VG/VG-	Good	w/o dj
1st ed	$35	$30	$25	$18	$15	$10	70%

Kane and Abel 1979

"SIMON & SCHUSTER/NEW YORK" on title page. No date on title page. Copyright page - 13th (of 19) line - "1 2 3 4 5 6 7 8 9 10". DJ price - $13.95 Quarter bound - black cloth with gold paper and no top stain. Gold pastedowns.

	F/F	F/NF	NF/VG+	VG+/VG	VG/VG-	Good	w/o dj
1st ed	$30	$25	$20	$18	$15	$10	80%

The Prodigal Daughter 1982

"THE LINDEN PRESS/SIMON & SCHUSTER/NEW YORK 1982" on title page. Copyright page - 15th (of 25) line - "10 9 8 7 6 5 4 3 2 1". DJ price - $15.95 Quarter bound - black cloth with black paper and no top stain. Black pastedowns.

	F/F	F/NF	NF/VG+	VG+/VG	VG/VG-	Good	w/o dj
1st ed	$25	$20	$15	$12	$10	$8	80%

A Quiver Full of Arrows 1982

"THE LINDEN PRESS/SIMON & SCHUSTER/NEW YORK 1982" on title page. Copyright page - 17th (of 23) line - "10 9 8 7 6 5 4 3 2 1". DJ price - $9.95 Quarter bound - red-orange cloth with gray paper and no top stain. Gray pastedowns.

	F/F	F/NF	NF/VG+	VG+/VG	VG/VG-	Good	w/o dj
1st ed	$20	$17	$13	$10	$8	$6	80%

First Among Equals 1984

"The Linden Press/Simon & Schuster/NEW YORK/1984" on title page. Copyright page - 19th (of 25) line - "1 3 5 7 9 10 8 6 4 2". DJ price - $16.95 Quarter bound - purple cloth with gray paper and no top stain. Gray pastedowns.

	F/F	F/NF	NF/VG+	VG+/VG	VG/VG-	Good	w/o dj
1st ed	$20	$17	$13	$10	$8	$6	80%

A Matter of Honor 1986

"THE LINDEN PRESS/SIMON & SCHUSTER/NEW YORK/1986" on title page. Copyright page - 15th (of 25) line - "1 3 5 7 9 10 8 6 4 2". DJ price - $18.95 Quarter bound - red cloth with gray paper and no top stain. Gray pastedowns.

	F/F	F/NF	NF/VG+	VG+/VG	VG/VG-	Good	w/o dj
1st ed	$15	$12	$10	$8	$6	$4	80%

A Twist in the Tale 1988

"SIMON & SCHUSTER/New York London Toronto Sydney Tokyo" on title page.
Copyright page - 15th (of 27) line - "1 3 5 7 9 10 8 6 4 2". DJ price - $17.95
Quarter bound - maroon cloth with maroon paper and no top stain. Speckled pastedowns.

	F/F	F/NF	NF/VG+	VG+/VG	VG/VG-	Good	w/o dj
1st ed	$15	$12	$10	$8	$6	$4	80%

As the Crow Flies 1991

"Harper Collins *Publishers*" on title page.
Copyright page - 6th (of 10) line - "FIRST EDITION". Last line - "91 92 93 94 95 MAC/RRD 10
9 8 7 6 5 4 3 2 1". DJ price - USA $22.95/CANADA $27.95.
Quarter bound - gold cloth with brown paper and no top stain. Gold pastedowns.

	F/F	F/NF	NF/VG+	VG+/VG	VG/VG-	Good	w/o dj
1st ed	$15	$12	$10	$8	$6	$4	75%

Honor Among Thieves 1993

"Harper Collins *Publishers*" on title page.
Copyright page - 12th (of 23) line - "FIRST EDITION". Last line - "93 94 95 96 97 #/HC 10 9 8
7 6 5 4 3 2 1". DJ price - USA $23.00/CANADA $29.95.
Quarter bound - dark blue cloth with blue paper and no top stain. Gray pastedowns.

	F/F	F/NF	NF/VG+	VG+/VG	VG/VG-	Good	w/o dj
1st ed	$15	$12	$10	$8	$6	$4	75%

Jean M. Auel

U.S. novelist, born in Chicago. Author of the four-book Earth's Children series which follows Ayla through the trials of one of the "Others" being raises by a clan of cavemen. The a prelude to the downfall of Neanderthal at the hands of Cro-Magnon is played out in Ayla's actions to liberate herself from Clan rules in *The Clan of the Cave Bear*. In *The Valley of Horses* Ayla, banished from the Clan, meets another one of the the Others and establishes her own self-worth. Ayla acceptance into the world of the Others is chronicled in the remaining books of the series.

The Clan of the Cave Bear 1980   First printing 75,000 copies

"CROWN PUBLISHING, INC. NEW YORK" on title page.   No date on title page.
Copyright page bottom two (of 22) lines - "10 9 8 7 6 5 4 3 2 1/First Edition".
DJ price - $12.95 (no different for early later editions).
Quarter bound - yellow cloth with green paper and no top stain. Pastedowns map.

	F/F	F/NF	NF/VG+	VG+/VG	VG/VG-	Good	w/o dj
1st ed	$80	$70	$60	$55	$50	$40	70%

The Valley of Horses 1982   First printing 100,000 copies

"Crown Publishing, Inc. New York" on title page.   No date on title page.
Copyright page bottom two (of 21) lines - "10 9 8 7 6 5 4 3 2 1/First Edition".

DJ price - $15.95 (no different for early later editions).
Quarter bound - cream cloth with blue paper and no top stain. Pastedowns map.

	F/F	F/NF	NF/VG+	VG+/VG	VG/VG-	Good	w/o dj
1st ed	$35	$30	$25	$18	$15	$10	70%

The Mamouth Hunters 1985   First printing 500,000 copies

"Crown Publishing, Inc. New York" on title page.   No date on title page.
Copyright page bottom two (of 19) lines - "10 9 8 7 6 5 4 3 2 1/First Edition".
DJ price - $19.95 (no different for early later editions).
Quarter bound - cream cloth with burnt orange paper and no top stain. Pastedowns map.

	F/F	F/NF	NF/VG+	VG+/VG	VG/VG-	Good	w/o dj
1st ed	$15	$12	$10	$8	$6	$4	60%

The Plains of Passage 1990

"Crown Publishing, Inc. New York" on title page.   No date on title page.
Copyright page bottom two (of 23) lines - "10 9 8 7 6 5 4 3 2 1/First Edition".
DJ price - $24.95/(Canada: $31.95) (no different for early later editions).
Quarter bound - purple cloth with gold paper and no top stain. Pastedowns map.

	F/F	F/NF	NF/VG+	VG+/VG	VG/VG-	Good	w/o dj
1st ed	$12	$10	$8	$6	$ 5	$4	50%

Peter Benchley

Jaws 1974

"1974/DOUBLEDAY & COMPANY, INC., GARDEN CITY, NEW YORK" on title page.
Copyright page - last (of 9) line - "First Edition".   DJ price - $6.95.
Full bound - black cloth with no top stain and blue pastedowns.

	F/F	F/NF	NF/VG+	VG+/VG	VG/VG-	Good	w/o dj
1st ed	$45	$35	$25	$20	$15	$10	70%

The Deep 1976

"DOUBLEDAY & COMPANY, INC., GARDEN CITY, NEW YORK/1976" on title page.
Copyright page - last (of 9) line - "FIRST EDITION".   DJ price - $7.95.
Quarter bound - black cloth with green cloth sides and no top stain. White pastedowns.

	F/F	F/NF	NF/VG+	VG+/VG	VG/VG-	Good	w/o dj
1st ed	$30	$25	$20	$15	$12	$8	70%

The Island 1979

"*Doubleday & Company, Inc., Garden City, New York/1979*" on title page.
Copyright page - last (of 11) line - "FIRST EDITION".   DJ price - $8.95.
Quarter bound - green cloth with orange sides and no top stain. White pastedowns.

	F/F	F/NF	NF/VG+	VG+/VG	VG/VG-	Good	w/o dj

1st ed		$20	$18	$15	$12	$10	$6	80%

William Blatty

The Exorcist 1971

"HARPER & ROW PUBLISHERS/NEW YORK, EVANSTON, SAN FRANCISCO, LONDON" on title page. Copyright page - 8th (of 10) line - "FIRST EDITION". DJ price - $6.95 with "0571" on bottom front flap. Quarter bound - maroon cloth with maroon sides and no top stain. Tan pastedowns.

		F/F	F/NF	NF/VG+	VG+/VG	VG/VG-	Good	w/o dj
1st ed		$65	$50	$40	$35	$25	$10	70%

Lawrence Block

Lawrence Block wrote his first paperback novels under the pen name of Sheldon Lord. These are all highly collectible and are all priced according to the following table.

Sheldon Lord Novels

Carla 1958 Midwood Publishers #8 PBO
A Strange Kind of Love 1958 Midwood Publishers #9 PBO
Born to Be Bad 1959 Midwood Publishers #14 PBO
69 Barrow Street 1959 Midwood Publishers #24 PBO
Of Shame and Joy 1960 Midwood Publishers #29 PBO
A Woman Must Love 1960 Midwood Publishers #33 PBO
Kept 1960 Midwood Publishers #35 PBO
Candy 1960 Midwood Publishers #40 PBO
A Girl Called Honey 1960 Midwood Publishers #41 PBO
So Willing 1960 Midwood Publishers #48 PBO
Puta 1963 Midwood Publishers #165 PBO
Pads Are For Passion 1961 Beacon Publishers #B387 PBO
Sex Is A Woman 1964 Beacon Publishers PBO
The Sex Shuttle 1964 Beacon Publishers PBO

	Fine	VG+	VG-	Good
1st PBO ed	$40	$15	$7	$3

Lawrence Block Novels

Mona 1961 Gold Medal # S1084 PBO
Death Pulls a Doublecross 1961 Gold Medal # S1162 PBO

	Fine	VG+	VG-	Good
1st PBO ed	$60	$25	$10	$5

The Girl In the Long Green Heart 1965 Gold Medal # K1555 PBO

	Fine	VG+	VG-	Good
1st PBO ed	$30	$12	$6	$3

Deadly Honeymoon 1967 A Cock Robin Mystery

"THE MACMILLIAN COMPANY, NEW YORK" on title page. No date on title page.
Copyright page - 10th (of 13) line - "FIRST PRINTING". DJ price - $4.50. Full bound - dark
green cloth with no top stain and white pastedowns.

	F/F	F/NF	NF/VG+	VG+/VG	VG/VG-	Good	w/o dj
1st ed	$250	$200	$150	$90	$75	$30	70%

After The First Death 1969 A Cock Robin Mystery

"THE MACMILLIAN COMPANY/New York" on title page. No date on title page.
Copyright page - 8th (of 11) line - "FIRST PRINTING". DJ price - $4.50. Full bound - navy
blue cloth with no top stain and white pastedowns.

	F/F	F/NF	NF/VG+	VG+/VG	VG/VG-	Good	w/o dj
1st ed	$225	$175	$125	$90	$75	$30	70%

The Specialist 1969 Gold Medal PBO

	Fine	VG+	VG-	Good
1st PBO ed	$25	$10	$6	$3

The Devil Knows You're Dead 1993

"WILLIAM MORROW AND COMPANY, INC./NEW YORK" on title page. No date on title
page. Copyright page - 21st and 22nd (of 22) lines - "First Edition/1 2 3 4 5 6 7 8 9 10".
Quarter bound - black cloth with gray sides and no top stain. Blue pastedowns.

	F/F	F/NF	NF/VG+	VG+/VG	VG/VG-	Good	w/o dj
1st ed	$15	$12	$10	$6	$5	$2	90%

Evan Tanner Mysteries

The Thief Who Couldn't Sleep 1966 Gold Medal # D1722 PBO
The Canceled Czech 1967 Gold Medal PBO
Tanner's Twelve Swingers 1967 Gold Medal PBO
Two For Tanner 1968 Gold Medal PBO
Tanner's Tiger 1968 Gold Medal PBO
Here Comes a Hero 1968 Gold Medal PBO

	Fine	VG+	VG-	Good
1st PBO ed	$30	$12	$6	$3

Me Tanner, You Jane 1970 A Cock Robin Mystery

"The MacMillan Company" on title page. No date on title page. Copyright page - 8th (of 12)
line - "First Printing". DJ price - $4.50. Full bound - tan cloth with no top stain and white

pastedowns.

		F/F	F/NF	NF/VG+	VG+/VG	VG/VG-	Good	w/o dj
1st ed		$100	$85	$60	$40	$25	$10	70%

Bernie Rhodenbarr Mysteries

Burglars Can't Be Choosers 1977

"Random House: New York" on title page. No date on title page. Copyright page - 13th and 14th (of 14) lines - "9 8 7 6 5 4 3 2/First Edition". DJ price - $6.95. Quarter bound - black cloth with gold sides and no top stain. White pastedowns.

		F/F	F/NF	NF/VG+	VG+/VG	VG/VG-	Good	w/o dj
1st ed		$75	$65	$50	$35	$25	$10	70%

The Burglar in the Closet 1978

"Random House New York" on title page. No date on title page. Copyright page - 15th and 16th (of 16) lines - "9 8 7 6 5 4 3 2/First Edition". DJ price - $6.95. Quarter bound - black cloth with light blue-gray sides and no top stain. White pastedowns.

		F/F	F/NF	NF/VG+	VG+/VG	VG/VG-	Good	w/o dj
1st ed		$75	$65	$50	$35	$25	$10	70%

The Burglar Who Liked to Quote Kipling 1979

"Random House: New York" on title page. No date on title page. Copyright page - 14th and 15th (of 15) lines - "9 8 7 6 5 4 3 2/First Edition". DJ price - $7.95. Quarter bound - black cloth with burnt-orange sides and no top stain. White pastedowns.

		F/F	F/NF	NF/VG+	VG+/VG	VG/VG-	Good	w/o dj
1st ed		$60	$50	$35	$25	$20	$10	70%

The Burglar Who Studied Spinoza 1980

"Random House: New York" on title page. No date on title page. Copyright page - 14th and 15th (of 15) lines - "9 8 7 6 5 4 3 2/First Edition". DJ price - $8.95. Quarter bound - black cloth with burnt-orange sides and no top stain. White pastedowns.

		F/F	F/NF	NF/VG+	VG+/VG	VG/VG-	Good	w/o dj
1st ed		$40	$35	$30	$20	$15	$8	80%

The Burglar Who Painted Like Mondrian 1983

"ARBOR HOUSE/NEW YORK" on title page. No date on title page. Copyright page - 8th (of 11) line - "10 9 8 7 6 5 4 3 2 1". DJ price - $14.50. Quarter bound - white cloth with red sides and no top stain. White pastedowns.

		F/F	F/NF	NF/VG+	VG+/VG	VG/VG-	Good	w/o dj
1st ed		$35	$30	$25	$15	$10	$6	80%

The Burglar Who Traded Ted Williams 1994

"A Dutton Book" on title page. No date on title page. Copyright page - 18th and 19th (of 44) lines - "First Printing, May, 1994/10 9 8 7 6 5 4 3 2 1". DJ price - U.S. $19.95/Canada $27.99. Quarter bound - black cloth with purple sides and no top stain. White pastedowns.

		F/F	F/NF	NF/VG+	VG+/VG	VG/VG-	Good	w/o dj
1st ed		$15	$12	$10	$6	$5	$2	90%

The Burglar Who Thought He Was Bogart 1995

"A DUTTON BOOK" on title page. No date on title page. Copyright page - 17th and 18th (of 42) lines - "First Printing, June, 1995/10 9 8 7 6 5 4 3 2 1". DJ price - U.S. $21.95/Canada $29.99. Quarter bound - blue cloth with light blue sides and no top stain. White pastedowns.

		F/F	F/NF	NF/VG+	VG+/VG	VG/VG-	Good	w/o dj
1st ed		$15	$12	$10	$6	$5	$2	90%

Matthew Scudder Mysteries

The Sins of the Father 1976 Dell 1992 Dark Harvest Hard Cover

		Fine	VG+	VG-	Good
1st PBO ed		$50	$25	$10	$5

		F/F	F/NF	NF/VG+	VG+/VG	VG/VG-	Good	w/o dj
1st ed		$25	$20	$15	$10	$7	$4	90%

Time to Murder and Create 1977 Dell 1993 Dark Harvest Hard Cover

		Fine	VG+	VG-	Good
1st PBO ed		$45	$25	$10	$5

		F/F	F/NF	NF/VG+	VG+/VG	VG/VG-	Good	w/o dj
1st ed		$25	$20	$15	$10	$7	$4	90%

In the Midst of Death 1976 Dell

		Fine	VG+	VG-	Good
1st PBO ed		$40	$20	$8	$4

A Stab In the Dark 1981

"ARBOR HOUSE/NEW YORK" on title page. No date on title page. Copyright page - last (of 11) line - "10 9 8 7 6 5 4 3 2 1". DJ price - $10.95. Quarter bound - black cloth with gray sides and no top stain. White pastedowns.

		F/F	F/NF	NF/VG+	VG+/VG	VG/VG-	Good	w/o dj
1st ed		$450	$375	$300	$200	$150	$35	60%

Eight Million Ways to Die 1982

"ARBOR HOUSE" on title page. No date on title page. Copyright page - 9th (of 13) line - "10

9 8 7 6 5 4 3 2 1". DJ price - $13.50. Quarter bound - red cloth with black sides and no top stain. White pastedowns.

	F/F	F/NF	NF/VG+	VG+/VG	VG/VG-	Good	w/o dj
1st ed	$300	$250	$200	$150	$100	$20	70%

When the Sacred Ginmill Closes 1986

"*ARBOR HOUSE/NEW YORK*" on title page. No date on title page. Copyright page - 17 lines with no mention of edition number. DJ price - $15.95. Quarter bound - burnt-orange cloth with brown sides and no top stain. Burnt-orange pastedowns.

	F/F	F/NF	NF/VG+	VG+/VG	VG/VG-	Good	w/o dj
1st ed	$30	$25	$20	$15	$10	$6	80%

Out on the Cutting Edge 1989

"William Morrow and Company, Inc./New York" on title page. No date on title page. Copyright page - 22nd and 23rd (of 24) lines - "First Edition/1 2 3 4 5 6 7 8 9 10". DJ price - $17.95. Quarter bound - white cloth with white sides and no top stain. Blue pastedowns.

	F/F	F/NF	NF/VG+	VG+/VG	VG/VG-	Good	w/o dj
1st ed	$20	$15	$10	$6	$5	$2	90%

A Ticket to the Boneyard 1990

"WILLIAM MORROW AND COMPANY, INC./NEW YORK" on title page. No date on title page. Copyright page - 21st and 22nd (of 23) lines - "First Edition/1 2 3 4 5 6 7 8 9 10". DJ price - $18.95. Quarter bound - brown cloth with dark brown sides and no top stain. Red pastedowns.

	F/F	F/NF	NF/VG+	VG+/VG	VG/VG-	Good	w/o dj
1st ed	$15	$12	$10	$6	$5	$2	90%

A Dance at the Slaughterhouse 1991

"WILLIAM MORROW AND COMPANY, INC./NEW YORK" on title page. No date on title page. Copyright page - 19th and 20th (of 21) lines - "First Edition/1 2 3 4 5 6 7 8 9 10". DJ price - $19.00. Quarter bound - brown cloth with burnt-orange sides and no top stain. Burnt-orange pastedowns.

	F/F	F/NF	NF/VG+	VG+/VG	VG/VG-	Good	w/o dj
1st ed	$15	$12	$10	$6	$5	$2	90%

A Walk Among the Tombstones 1992

"WILLIAM MORROW AND COMPANY, INC./NEW YORK" on title page. No date on title page. Copyright page - 19th and 20th (of 21) lines - "First Edition/1 2 3 4 5 6 7 8 9 10". DJ price - $19.00. Quarter bound - red cloth with light violet sides and no top stain. Light orange pastedowns.

	F/F	F/NF	NF/VG+	VG+/VG	VG/VG-	Good	w/o dj
1st ed	$15	$12	$10	$6	$5	$2	90%

A Long Line of Dead Men 1994

"WILLIAM MORROW AND COMPANY, INC./NEW YORK" on title page. No date on title page. Copyright page - 22nd and 23rd (of 23) lines - "First Edition/1 2 3 4 5 6 7 8 9 10". DJ price - $20.00. Quarter bound - red cloth with black sides and no top stain. Red pastedowns.

		F/F	F/NF	NF/VG +	VG+/VG	VG/VG-	Good	w/o dj
1st ed		$15	$12	$10	$6	$5	$2	90%

Short Stories

Sometimes They Bite 1983

"ARBOR HOUSE NEW YORK" on title page. No date on title page. Copyright page - 10th (of 14) line - "10 9 8 7 6 5 4 3 2 1". DJ price - $14.50. Quarter bound - black cloth with lime green sides and no top stain. White pastedowns.

		F/F	F/NF	NF/VG +	VG+/VG	VG/VG-	Good	w/o dj
1st ed		$35	$30	$25	$15	$10	$6	80%

Like A Lamb To Slaughter 1984

"ARBOR HOUSE/NEW YORK" on title page. No date on title page. Copyright page - 13th (of 17) line - "10 9 8 7 6 5 4 3 2 1". DJ price - $15.95. Quarter bound - gray cloth with black sides and no top stain. White pastedowns.

		F/F	F/NF	NF/VG +	VG+/VG	VG/VG-	Good	w/o dj
1st ed		$25	$20	$15	$10	$8	$5	80%

Some Days You Get The Bear 1994

"WILLIAM MORROW AND COMPANY, INC./NEW YORK" on title page. No date on title page. Copyright page - 23rd and 24th (of 25) lines - "First Edition/1 2 3 4 5 6 7 8 9 10". DJ price - $20.00. Quarter bound - purple cloth with light gray sides and no top stain. Light gray pastedowns.

		F/F	F/NF	NF/VG +	VG+/VG	VG/VG-	Good	w/o dj
1st ed		$15	$12	$10	$6	$5	$2	90%

Ray Bradbury

Dark Carnival 1947

		F/F	F/NF	NF/VG +	VG+/VG	VG/VG-	Good	w/o dj
1st ed		$750	$550	$400	$300	$250	$150	33%

The Martian Chronicles 1950

		F/F	F/NF	NF/VG +	VG+/VG	VG/VG-	Good	w/o dj
1st ed		$650	$475	$350	$250	$200	$125	33%

The Illustrated Man 1951

"GARDEN CITY, NEW YORK, 1951/DOUBLEDAY & COMPANY, INC." on title page.
Copyright page - last (of 5) line - "FIRST EDITION". DJ price - $2.75.
. Full bound - tan cloth with no top stain and white pastedowns.

		F/F	F/NF	NF/VG+	VG+/VG	VG/VG-	Good	w/o dj
1st ed		$650	$475	$350	$250	$200	$125	33%

Fahrenheit 451 1953

		F/F	F/NF	NF/VG+	VG+/VG	VG/VG-	Good	w/o dj
1st ed		$800	$650	$500	$375	$300	$150	33%

The Golden Apples of the Sun 1953

		F/F	F/NF	NF/VG+	VG+/VG	VG/VG-	Good	w/o dj
1st ed		$650	$475	$350	$250	$200	$125	33%

The October Country 1955

		F/F	F/NF	NF/VG+	VG+/VG	VG/VG-	Good	w/o dj
1st ed		$500	$350	$250	$175	$150	$100	33%

Switch on the Night

		F/F	F/NF	NF/VG+	VG+/VG	VG/VG-	Good	w/o dj
1st ed		$500	$350	$250	$175	$150	$100	33%

Dandelion Wine 1957

		F/F	F/NF	NF/VG+	VG+/VG	VG/VG-	Good	w/o dj
1st ed		$500	$350	$250	$175	$150	$100	33%

A Medicine for Melancholy 1959

Copyright page - last line -"First Edition". DJ price - $3.75.
Full bound - black cloth with no top stain and white pastedowns.

		F/F	F/NF	NF/VG+	VG+/VG	VG/VG-	Good	w/o dj
1st ed		$450	$325	$225	$150	$125	$80	33%

Something Wicked This Way Comes 1962

		F/F	F/NF	NF/VG+	VG+/VG	VG/VG-	Good	w/o dj
1st ed		$400	$300	$200	$125	$100	$80	33%

R is for Rocket 1962

Copyright page - last (of 5) line -"FIRST EDTION". DJ price - $2.95.
Full bound - dark blue cloth with no top stain and white pastedowns.

	F/F	F/NF	NF/VG+	VG+/VG	VG/VG-	Good	w/o dj

1st ed		$350	$250	$200	$125	$100	$80	33%

The Anthem Sprinters

		F/F	F/NF	NF/VG+	VG+/VG	VG/VG-	Good	w/o dj
1st ed		$300	$225	$150	$100	$60	$40	40%

The Machinies of Joy 1964

		F/F	F/NF	NF/VG+	VG+/VG	VG/VG-	Good	w/o dj
1st ed		$250	$200	$125	$75	$50	$30	50%

I Sing the Body Electric 1969

		F/F	F/NF	NF/VG+	VG+/VG	VG/VG-	Good	w/o dj
1st ed		$45	$40	$35	$25	$20	$13	50%

The Halloween Tree 1972

		F/F	F/NF	NF/VG+	VG+/VG	VG/VG-	Good	w/o dj
1st ed		$35	$30	$25	$20	$15	$10	75%

When Elephants Last in the Dooryard Bloomed 1973

		F/F	F/NF	NF/VG+	VG+/VG	VG/VG-	Good	w/o dj
1st ed		$35	$30	$25	$20	$15	$10	75%

Long After Midnight 1976

		F/F	F/NF	NF/VG+	VG+/VG	VG/VG-	Good	w/o dj
1st ed		$25	$20	$15	$12	$10	$8	75%

The Haunted Computer and Android Pope 1981

		F/F	F/NF	NF/VG+	VG+/VG	VG/VG-	Good	w/o dj
1st ed		$25	$20	$15	$12	$10	$8	75%

Death Is A Lonely Business 1985

"ALFRED A. KNOPF NEW YORK 1985" on page opposite title page.
Copyright page - last (of 21) line - "FIRST TRADE EDITION". DJ price - $15.95.
Quarter bound - black cloth with tan sides and no top stain. White pastedowns.

		F/F	F/NF	NF/VG+	VG+/VG	VG/VG-	Good	w/o dj
1st ed		$25	$20	$15	$12	$10	$8	75%

Death Has Lost Its Charm for Me 1987

		F/F	F/NF	NF/VG+	VG+/VG	VG/VG-	Good	w/o dj
1st ed		$20	$17	$12	$10	$8	$6	75%

The Toynbee Convector 1988

"ALFRED A. KNOPF/NEW YORK [1988]" on title page.
Copyright page - last (of 24) line -*"First Edition"*. DJ price - $17.95.
Quarter bound - black cloth with black sides and no top stain. White pastedowns.

		F/F	F/NF	NF/VG+	VG+/VG	VG/VG-	Good	w/o dj
1st ed		$20	$17	$12	$10	$8	$6	75%

A Graveyard for Lunatics 1990

"ALFRED A. KNOPF/NEW YORK/1990" on page opposite title page.
Copyright page - last (of 17) line - "First Edition". DJ price - $18.95.
Quarter bound -dark blue cloth with tan sides and no top stain. White pastedowns.

		F/F	F/NF	NF/VG+	VG+/VG	VG/VG-	Good	w/o dj
1st ed		$20	$17	$12	$10	$8	$6	75%

James Lee Burke

Half of Paradise 1965

		F/F	F/NF	NF/VG+	VG+/VG	VG/VG-	Good	w/o dj
1st ed		$1,000	$900	$700	$400	$300	$75	60%

To the Bright and Shining Sun 1970

		F/F	F/NF	NF/VG+	VG+/VG	VG/VG-	Good	w/o dj
1st ed		$800	$700	$500	$350	$275	$75	60%

Lay Down My Sword and Shield 1971

		F/F	F/NF	NF/VG+	VG+/VG	VG/VG-	Good	w/o dj
1st ed		$750	$650	$450	$325	$250	$75	60%

The Lost Get-Back Boogie 1986

"LOUISIANA STATE UNIVERSITY PRESS/Baton Rouge and London/1986" on title page.
Copyright page - 12th (of 18) line "10 9 8 7 6 5 4 3 2 1". DJ price - $16.95.
Note: Chapter One was copyright in 1978.

		F/F	F/NF	NF/VG+	VG+/VG	VG/VG-	Good	w/o dj
1st ed		$60	$50	$40	$30	$20	$10	70%

Neon Rain 1987

"HENRY HOLT AND COMPLANY NEW YORK" on title page. No date on title page.
Copyright page - 14th and 17th (of 18) lines "First Edition/10 9 8 7 6 5 4 3 2 1". DJ price -
$16.95. Quarter bound - black cloth with gray sides and no top stain. White pastedowns.

		F/F	F/NF	NF/VG+	VG+/VG	VG/VG-	Good	w/o dj
1st ed		$150	$125	$90	$70	$60	$20	70%

Heaven's Prisoners 1988

"HENRY HOLT AND COMPLANY/NEW YORK" on title page. No date on title page.
Copyright page - 16th and 19th (of 20) lines "First Edition/10 9 8 7 6 5 4 3 2 1". DJ price -
$17.95. Quarter bound - black cloth with gray sides and no top stain. White pastedowns.

		F/F	F/NF	NF/VG+	VG+/VG	VG/VG-	Good	w/o dj
1st ed		$90	$75	$45	$35	$30	$15	70%

Black Cherry Blues 1989   First printing 35,000 copies

"Little, Brown and Company/BOSTON TORONTO LONDON" on title page. No date on
title page. Copyright page - 8th and 24th (of 29) lines "FIRST EDITION/10 9 8 7 6 5 4 3 2 1".
DJ price - $17.95/$21.95 in Canada. Quarter bound - red cloth with gray sides and no top
stain. Cream pastedowns.

		F/F	F/NF	NF/VG+	VG+/VG	VG/VG-	Good	w/o dj
1st ed		$50	$45	$30	$20	$15	$6	80%

Tom Clancy

The Hunt for Red October 1984

"Naval Institute Press/Annapolis, Maryland" on title page. No date on title page.
Copyright page - 18 lines with no mention of edition or printing number. Later printings
have a 19th line added at the bottom of the page such as "84 85 86 87 88 10 9 8 7 6 5 4 3 2".
DJ has no price on it. Full bound - deep red with no top stain and gray pastedowns.

		F/F	F/NF	NF/VG+	VG+/VG	VG/VG-	Good	w/o dj
1st ed		$650	$500	$400	$300	$250	$100	70%

Red Storm Rising 1986

"G.P. Putnam's Sons New York" on title page. No date on title page.
Copyright page - last (of 20) line - "1 2 3 4 5 6 7 8 9 10". DJ price - $19.95.
Quarter bound - black with black sides and no top stain. Gray pastedowns.

		F/F	F/NF	NF/VG+	VG+/VG	VG/VG-	Good	w/o dj
1st ed		$25	$20	$15	$12	$8	$5	80%

Patriot Games 1987

"G.P. PUTNAM'S SONS New York" on title page. No date on title page.
Copyright page - last (of 17) line - "1 2 3 4 5 6 7 8 9 10". DJ price - $19.95.
Quarter bound - gray with gray sides and no top stain. Gray pastedowns.

		F/F	F/NF	NF/VG+	VG+/VG	VG/VG-	Good	w/o dj
1st ed		$25	$20	$15	$12	$8	$5	80%

The Cardinal of the Kremlin 1988

"G.P. PUTNAM'S SONS NEW YORK" on title page. No date on title page.
Copyright page - last (of 19) line - "1 2 3 4 5 6 7 8 9 10". DJ price - $19.95/$27.95 CAN.
Quarter bound - black with black sides and no top stain. Gray pastedowns.

		F/F	F/NF	NF/VG+	VG+/VG	VG/VG-	Good	w/o dj
1st ed		$20	$17	$12	$10	$7	$4	80%

Clear and Present Danger 1989

"G.P. PUTNAM'S SONS/New York" on title page. No date on title page.
Copyright page - last (of 22) line - "1 2 3 4 5 6 7 8 9 10". DJ price - $21.95/$29.95 CAN.
Quarter bound - black with gray sides and no top stain. Black pastedowns.

		F/F	F/NF	NF/VG+	VG+/VG	VG/VG-	Good	w/o dj
1st ed		$15	$12	$10	$9	$7	$4	80%

Mary Higgins Clark

Where Are the Children? 1975

"SIMON AND SCHUSTER NEW YORK" on title page. No date on title page. Copyright
page - 10th (of 17) line - "1 2 3 4 5 6 7 8 9 10". DJ price $7.95. Full bound - brown with
speckles cloth with no top stain and light tan pastedowns.

		F/F	F/NF	NF/VG+	VG+/VG	VG/VG-	Good	w/o dj
1st ed		$100	$90	$75	$50	$40	$20	70%

A Stranger Is Watching 1977

"SIMON AND SCHUSTER   NEW YORK" on title page. No date on title page. Copyright
page - 13th (of 19) line - "1 2 3 4 5 6 7 8 9 10". DJ price $8.95. Quarter bound - navy blue cloth
with white sides with no top stain. White pastedowns.

		F/F	F/NF	NF/VG+	VG+/VG	VG/VG-	Good	w/o dj
1st ed		$50	$45	$40	$30	$25	$10	70%

The Cradle Will Fall 1980

"SIMON AND SCHUSTER   NEW YORK" on title page. No date on title page. Copyright
page - 17th (of 23) line - "1 2 3 4 5 6 7 8 9 10". DJ price $10.95. Quarter bound - forest green
cloth with speckled green sides and no top stain. Speckled green pastedowns.

		F/F	F/NF	NF/VG+	VG+/VG	VG/VG-	Good	w/o dj
1st ed		$35	$30	$25	$22	$18	$12	70%

A Cry in the Night

		F/F	F/NF	NF/VG+	VG+/VG	VG/VG-	Good	w/o dj
1st ed		$30	$25	$20	$18	$15	$10	70%

Stillwatch 1984

"SIMON AND SCHUSTER   NEW YORK" on title page. No date on title page. Copyright
page - 19th (of 25) line - "1 3 5 7 9 10 8 6 4 2". DJ price $14.95. Quarter bound - red-orange
cloth with brown sides with no top stain. Brown pastedowns.

33

	F/F	F/NF	NF/VG+	VG+/VG	VG/VG-	Good	w/o dj
1st ed	$25	$22	$18	$15	$12	$8	70%

Weep No More, My Lady 1987

"SIMON AND SCHUSTER NEW YORK" on title page. No date on title page. Copyright page - 18th (of 24) line - "10 9 8 7 6 5 4 3 2 1". DJ price $17.95. Quarter bound - black cloth with steel-blue sides with no top stain. Gray pastedowns.

	F/F	F/NF	NF/VG+	VG+/VG	VG/VG-	Good	w/o dj
1st ed	$18	$16	$12	$9	$6	$3	80

While My Pretty One Sleeps 1989

"SIMON AND SCHUSTER/New York London/Toronto Sydney/Tokyo" on page opposite title page. No date on title page. Copyright page - 18th (of 24) line - "10 9 8 7 6 5 4 3 2 1". DJ price $19.95. Quarter bound - gray cloth with speckled gray sides with no top stain. Speckled gray pastedowns.

	F/F	F/NF	NF/VG+	VG+/VG	VG/VG-	Good	w/o dj
1st ed	$15	$14	$10	$8	$6	$3	80%

The Anastasia Syndrome 1989

"SIMON AND SCHUSTER/New York London Toronto Sydney Tokyo" on title page. No date on title page. Copyright page - 19th (of 34) line - "1 3 5 7 9 10 8 6 4 2". DJ price $19.95. Quarter bound - marroon cloth with gray sides with no top stain. Gray pastedowns.

	F/F	F/NF	NF/VG+	VG+/VG	VG/VG-	Good	w/o dj
1st ed	$15	$14	$10	$8	$6	$3	80%

Loves Music, Loves to Dance 1991

"SIMON & SCHUSTER NEW YORK LONDON TORONTO SYDNEY TOKYO SINGAPORE" on title and opposing pages. No date on title page. Copyright page - 18th (of 34) line - "1 2 3 4 5 6 7 8 9 10". DJ price $21.95. Quarter bound - black cloth with red sides with no top stain. Red pastedowns.

	F/F	F/NF	NF/VG+	VG+/VG	VG/VG-	Good	w/o dj
1st ed	$15	$14	$10	$8	$6	$3	80%

All Around the Town 1992

"SIMON & SCHUSTER NEW YORK LONDON TORONTO SYDNEY TOKYO SINGAPORE" on title and opposing pages. No date on title page. Copyright page - 18th (of 21) line - "1 3 5 7 9 10 8 6 4 2". DJ price $22.00. Quarter bound - marroon cloth with cream sides with no top stain. Cream pastedowns.

	F/F	F/NF	NF/VG+	VG+/VG	VG/VG-	Good	w/o dj
1st ed	$15	$14	$10	$8	$6	$3	80%

I'll Be Seeing You 1993

"SIMON & SCHUSTER NEW YORK LONDON TORONTO SYDNEY TOKYO SINGAPORE" on title and opposing pages. No date on title page. Copyright page - 18th (of

20) line - "1 3 5 7 9 10 8 6 4 2". DJ price $23.00. Quarter bound - dark blue cloth with dark blue sides with no top stain. Dark blue pastedowns.

	F/F	F/NF	NF/VG+	VG+/VG	VG/VG-	Good	w/o dj
1st ed	$15	$14	$10	$8	$6	$3	80%

Remember Me 1994

"SIMON & SCHUSTER   NEW YORK LONDON TORONTO SYDNEY TOKYO SINGAPORE" on title and opposing pages. No date on title page. Copyright page - 17th (of 19) line - "1 3 5 7 9 10 8 6 4 2". DJ price U.S. $23.50/Can. $29.50. Quarter bound - black cloth with black sides with no top stain. Red pastedowns.

	F/F	F/NF	NF/VG+	VG+/VG	VG/VG-	Good	w/o dj
1st ed	$15	$14	$10	$8	$6	$3	80%

Arthur Clarke

2001: A Space Odyssey 1968

"THE NEW AMERICAN LIBRARY" on title page. No date on title page. Copyright page - 4th (of 8) line - "FIRST PRINTING". DJ price - $4.95. Quarter bound - black cloth with light blue sides. Light blue space craft and figure on black background on pastedowns.

	F/F	F/NF	NF/VG+	VG+/VG	VG/VG-	Good	w/o dj
1st ed	$400	$250	$175	$125	$100	$60	50%

Rendezvous with RAMA 1973

"Harcourt Brace Jovanovich, Inc. New York" on title page. No date on title page. Copyright page - 8th and 9th (of 15) lines - "First edition/B C D E". DJ price - $6.95. Full bound - black cloth with no top stain and yellow pastedowns.

	F/F	F/NF	NF/VG+	VG+/VG	VG/VG-	Good	w/o dj
1st ed	$75	$65	$50	$30	$25	$15	60%

RAMA II 1989

"BANTAM BOOKS/NEW YORK TORONTO LONDON SYDNEY AUCKLAND" on title page. No date on title page. Copyright page - last (of 28) line - "D H 0 9 8 7 6 5 4 3 2 1". DJ price - "IN U.S./$18.95/IN CANADA/$23.95".
Quarter bound - black cloth with black paper and no top stain. White pastedowns.

	F/F	F/NF	NF/VG+	VG+/VG	VG/VG-	Good	w/o dj
1st ed	$25	$20	$15	$12	$10	$8	50%

Garden of RAMA 1991

"BANTAM BOOKS/NEW YORK TORONTO LONDON SYDNEY AUCKLAND" on title page. No date on title page. Copyright page - last (of 27) line - "BVG 0 9 8 7 6 5 4 3 2 1". DJ price - "IN U.S./$20.00/IN CANADA/$25.00".
Quarter bound - violet cloth with blue paper and no top stain. White pastedowns.

F/F	F/NF	NF/VG+	VG+/VG	VG/VG-	Good	w/o dj

1st ed		$25	$20	$15	$12	$10	$8	50%

James Clavell

King Rat 1962

"LITTLE, BROWN AND COMPANY/BOSTON TORONTO" on title page. No date on title page. Copyright page - 7th (of 10) line - "FIRST EDITION". DJ price - $5.75.
Full bound - cream cloth with olive green top stain and white pastedowns.

		F/F	F/NF	NF/VG+	VG+/VG	VG/VG-	Good	w/o dj
1st ed		$200	$175	$150	$100	$75	$50	50%

Tai-Pan 1966

"ATHENEUM (1966) NEW YORK" on title page. Copyright page - last (of 7) line - "First Edition". DJ price $6.95. Quarter bound - tan cloth with red sides and light orange top stain. Maps on yellow background on pastedowns.

		F/F	F/NF	NF/VG+	VG+/VG	VG/VG-	Good	w/o dj
1st ed		$100	$80	$65	$50	$40	$25	50%

Shogun 1975

"ATHENEUM (1975) NEW YORK" on title page. Copyright page - last (of 9) line - "First Edition". DJ price - $12.50. Quarter bound - green cloth with blue paper and yellow top stain. Maps on pastedowns with beige background.

		F/F	F/NF	NF/VG+	VG+/VG	VG/VG-	Good	w/o dj
1st ed		$100	$80	$65	$50	$40	$25	50%

Noble House 1981

"DELACORTE PRESS/NEW YORK" on title page. No date on title page.   Copyright page - 12th (of 18) line - "First Printing".   DJ price - $19.95.
Full bound - red cloth with gold top stain and black pastedowns.

		F/F	F/NF	NF/VG+	VG+/VG	VG/VG-	Good	w/o dj
1st ed		$25	$20	$15	$12	$10	$7	80%

Stephen Coonts (1946-)

The Flight of the Intruder 1986

This story of naval aviators in the Vietnam War was the basis for the 1991 film starring Danny Glover.

"Naval Institute Press, Annapolis, Maryland" on title page.   No date on title page.
Copyright page - 21st (of 24) line - "10 9 8 7 6 5 4 3 2 1". DJ price - $15.95.
Quarter bound - black cloth with light gray paper and no top stain. Black pastedowns.

		F/F	F/NF	NF/VG+	VG+/VG	VG/VG-	Good	w/o dj
1st ed		$35	$30	$25	$20	$10	$5	80%

Final Flight 1988

The return of naval aviator Jake Grafton, but with the locale changed to the Mediterranean.

"Doubleday/NEW YORK LONDON TORONTO SYDNEY AUCKLAND" on title page. No date on title page. Copyright page - 26th, 27th, and 28th (of 28) lines - "October 1988/First Edition/BG". DJ price - U.S. $19.95/Canada $24.95. Quarter bound - black cloth with blue paper and no top stain. Map on pastedown.

		F/F	F/NF	NF/VG+	VG+/VG	VG/VG-	Good	w/o dj
1st ed		$20	$15	$12	$10	$8	$5	80%

The Minotaur 1986

"Doubleday - New York, London, Toronto, Sydney, Auckland" on title page. No date on title page. Copyright page - 26th, 27th, and 28th (of 28) lines - "October 1989 / FIRST EDITION / BG". DJ price - U.S. $19.95/Canada $24.95.
Quarter bound - black cloth with black paper and no top stain. Red pastedowns.

		F/F	F/NF	NF/VG+	VG+/VG	VG/VG-	Good	w/o dj
1st ed		$20	$15	$12	$10	$8	$5	80%

Bernard Cornwell

Sharpe's Eagle 1981

"THE VIKING PRESS NEW YORK" on title page. No date on title page. Copyright page - 13 lines plus Viking ship symbol at bottom. Fourth line - "First published in 1981 by The Viking Press".
DJ price - $12.95. "0481" on lower right corner of front dj flap.
Quarter bound - tan cloth with brown sides and no top stain. Tan pastedowns.

		F/F	F/NF	NF/VG+	VG+/VG	VG/VG-	Good	w/o dj
1st ed		$60	$50	$40	$30	$25	$6	70%

Sharpe's Gold 1982

"THE VIKING PRESS NEW YORK" on title page. No date on title page. Copyright page - 13 lines plus viking ship symbol at bottom. Third line - "Published in 1982 by The Viking Press". DJ price - $13.95. "0182" on lower right corner of front dj flap.
Quarter bound - tan cloth with dark brown sides and no top stain. Speckled tan pastedowns.

		F/F	F/NF	NF/VG+	VG+/VG	VG/VG-	Good	w/o dj
1st ed		$50	$40	$30	$25	$20	$5	70%

Sharpe's Company 1982

"The Viking Press New York" on title page. No date on title page. Copyright page - no mention of edition number - 3rd (of 12) line - "Published in 1982 by the Viking Press". DJ price - $14.95.
Quarter bound - tan cloth with burnt orange sides and no top stain. Tan pastedowns.

		F/F	F/NF	NF/VG+	VG+/VG	VG/VG-	Good	w/o dj
1st ed		$40	$35	$25	$15	$10	$5	70%

Sharpe's Sword 1983

"THE VIKING PRESS   NEW YORK" on title page. No date on title page. Copyright page -
no mention of edition number - 3rd (of 12) line - "Published in 1983 by the Viking Press".
DJ price - $15.95.
Quarter bound - gold cloth with tan sides and no top stain. White pastedowns.

		F/F	F/NF	NF/VG+	VG+/VG	VG/VG-	Good	w/odj
1st ed		$40	$35	$25	$15	$10	$5	70%

Sharpe's Enemy 1984

"THE VIKING PRESS   NEW YORK" on title page. No date on title page. Copyright page -
3rd (of 12) line - "First published in 1984 by The Viking Press".
DJ price - $16.95. "03163084" on lower right corner of front dj flap.
Quarter bound - black cloth with light tan sides and no top stain. White pastedowns.

		F/F	F/NF	NF/VG+	VG+/VG	VG/VG-	Good	w/odj
1st ed		$40	$35	$25	$15	$10	$5	70%

Sharpe's Honour 1985

"VIKING" on title page. No date on title page. Copyright page - 5th (of 24) line - "First
American Edition". DJ price - $16.95.
Quarter bound - white cloth with brown sides and no top stain. White pastedowns.

		F/F	F/NF	NF/VG+	VG+/VG	VG/VG-	Good	w/odj
1st ed		$35	$30	$25	$15	$10	$5	80%

Sharpe's Regiment 1986

"VIKING" on title page. No date on title page. Copyright page - 5th (of 18) line - "First
American Edition". DJ price - $16.95.
Quarter bound - white cloth with purple sides and no top stain. White pastedowns.

		F/F	F/NF	NF/VG+	VG+/VG	VG/VG-	Good	w/odj
1st ed		$35	$30	$25	$15	$10	$5	80%

Sharpe's Siege 1987

		F/F	F/NF	NF/VG+	VG+/VG	VG/VG-	Good	w/odj
1st ed		$35	$30	$25	$15	$10	$5	80%

Sharpe's Rifles 1988

"VIKING" on title page. No date on title page. Copyright page - 15th (of 38) line - "First
American Edition".   DJ price $17.95. "09173088" on lower right corner of front dj flap.
Quarter bound - black cloth with gold sides and no top stain. White pastedowns.

		F/F	F/NF	NF/VG+	VG+/VG	VG/VG-	Good	w/odj
1st ed		$35	$30	$25	$15	$10	$5	80%

Sharpe's Revenge 1989

"VIKING" on title page. No date on title page. Copyright page - 15th (of 36) line - "First

American Edition". 17th line - "1 3 5 7 9 10 8 6 4 2". DJ price $17.95.
Quarter bound - black cloth with orange sides and no top stain. White pastedowns.

		F/F	F/NF	NF/VG +	VG +/VG	VG/VG -	Good	w/o dj
1st ed		$35	$30	$25	$15	$10	$5	80%

Waterloo 1990

"VIKING" on title page. No date on title page. Copyright page - 13th (of 39) line - "First
American Edition". 16th line - "1 3 5 7 9 10 8 6 4 2". DJ price $18.95. "0690" on lower right
corner of front dj flap. Quarter bound - black cloth with orange sides and no top stain.
White pastedowns.

		F/F	F/NF	NF/VG +	VG +/VG	VG/VG -	Good	w/o dj
1st ed		$25	$20	$15	$10	$7	$5	80%

Sharpe's Devil 1992

"Harper Collins *Publishers*" on title page. No date on title page. Copyright page - 10th (of 22)
line - "FIRST EDITION". 22nd line "92 93 94 95 96 ♦ / HC 10 9 8 7 6 5 4 3 2 1".
DJ price USA $20.00/CANADA $26.75". "0692P" on lower right corner of front dj flap.
Quarter bound - navy blue cloth with red sides and no top stain. White pastedowns.

		F/F	F/NF	NF/VG +	VG +/VG	VG/VG -	Good	w/o dj
1st ed		$25	$20	$15	$10	$7	$5	80%

Patricia Cornwell

A Time for Remembering 1983   The Ruth Bell Graham Story

"HARPER & ROW, PUBLISHERS, SAN FRANCISCO/Cambridge, Hagerstown, New York,
Philadelphia/London, Mexico City, Sao Paulo, Sydney" on title page. No date on title page.
Copyright page - 15th (of 25) line - "FIRST EDITION". Last line - "83 84 85 86 87 10 9 8 7 6 5 4
3 2 1". DJ price $13.95. Full bound - tan cloth no top stain and red pastedowns.

		F/F	F/NF	NF/VG +	VG +/VG	VG/VG -	Good	w/o dj
1st ed		$150	$125	$80	$60	$40	$15	80%

Post-Mortem 1990

"CHARLES SCRIBNER'S SONS/NEW YORK" on title page. No date on title page.
Copyright page - 23rd (of 24) line - "10 9 8 7 6 5 4 3 2 1". DJ price $16.95/$23.75 IN CANADA.
Quarterbound - navy cloth with red sides and no top stain. White pastedowns.

		F/F	F/NF	NF/VG +	VG +/VG	VG/VG -	Good	w/o dj
1st ed		$600	$500	$400	$300	$200	$75	80%

Body of Evidence 1991

"CHARLES SCRIBNER'S SONS *New York* /COLLIER MACMILLAN CANADA *Toronto*
/MAXWELL MACMILLAN INTERNATIONAL *New York Oxford Singapore Sydney*" on
title page. No date on title page. Copyright page - 26th (of 27) line - "10 9 8 7 6 5 4 3 2 1". DJ
price $24.95 IN CANADA $18.95. Quarterbound - black cloth with gray sides and no top
stain. Red pastedowns.

	F/F	F/NF	NF/VG+	VG+/VG	VG/VG-	Good	w/o dj
1st ed	$85	$70	$50	$35	$25	$10	90%

All That Remains 1992

"CHARLES SCRIBNER'S SONS *New York* /COLLIER MACMILLAN CANADA *Toronto* /MAXWELL MACMILLAN INTERNATIONAL *New York Oxford Singapore Sydney*" on title page. No date on title page. Copyright page - 28th (of 29) line - "10 9 8 7 6 5 4 3 2 1". Quarterbound - black cloth with gray sides and no top stain. Red pastedowns. DJ price $25.95 IN CANADA $20.00. (Same dj for later editions)

	F/F	F/NF	NF/VG+	VG+/VG	VG/VG-	Good	w/o dj
1st ed	$35	$30	$20	$12	$10	$7	90%

Cruel and Unusual 1993

"CHARLES SCRIBNER'S SONS *New York* /MAXWELL MACMILLAN CANADA *Toronto* /MAXWELL MACMILLAN INTERNATIONAL *New York Oxford Singapore Sydney*" on title page. No date on title page. Copyright page - 31st (of 32) line - "10 9 8 7 6 5 4 3 2 1". Quarterbound - black cloth with gray sides and no top stain. Red pastedowns. DJ price $21.00/$26.95 IN CANADA. (Same dj for later editions)

	F/F	F/NF	NF/VG+	VG+/VG	VG/VG-	Good	w/o dj
1st ed	$20	$12	$10	$8	$6	$4	90%

Body Farm 1994

"CHARLES SCRIBNER'S SONS/New York London Totonto Sydney Tokyo Singapore" on title page. No date on title page. Copyright page - 13th (of 24) line - "1 3 5 7 9 10 8 6 4 2". DJ price U.S. $23.00 /Can. $30.00. Quarterbound - black cloth with tan sides and no top stain. Gray pastedowns.

	F/F	F/NF	NF/VG+	VG+/VG	VG/VG-	Good	w/o dj
1st ed	$20	$12	$10	$8	$6	$4	90%

From Potter's Field 1995

"Scribner/New York London Totonto Sydney Tokyo Singapore" on title page. No date on title page. Copyright page - 14th (of 24) line - "10 9 8 7 6 5 4 3 2 1". DJ price U.S. $24.00 /Can. $32.50. Quarterbound - dark gray cloth with light gray sides and no top stain. Blue pastedowns.

	F/F	F/NF	NF/VG+	VG+/VG	VG/VG-	Good	w/o dj
1st ed	$15	$12	$10	$8	$6	$4	90%

Michael Crichton (1942-)

U.S. novelist, born in Chicago and educated at Harvard Medical School. His style of writing reflects his scientific and medical background. Several of his novels have been made into major motion pictures - most notably Jurassic PArk, Rising Sun and Congo. Crichton has written under the pseudonym of John Lange, Jeffrey Hudson, and Michael Douglas.

The Andromeda Strain 1969

"ALFRED A. KNOPF/NEW YORK 1969" on title page.
Copyright page - 3rd (of 13) line - "FIRST EDITION". DJ price - $5.95.
Quarter bound - cream cloth with black paper and gray top stain. Black pastedowns.

		F/F	F/NF	NF/VG+	VG+/VG	VG/VG-	Good	w/o dj
1st ed		$150	$100	$75	$50	$35	$15	70%

Venom Business 1969 Written as John Lange.

"THE WORLD PUBLISHING COMPANY/NEW YORK AND CLEVELAND" on title page.
Copyright page - 5th (of 18) line -"First printing - May, 1969". DJ price - $5.95.
Quarter bound - yellow with green sides and no top stain. Black pastedowns.

		F/F	F/NF	NF/VG+	VG+/VG	VG/VG-	Good	w/o dj
1st ed		$150	$125	$90	$60	$45	$30	50%

Five Patients 1970

"Alfred A. Knopf/New York 1970" on title page. Copyright page - last (of 13) line - "First Edition". DJ price - $5.95. Full bound - red cloth with gray top stain and white pastedowns.

		F/F	F/NF	NF/VG+	VG+/VG	VG/VG-	Good	w/o dj
1st ed		$75	$60	$50	$35	$25	$15	70%

Dealing or the Berkeley-to-Boston Forty-Brick Lost-Bag Blues 1970 Written as Michael Douglas

"Alfred A. Knopf/New York/1971" on title page. Copyright page indicates a copyright date of 1970. Copyright page - last (of 12) line - "FIRST EDITION". DJ price - $5.95.
Quarter bound - gold cloth with cream sides and light green top stain. Gold pastedowns.

		F/F	F/NF	NF/VG+	VG+/VG	VG/VG-	Good	w/o dj
1st ed		$85	$75	$60	$45	$35	$20	50%

The Terminal Man 1972

"Alfred A. Knopf, New York, 1972" on title page. Copyright page - last (of 18) line - "FIRST EDITION". DJ price - $6.95. Quarter bound -gold cloth with gray paper and yellow top stain. Gray pastedowns with drawing of brain.

		F/F	F/NF	NF/VG+	VG+/VG	VG/VG-	Good	w/o dj
1st ed		$60	$50	$40	$30	$20	$10	70%

Binary 1972 Written as John Lange

"New York: Alfred A. Knopf/1972" on title page. Copyright page - last (of 14) line - "First Edition". DJ price - $5.95 at top, 7/72 at bottom of front flap. Quarter bound - red spine with tan sides and red top stain. White pastedowns.

		F/F	F/NF	NF/VG+	VG+/VG	VG/VG-	Good	w/o dj
1st ed		$75	$60	$50	$35	$25	$15	70%

The Great Train Robbery 1975

"ALFRED A. KNOPF/NEW YORK/1975" on title page.

Copyright page - last (of 17) line - "FIRST EDITION". DJ price - $7.95.
Quarter bound - brown cloth with green paper and green-gray top stain. White pastedowns.

		F/F	F/NF	NF/VG+	VG+/VG	VG/VG-	Good	w/o dj
1st ed		$50	$40	$35	$30	$25	$15	70%

Eaters of the Dead 1976

"Alfred A. Knopf, New York, 1976" on title page. Copyright page - last (of 23) line - "FIRST
EDITION". DJ price - $6.95. Quarter bound - black cloth with tan paper and red top stain.
White pastedowns. Note: The book club edition indicates First Edition on the copyright page but is
distinguished from a true first edition by the book club indentation on the rear board.

		F/F	F/NF	NF/VG+	VG+/VG	VG/VG-	Good	w/o dj
1st ed		$75	$60	$45	$35	$25	$15	70%

Jasper Johns 1977

		F/F	F/NF	NF/VG+	VG+/VG	VG/VG-	Good	w/o dj
1st ed		$100	$75	$60	$45	$35	$20	50%

Congo 1980

"ALFRED A. KNOPF New York 1980" on title page.
Copyright page - last (of 16) line - "FIRST TRADE EDITION". DJ price - $10.95.
Quarter bound - red cloth with black paper and no top stain. White pastedowns.

		F/F	F/NF	NF/VG+	VG+/VG	VG/VG-	Good	w/o dj
1st ed		$70	$55	$40	$30	$20	$15	70%

Electronic Life 1983

"Alfred A. Knopf, New York 1983" on title page. Copyright page - last (of 24) line - "FIRST
EDITION". DJ price - $12.95. Quarter bound - black cloth with gray paper and no top stain.
White pastedowns.

		F/F	F/NF	NF/VG+	VG+/VG	VG/VG-	Good	w/o dj
1st ed		$40	$35	$30	$20	$15	$8	70%

Sphere 1987

"ALFRED A. KNOPF NEW YORK 1987" on title page. Copyright page - last (of 14) line -
"FIRST EDITION". DJ price - $17.95. Quarter bound - green cloth with blue paper and no
top stain. White pastedowns.

		F/F	F/NF	NF/VG+	VG+/VG	VG/VG-	Good	w/o dj
1st ed		$15	$12	$10	$8	$6	$4	80%

Jurassic Park 1990

"ALFRED A. KNOPF *New York* 1990" on title page. Copyright page - 11th (of 13) line -
"First Trade Edition". DJ price - U.S.A. $19.95/Canada $26.00
Quarter bound - dark blue cloth with light blue paper and no top stain. White pastedowns.

		F/F	F/NF	NF/VG+	VG+/VG	VG/VG-	Good	w/o dj
1st ed		$40	$35	$25	$20	$15	$10	80%

Rising Sun 1990

"ALFRED A. KNOPF *New York* 1992" on title page. Copyright page - 19th (of 30) line
"First Trade Edition". DJ price - U.S.A. $22.00/Canada $28.00.
Quarter bound - black cloth with orange paper and no top stain. White pastedowns.

		F/F	F/NF	NF/VG+	VG+/VG	VG/VG-	Good	w/o dj
1st ed		$15	$12	$10	$8	$6	$4	80%

Clive Cussler

The Mediterranean Caper 1973 U.K. 1973 U.S.

Author's first book published in U.K. as *May Day*. First published in U.S. in paperback by
Pyramid Books in 1973. #V3179 Price $1.25. Copyright page - "First printing November
1973. Page edges stained green.

	Fine	VG+	VG-	Good
1st US ed wrapps	$50	$35	$20	$10

Raise the Titanic! 1976

"The Viking Press New York" on title page. Copyright page - 5th (of 17) line - "First
published in 1976 by The Viking Press."   No other mention of printing number. DJ price -
$8.95. Quarter bound - lime green cloth with blue sides and no top stain. Blue pastedowns.

		F/F	F/NF	NF/VG+	VG+/VG	VG/VG-	Good	w/o dj
1st ed		$60	$45	$30	$25	$15	$8	60%

Vixon 03 1978

"The Viking Press New York" on title page. Copyright page - 3rd (of 14) line - "First
published in 1978 by The Viking Press."   No other mention of printing number. DJ price -
$9.95. Quarter bound - gray cloth with steel blue sides and no top stain. White pastedowns.

		F/F	F/NF	NF/VG+	VG+/VG	VG/VG-	Good	w/o dj
1st ed		$50	$40	$30	$25	$15	$8	60%

Night Probe 1981

"BANTAM BOOKS/Toronto/New York/London/Sydney" on title page. No date on title
page. Copyright page - last (20th) line - "0 9 8 7 6 5 4 3 2 1"   DJ price - $13.95.
Quarter bound - blue cloth, blue sides with no top stain and white pastedowns.

		F/F	F/NF	NF/VG+	VG+/VG	VG/VG-	Good	w/o dj
1st ed		$35	$25	$20	$15	$12	$8	80%

Pacific Vortex 1983 Published first as a Bantom paperback.

Cover "22866-8 * $3.95". Cover of first printings also contains "A BRAND-NEW DIRK PITT
THRILLER!/NEVER BEFORE PUBLISHED!" which is dropped from later printings. On rear
cover, at the bottom of the bar code box is "ISBN 0-553-22866-8". First page is color drawing
of skindiver. Copyright page - 2nd (of 17) *"A Bantam Book/January 1983"*. (No further
printings are indicted.) Last line - "H 0 9 8 7 6 5 4 3 2 1".

	Fine ·	VG+	VG-	Good
1st US ed wrapps	$15	$10	$7	$3

Deep Six 1984

"SIMON AND SCHUSTER/NEW YORK" on title page. No date on title page.
Copyright page - 19th (of 25) line - "10 9 8 7 6 5 4 3 2 1" DJ price - $18.95.
Quarter bound - dark blue with light blue sides and no top stain. White pastedowns.

	F/F	F/NF	NF/VG+	VG+/VG	VG/VG-	Good	w/o dj
1st ed	$20	$15	$12	$10	$8	$6	80%

Cyclops 1986

"SIMON AND SCHUSTER/NEW YORK" on title page. No date on title page.
Copyright page - 17th (of 28) line - "10 9 8 7 6 5 4 3 2 1" . DJ price - $18.95.
Quarter bound - black cloth with blue sides and no top stain. White pastedowns.

	F/F	F/NF	NF/VG+	VG+/VG	VG/VG-	Good	w/o dj
1st ed	$20	$15	$12	$10	$8	$6	80%

Treasure 1988

"SIMON AND SCHUSTER NEW YORK LONDON TORONTO SYDNEY TOKYO" on
title page. No date on title page. Copyright page - 18th (of 24) line - "10 9 8 7 6 5 4 3 2 1". DJ
price - $18.95. Quarter bound - dark blue with blue sides and no top stain. Blue pastedowns.

	F/F	F/NF	NF/VG+	VG+/VG	VG/VG-	Good	w/o dj
1st ed	$15	$12	$10	$8	$6	$4	80%

Dragon 1990

"Simon & Schuster" on page opposite title page. "New York London Toronto Sydney
Tokyo Singapore" on title page. No date on title page. Copyright page - 18th (of 29) line -
"10 9 8 7 6 5 4 3 2 1". DJ price - $21.95.
Quarter bound - red cloth with blue paper sides and no top stain. Blue pastedowns.

	F/F	F/NF	NF/VG+	VG+/VG	VG/VG-	Good	w/o dj
1st ed	$15	$12	$10	$8	$6	$4	80%

Sahara 1992

"Simon & Schuster New York London Toronto Sydney Tokyo Singapore" on title page.
No date on title page. Copyright page - 18th (of 39) line - "1 3 5 7 9 10 8 6 4 2".
DJ price - $23.00.
Quarter bound - dark blue cloth with blue paper sides and no top stain. Blue pastedowns.

	F/F	F/NF	NF/VG+	VG+/VG	VG/VG-	Good	w/o dj
1st ed	$15	$12	$10	$8	$6	$4	80%

Inca Gold 1994

"Simon & Schuster New York London Toronto Sydney Tokyo Singapore" on title page.

No date on title page. Copyright page - 17th (of 27) line - "10 9 8 7 6 5 4 3 2 1". DJ price - U.S. $24.00/Can. $30.00. Quarter bound - black cloth with red sides and no top stain. Red pastedowns.

	F/F	F/NF	NF/VG+	VG+/VG	VG/VG-	Good	w/o dj
1st ed	$15	$12	$10	$8	$6	$4	80%

Len Deighton

The Ipcress File   1962 U.K.   1963 U.S.

	F/F	F/NF	NF/VG+	VG+/VG	VG/VG-	Good	w/o dj
1st US ed	$150	$125	$100	$80	$60	$30	60%
1st UK ed	$400	$350	$275	$200	$150	$60	60%

Horse Under Water   1963 U.K.   1968 U.S.

"NEW YORK/G.P. *Putnam's Sons*" on title page. No date on title page. Copyright page - 2nd (of 7) line - "FIRST AMERICAN EDITION 1968". Last line - "PRINTED IN THE UNITED STATES OF AMERICA". Uncut page edges. DJ price $4.95. Full bound - blue cloth with no top stain and orange pastedowns.

"JONATHAN CAPE/THIRTY BEDFORD SQUARE/LONDON" on title page. No date on title page. Copyright page - 1st (of 6) line - "FIRST PUBLISHED 1963". DJ price 16s. Full bound - red cloth with no top stain and crossword puzzle on pastedowns.

	F/F	F/NF	NF/VG+	VG+/VG	VG/VG-	Good	w/o dj
1st US ed	$50	$40	$30	$25	$20	$10	70%
1st UK ed	$300	$250	$175	$125	$100	$50	60%

Funeral in Berlin   1964 U.K.   1965 U.S.

"NEW YORK/G.P. *Putnam's Sons*" on title page. No date on title page. Copyright page - 1st (of 7) line - "FIRST AMERICAN EDITION 1965". Last line - "MANUFACTURED IN THE UNITED STATES OF AMERICA". Later printings have printing number, such as *"Fifth Printing"*, on top of front dj flap and an 8th line that such as "Fifth Impression" on the copyright page. Uncut page edges. DJ price $4.95. Quarter bound - black cloth with white sides and red top stain. Red pastedowns

	F/F	F/NF	NF/VG+	VG+/VG	VG/VG-	Good	w/o dj
1st US ed	$75	$70	$60	$50	$40	$20	70%
1st UK ed	$200	$175	$125	$90	$70	$40	60%

Len Deighton's French Cook Book   1965 Paperback Original First Edition

"LONDON/PENGUIN BOOKS LIMITED" on title page. Copyright page - 4th (of 12) line - "First published 1965". A Penguin Book PH117. 10'6

	Fine	VG+	VG-	Good
1st UK ed	$60	$35	$20	$5

The Billion Dollar Brain   1966 U.K.   1966 U.S.

"*G.P. Putnam's Sons New York*" on title page. No date on title page. Copyright page - 7th (of 8) line - "*First Impression*" . DJ with blue ink and DJ price $4.95. Full bound - red cloth with no top stain and gold pastedowns.

"Jonathan Cape/Thirty Bedford Square London" on title page. No date on title page. Copyright page - 1st (of 9) line - "FIRST PUBLISHED 1966". DJ very fragile silver foil with price 21s. Full bound - navy blue cloth with no top stain and computer programming page on pastedowns.

	F/F	F/NF	NF/VG+	VG+/VG	VG/VG-	Good	w/o dj
1st US ed	$60	$50	$40	$30	$25	$15	70%
1st UK ed	$150	$125	$100	$75	$60	$30	60%

An Expensive Place to Die 1967

	F/F	F/NF	NF/VG+	VG+/VG	VG/VG-	Good	w/o dj
1st ed	$55	$45	$30	$25	$20	$10	70%

Bomber 1970

"HARPER & ROW, PUBLISHERS/NEW YORK AND EVANSTON" on title page. No date on title page. Copyright page - 9th (of 10) line - "FIRST U.S. EDITION 1968". DJ price $7.95. Quarter bound - black cloth with lime green sides and green top stain. Olive pastedowns.

	F/F	F/NF	NF/VG+	VG+/VG	VG/VG-	Good	w/o dj
1st ed	$45	$35	$25	$20	$15	$7	70%

Declarations of War 1971 in U.S. as Eleven Declarations of War 1974

"New York and London/Harcourt Brace Jovanovich" on title page. No date on title page. Copyright page - 15th and 16th (of 16) lines - "First edition/BCDE" DJ price $6.95. Quarter bound - black cloth with yellow sides and no top stain. White pastedowns.

"Jonathan Cape Thirty Bedford Square London" on title page. No date on title page. Copyright page - 1st (of 8) line - "FIRST PUBLISHED 1971". Wrap around pictorial dj. Full bound - black cloth with red top stain and red pastedowns.

	F/F	F/NF	NF/VG+	VG+/VG	VG/VG-	Good	w/o dj
1st US ed	$30	$25	$20	$15	$12	$8	70%
1st UK ed	$100	$90	$75	$50	$35	$20	60%

Yesterday's Spy 1975

"HARCOURT BRACE JOVANOVICH NEW YORK AND LONDON" on title page. No date on title page. Copyright page - 15th and 16th (of 16) lines - "First American edition/BCDE". DJ price $7.95. Quarter bound - brown cloth with orange sides and orange top stain. Brown speckled pastedowns.

"JONATHAN CAPE/THIRTY BEDFORD SQUARE LONDON" on title page. No date on title page. Copyright page - 1st (of 7) line - "FIRST PUBLISHED 1975". DJ price - £2.75. Full bound - brown cloth with dark brown top stain and cream pastedowns.

	F/F	F/NF	NF/VG+	VG+/VG	VG/VG-	Good	w/o dj
1st US ed	$20	$18	$15	$12	$10	$5	80%

	F/F	F/NF	NF/VG+	VG+/VG	VG/VG-	Good	w/o dj
1st UK ed	$60	$50	$40	$25	$20	$10	70%

Catch a Falling Spy 1976

"Harcourt Brace Jovanovich/New York and London" on title page. No date on title page. Copyright page - 15th and 16th (of 16) lines - "First American Edition/BCDE". DJ price $7.95. Quarter bound - brown cloth with orange sides and red-orange top stain. Speckled tan pastedowns.

	F/F	F/NF	NF/VG+	VG+/VG	VG/VG-	Good	w/o dj
1st ed	$25	$20	$15	$12	$10	$5	80%

SS-GB   U.K. 1978   U.S. 1979

"ALFRED A KNOPF/NEW YORK/1979" on title page. Copyright page - 28th (of 28) line - "First American Edition". DJ price $9.95. Quarter bound - cream cloth with blue sides and light blue top stain. White pastedowns.

"JONATHAN CAPE/THIRTY BEDFORD SQUARE LONDON" on title page. No date on title page. Copyright page - 1st (of 19) line - "First published 1978". DJ price - £4.95. Full bound - black cloth with red top stain and red pastedowns.

	F/F	F/NF	NF/VG+	VG+/VG	VG/VG-	Good	w/o dj
1st US ed	$20	$18	$15	$12	$10	$5	80%
1st UK ed	$50	$40	$30	$20	$15	$10	70%

Mexico Set 1984

Copyright page - 16th (of 27) line - "First published 1984". DJ price - £8.95. Full bound - black cloth with no top stain and red pastedowns.

	F/F	F/NF	NF/VG+	VG+/VG	VG/VG-	Good	w/o dj
1st US ed	$12	$10	$8	$6	$4	$2	80%
1st UK ed	$25	$20	$15	$10	$8	$5	80%

London Match 1985

Copyright page - 10th (of 16) line - "First published 1985". DJ price - £9.95. Full bound - black cloth with no top stain and red pastedowns.

	F/F	F/NF	NF/VG+	VG+/VG	VG/VG-	Good	w/o dj
1st US ed	$12	$10	$8	$6	$4	$2	80%
1st UK ed	$25	$20	$15	$10	$8	$5	80%

Allan W. Eckert

The Frontiersman 1967   First volume in the four book series "The Winning of America.

"LITTLE, BROWN AND COMPANY BOSTON TORONTO" on title page. No date on title page. Copyright page - 9th (of 12) line - "FIRST EDITION". DJ price - $8.95. Full bound - green cloth with no top stain and map with green top and bottom stripes on pastedowns.

	F/F	F/NF	NF/VG+	VG+/VG	VG/VG-	Good	w/o dj

1st ed		$35	$30	$25	$18	$15	$10	70%

Wilderness Empire 1969 Second volume in the four book series "The Winning of America.

"LITTLE, BROWN AND COMPANY BOSTON TORONTO" on title page. No date on title page. Copyright page - 9th (of 12) line - "FIRST EDITION". DJ price - $8.95. Full bound - maroon cloth with no top stain and map with maroon picture frame on pastedowns.

		F/F	F/NF	NF/VG+	VG+/VG	VG/VG-	Good	w/odj
1st ed		$30	$25	$20	$15	$12	$9	70%

The Conquerors 1970 Third volume in the four book series "The Winning of America.

"LITTLE, BROWN AND COMPANY BOSTON TORONTO" on title page. No date on title page. Copyright page - 10th (of 13) line - "FIRST EDITION". DJ price $10.00. Full bound - green cloth with no top stain and map with green picture frame on pastedowns.

		F/F	F/NF	NF/VG+	VG+/VG	VG/VG-	Good	w/odj
1st ed		$30	$25	$20	$15	$12	$9	70%

The Wilderness War 1978 Fourth volume in the four book series "The Winning of America.

"LITTLE, BROWN AND COMPANY BOSTON TORONTO" on title page. Copyright page - 8th (of 23) line - "FIRST EDITION". Full bound - green cloth with no top stain and map on pastedowns.

		F/F	F/NF	NF/VG+	VG+/VG	VG/VG-	Good	w/odj
1st ed		$30	$25	$20	$15	$12	$9	70%

The Great Auk 1963

"LITTLE, BROWN AND COMPANY BOSTON TORONTO" on title page. Copyright page - 7th (of 10) line - "FIRST EDITION". Full bound - light blue cloth with light blue top stain and map on pastedowns.

		F/F	F/NF	NF/VG+	VG+/VG	VG/VG-	Good	w/odj
1st ed		$40	$30	$20	$15	$12	$9	60%

The Court Martial of Daniel Boone 1973

"Little, Brown and Company/Boston/Toronto" on title page. No date on title page. Copyright page - 8th and 9th (of 18) lines - "FIRST EDITION/T10/73". Quarter bound - navy blue cloth with gold sides and no top stain. Map of Kentucky on pastedowns.

		F/F	F/NF	NF/VG+	VG+/VG	VG/VG-	Good	w/odj
1st ed		$30	$25	$20	$15	$12	$9	70%

F. Scott Fitzgerald (1896-40)

U.S. novelist, author of eleven complete novels, all worth of preservation.

The Evil Eye 1915 A Musical Comedy in Two Acts. Cincinnati, New York and London: The John Church Co. Cloth backed flexible illustrated boards.

		Fine	NF	VG+	VG	VG-	Good
1st ed		$3,000	$2,200	$1,300	$1,000	$700	$300

Princeton Bric-a-Brac 1917 Princeton University annual publication by the junior class in Fitzgerald's senior year contains his poems and several group photos with him shown. Issued without dust jacket.

		Fine	NF	VG+	VG	VG-	Good
1st ed		$300	$250	$175	$125	$100	$60

A Book of Princeton Verse 1919 Contains poems by Fitzgerald.

		Fine	NF	VG+	VG	VG-	Good
1st ed		$300	$250	$175	$125	$100	$60

This Side of Paradise 1920

		Fine	NF	VG+	VG	VG-	Good
1st ed		$1,000	$750	$500	$300	$250	$125

Flappers and Philosophers 1920 5,000 copies

		Fine	NF	VG+	VG	VG-	Good
1st ed		$600	$500	$300	$200	$175	$100

Tales of the Jazz Age 1922 First two printings both have "an" for "and" on page 236, line 6.

		Fine	NF	VG+	VG	VG-	Good
1st ed		$500	$400	$250	$175	$150	$75

The Beautiful and the Damned 1922 1st issue should not have the Scribner seal on the copyright page nor should it have leaf of ads at back. Titles in this leaf of ads should be on inside flap of dj. 1st issue dj is white lettering outlined in black and is extremely rare in any condition.

		F/F	F/NF	NF/VG+	VG+/VG	VG/VG-	Good	w/o dj
1st ed		$5,000	$4,000	$3,000	$2,000	$1,500	$750	10%

The Vegetable or From President to Postman 1923

		F/F	F/NF	NF/VG+	VG+/VG	VG/VG-	Good	w/o dj
1st ed		$1,500	$1,200	$900	$650	$500	$300	15%

The Great Gatsby 1925 Lines 9 and 10 on page 205 of 1st issue should read "sick in tired of it". Later issues correct this to "sick and tired of it".

		F/F	F/NF	NF/VG+	VG+/VG	VG/VG-	Good	w/o dj
1st ed		$6,000	$5,000	$4,000	$3,000	$2,200	$1,000	10%

All the Sad Young Men 1926

		F/F	F/NF	NF/VG+	VG+/VG	VG/VG-	Good	w/o dj
1st ed		$3,000	$2,500	$1,800	$1,200	$900	$500	10%

Taps at Reveille 1935 2nd state pages 349 - 352 are cancels. 1st and 2nd state dj.

Page 351 lines 29 - 30 on 2nd printing read "Oh, things like that happen".

		F/F	F/NF	NF/VG+	VG+/VG	VG/VG-	Good	w/o dj
1st ed		$2,700	$2,200	$1,500	$1,200	$1,000	$500	10%

The Last Tycoon 1941

		F/F	F/NF	NF/VG+	VG+/VG	VG/VG-	Good	w/o dj
1st ed		$750	$600	$500	$400	$300	$150	15%

The Crack-Up 1945

		F/F	F/NF	NF/VG+	VG+/VG	VG/VG-	Good	w/o dj
1st ed		$200	$150	$100	$85	$60	$40	25%

Ian Fleming (1908-64)

British novelist, born in London, educated at Eton and Sandhurst, Fleming authored 14 James Bond stories whose total worldwide sales exceed forty million copies. In 1939, at the age of 31, he went to Moscow as a special correspondent for The Times of London. Later that year he joined the British Naval Intelligence where he served throughout World War II. During the years he was writing the James Bond novels, Fleming divided his time between London and Jamaica.

Casino Royale 1953 U.K. 4,730 copies   1954 U.S.

"THE MACMILLAN COMPANY/1954" on title page. Copyright page - 1st (of 10) line - "COPYRIGHT 1953 BY". 9th line - "FIRST EDITION". Rear panel of dj "Casino Royale..../ was an immediate sensation..."
Full bound - dark green cloth with red print and no top stain. White pastedowns.

		F/F	F/NF	NF/VG+	VG+/VG	VG/VG-	Good	w/o dj
1st ed	U.S.	$300	$225	$175	$125	$100	$65	40%
1st ed	U.K.	$2,200	$1,800	$1,300	$900	$700	$350	20%

Live and Let Die 1954 U.K. 7,500 copies   1955 U.S.

"THE MACMILLAN COMPANY/NEW YORK" on title page. No date on title page. Copyright page - 6th (of 7) line - "FIRST PRINTING". A Cock Robin Thriller. DJ price - $3.00. Full bound - gold cloth with no top stain and white pastedowns.

		F/F	F/NF	NF/VG+	VG+/VG	VG/VG-	Good	w/o dj
1st ed	U.S.	$275	$200	$150	$125	$100	$50	33%
1st ed	U.K.	$1,050	$800	$600	$450	$375	$200	20%

Moonraker 1955 U.K. 1955 U.S.

		F/F	F/NF	NF/VG+	VG+/VG	VG/VG-	Good	w/o dj
1st ed	U.S.	$225	$175	$130	$110	$90	$45	33%
1st ed	U.K.	$900	$700	$550	$425	$350	$175	20%

Diamonds Are Forever 1956 U.K. 12,500 copies   1956 U.S.

"JONATHAN CAPE/THIRTY BEDFORD SQUARE/LONDON" on title page. No date on title page. Copyright page - 1st (of 4) line - "FIRST PUBLISHED 1956". DJ price 12s 6d. Full bound - black cloth with no top stain and white pastedowns.

"NEW YORK 1956/THE MACMILLAN COMPANY" on title page. Copyright page - 9th (of 11) line - "FIRST PRINTING". Full bound - gray cloth with no top stain and white pastedowns.

		F/F	F/NF	NF/VG+	VG+/VG	VG/VG-	Good	w/o dj
1st ed	U.S.	$200	$150	$125	$100	$80	$40	33%
1st ed	U.K.	$800	$600	$500	$400	$325	$150	20%

From Russia With Love 1957 U.K.   1957 U.S.

		F/F	F/NF	NF/VG+	VG+/VG	VG/VG-	Good	w/o dj
1st ed	U.S.	$175	$125	$110	$90	$75	$35	40%
1st ed	U.K.	$650	$500	$450	$375	$300	$125	25%

Dr. No 1958 U.K.   1958 U.S.

"JONATHAN CAPE/THIRTY BEDFORD SQUARE/LONDON" on title page. No date on title page. Copyright page - 1st (of 5) line - "FIRST PUBLISHED 1958". DJ price - 13s 6d. Full bound - black cloth with no top stain and white pastedowns.

"*New York* THE MACMILLAN COMPANY/1958" on title page. Copyright page - 6th (of 8) -"*First Printing*" .   DJ price - $3.50. Full bound - black cloth with no top stain and white pastedowns.

		F/F	F/NF	NF/VG+	VG+/VG	VG/VG-	Good	w/o dj
1st ed	U.S.	$125	$100	$80	$65	$50	$25	40%
1st ed	U.K.	$500	$400	$325	$250	$200	$75	25%

Goldfinger 1959 U.K.   1959 U.S.

"JONATHAN CAPE/THIRTY BEDFORD SQUARE/LONDON" on title page. No date on title page. Copyright page - 1st (of 6) line -"FIRST PUBLISHED 1959". DJ price - 15s. Full bound - black cloth with no top stain and white pastedowns.

"New York/THE MACMILLAN COMPANY/ 1959" on title page. Copyright page 1st - (of 3) line - "FIRST PUBLISHED 1959". Third line - "PRINTED IN GREAT BRITAIN". DJ price - $2.95 on top and $3.00 on bottom of front flap (both on diagonals). Full bound - black cloth with no top stain and white pastedowns.

		F/F	F/NF	NF/VG+	VG+/VG	VG/VG-	Good	w/o dj
1st ed	U.S.	$110	$80	$60	$50	$40	$15	40%
1st ed	U.K.	$450	$300	$225	$150	$125	$50	25%

For Your Eyes Only 1960 U.K.   1960 U.S.

"THE VIKING PRESS/NEW YORK" on title page. No date on title page. Copyright page - seven lines with on mention of printing number. Second line "PUBLISHED IN 1960 BY

51

THE VIKING PRESS, INC." Last line - "PRINTED IN THE U.S.A. BY THE VAIL-BALLOU PRESS". DJ with red spine background and price $3.50. Bound with yellow cloth on top and light green cloth on bottom. No top stain and white pastedowns.

"JONATHAN CAPE/THIRTY BEDFORD SQUARE LONDON" on title page. No date on title page. Copyright page - 1st (of 4) line - "FIRST PUBLISHED 1960". DJ price - 15s. Full bound - black cloth with no top stain and white pastedowns.

		F/F	F/NF	NF/VG+	VG+/VG	VG/VG-	Good	w/o dj
1st ed	U.S.	$90	$75	$60	$50	$40	$15	50%
1st ed	U.K.	$350	$250	$200	$125	$100	$40	33%

Thunderball 1961 U.K. 1961 U.S.

"NEW YORK The Viking Press 1961" on title page.
Copyright page - 3rd (of 6) line - "PUBLISHED IN 1961 BY THE VIKING PRESS, INC.".
DJ price - $3.95. Full bound - yellow with pink top stain and white pastedowns.

"JONATHAN CAPE/THIRTY BEDFORD SQUARE/LONDON" on title page. No date on title page. Copyright page - 1st (of 5) line - "FIRST PUBLISHED 1961". DJ price - 15s. Full bound - black cloth with no top stain and white pastedowns.

		F/F	F/NF	NF/VG+	VG+/VG	VG/VG-	Good	w/o dj
1st ed	U.S.	$75	$60	$50	$35	$25	$12	50%
1st ed	U.K.	$275	$200	$150	$100	$80	$30	33%

The Spy Who Loved Me 1962 U.K. 1962 U.S.

"JONATHAN CAPE/THIRTY BEDFORD SQUARE/LONDON" on title page. No date on title page. Copyright page - 1st (of 6) line - "FIRST PUBLISHED 1962". DJ price - 15s. Full bound - black cloth with no top stain and red pastedowns.

"The Viking Press/*New York*" on title page. No date on title page. Copyright page - 3rd (of 6) line - "FIRST PRUBLISHED IN 1962 BY THE VIKING PRESS, INC." DJ resembles UK-type Fleming dj. Full bound - light burnt-orange with light orange top stain and brown pastedowns.

		F/F	F/NF	NF/VG+	VG+/VG	VG/VG-	Good	w/o dj
1st ed	U.S.	$60	$50	$40	$30	$25	$10	50%
1st ed	U.K.	$225	$150	$125	$90	$75	$25	33%

On Her Majesty's Secret Service 1963 U.K. 1963 U.S.

"JONATHAN CAPE/THIRTY BEDFORD SQUARE/LONDON" on title page. No date on title page. Copyright page - 1st (of 9) line - "FIRST PUBLISHED 1963". DJ price - 16s. Full bound - black cloth with no top stain and white pastedowns.

"NEW AMERICAN LIBRARY" on title page. No date on title page. Copyright page - 1st (of 9) line - "First Printed, September, 1963." DJ price - $4.50. Quarter bound - black spine with light blue sides and yellow top stain. Light gold pastedowns.

		F/F	F/NF	NF/VG+	VG+/VG	VG/VG-	Good	w/o dj
1st ed	U.S.	$55	$45	$35	$25	$20	$10	50%
1st ed	U.K.	$175	$125	$100	$75	$60	$20	33%

Thrilling Cities 1963 U.K. 1964 U.S.

"NEW AMERICAN LIBRARY" on title page. No date on title page.
Copyright page - 2nd (of 13) line - "First publication in the United States, 1964."
7th and 8th lines - "Published simultaneously in Canada by/Nelson, Foster& Scott, Ltd."
DJ price - $4.95. On rear panel of 1st issue dj, author is refered to in the present tense (author died shortly after book was published). On later dj's the tense is changed to past tense.
Full bound - yellow cloth with orange top stain. Orange pastedowns (white in later printings).

		F/F	F/NF	NF/VG+	VG+/VG	VG/VG-	Good	w/o dj
1st ed	U.S.	$30	$25	$20	$15	$12	$10	33%
1st ed	U.K.	$50	$40	$30	$25	$20	$15	33%

You Only Live Twice 1964 U.K. 1964 U.S.

"Jonathan Cape" on title page. No date on title page. Copyright page - 1st (of 9) line - "First published 1964". Full bound - black cloth with no top stain. Pastedowns woodgrain.

"NEW AMERICAN LIBRARY" on title page. No date on title page.
Copyright page - 1st (of 10) line - "FIRST PRINTING". DJ price - $4.50.
Full bound - yellow cloth with red top stain and red pastedowns.

		F/F	F/NF	NF/VG+	VG+/VG	VG/VG-	Good	w/o dj
1st ed	U.S.	$50	$40	$30	$25	$20	$10	50%
1st ed	U.K.	$100	$85	$60	$50	$45	$15	40%

Chitty Chitty Bang Bang 1964

"Random House New York" on title page. No date on title page. Copyright page - 1st (of 7) line - "FIRST PRINTING". DJ price - $3.50. Rear panel of DJ shows back of car with "A Random House Book" at bottom. Full bound - red with gold lettering and black top stain. Green and black pictorial pastedowns.

		F/F	F/NF	NF/VG+	VG+/VG	VG/VG-	Good	w/o dj
1st ed		$75	$60	$50	$35	$25	$10	70%

Ian Fleming Introduces Jamaica 1965

"HAWTHORN/BOOKS, INC./PUBLISHERS -- NEW YORK" on title page. No date on title page. Copyright page - 13 lines with no mention of printing or edition number. Printed in the Netherlands. DJ price - $6.95. Full bound - orange with gold lettering on spine and yellow top stain. Map of Jamaica with orange background frame on pastedowns.

		F/F	F/NF	NF/VG+	VG+/VG	VG/VG-	Good	w/o dj
1st ed		$45	$40	$30	$25	$20	$10	70%

Man with the Golden Gun 1965 U.K. 1965 U.S.

"JONATHAN CAPE/THIRTY BEDFORD SQUARE LONDON" on title page. No date on title page. Copyright page - 1st (of 4) line - "First published 1965". DJ price - 18s.
Full bound - black cloth with no top stain. Pastedowns green background, white streaks.
Note: The true first issue of this book shows a gilt highlighted gun on the front board. The print run of this book was so limited that the first readily available U.K. edition of the book (shown above) is actually the second issue.

"PUBLISHED BY THE NEW AMERICAN LIBRARY" on title page. No date on title page.
Copyright page - 5th (of 9) line -"FIRST EDITION". DJ price - $4.50.
Full bound - black paper with light yellow top stain and gold pastedowns.

		F/F	F/NF	NF/VG+	VG+/VG	VG/VG-	Good	w/o dj
1st ed	U.S.	$35	$30	$25	$20	$17	$10	60%
1st ed	U.K.	$70	$60	$50	$40	$35	$15	50%

<u>Octopussy and The Living Daylights</u> 1966 U.K.   <u>Octopussy</u> 1966 U.S.

"THE NEW AMERICAN LIBRARY" on title page. No date on title page.
Copyright page - 17th (of 23) line - "FIRST PRINTING". DJ price - $3.50.
Full bound - black cloth with no top stain and gold pastedowns.

"Jonathan Cape/Thirty Bedford Square/London" on title page. No date on title page.
Copyright page - 1st (of 9) line - "First published 1966". DJ price - 16s.
Full bound - black cloth with no top stain. Pastedowns gray marble.

		F/F	F/NF	NF/VG+	VG+/VG	VG/VG-	Good	w/o dj
1st ed	U.S.	$30	$25	$20	$15	$12	$10	60%
1st ed	U.K.	$60	$50	$40	$30	$25	$10	50%

Ken Follett (1949-)

Eye of the Needle 1978

"ARBOR HOUSE/*New York*" on title page. No date on title page.
Copyright page - seven lines with no mention of printing number. Later printings have an
8th line added at the top of the others such as "SECOND PRINTING".
DJ price - $8.95 with "7-78" on the bottom of the rear dj flap.
Quarter bound - black cloth with red sides. No top stain. Tan pastedowns.

		F/F	F/NF	NF/VG+	VG+/VG	VG/VG-	Good	w/o dj
1st ed		$50	$40	$30	$20	$12	$6	70%

Triple 1979

"ARBOR HOUSE/NEW YORK" on title page. No date on title page.
Copyright page - eight lines with no mention of printing number. DJ price - $10.95 (no
different for later printings).   Later printings have a ninth line such as "SECOND
PRINTING". Quarter bound - red cloth with black sides. No top stain. White pastedowns.

		F/F	F/NF	NF/VG+	VG+/VG	VG/VG-	Good	w/o dj
1st ed		$20	$15	$12	$10	$8	$5	80%

The Key to Rebecca 1980

"WILLIAM MORROW AND COMPANY, INC./*New York   1980*" on title page.
Copyright page - 15th and 16th (of 16) lines - "First Edition/1 2 3 4 5 6 7 8 9 10". DJ price -
$12.95. Quarter bound -white cloth with cream sides and red top stain. Red pastedowns.

		F/F	F/NF	NF/VG+	VG+/VG	VG/VG-	Good	w/o dj
1st ed		$15	$12	$10	$8	$6	$4	80%

The Man from St. Petersburg 1982

"WILLIAM MORROW AND COMPANY, INC./NEW YORK 1982" on title page.
Copyright page - 19th and 20th (of 21) lines - "First Edition/1 2 3 4 5 6 7 8 9 10". DJ price -
$14.50. Quarter bound -brown cloth with cream sides and no top stain. Brown pastedowns.

	F/F	F/NF	NF/VG+	VG+/VG	VG/VG-	Good	w/o dj
1st ed	$15	$12	$10	$8	$6	$4	80%

On Wings of Eagles 1983

"William Morrow and Company, Inc. New York/1983" on title page. Copyright page - 26th
and 27th (of 28) lines - "First Edition/1 2 3 4 5 6 7 8 9 10". DJ price - $16.95.
Quarter bound -blue cloth with cream sides and no top stain. Maps on pastedowns.

	F/F	F/NF	NF/VG+	VG+/VG	VG/VG-	Good	w/o dj
1st ed	$25	$20	$15	$12	$8	$5	80%

Lie Down with Lions 1986

"WILLIAM MORROW AND COMPANY, INC. NEW YORK" on title page. No date on
title page. Copyright page - 21st and 22nd (of 23) lines - "First Edition/1 2 3 4 5 6 7 8 9 10".
DJ price - $18.95. Quarter bound -red cloth with cream sides and no top stain. Maps on
pastedowns.

	F/F	F/NF	NF/VG+	VG+/VG	VG/VG-	Good	w/o dj
1st ed	$15	$12	$10	$8	$6	$4	80%

Pillars of the Earth 1989

"WILLIAM MORROW AND COMPANY, INC./NEW YORK" on title page. No date on title
page. Copyright page - 19th and 20th (of 21) lines - "First Edition/1 2 3 4 5 6 7 8 9 10".
DJ price - $22.95.
Quarter bound -brown cloth with brown sides and no top stain. Mottled tan pastedowns.

	F/F	F/NF	NF/VG+	VG+/VG	VG/VG-	Good	w/o dj
1st ed	$15	$12	$10	$8	$6	$4	80%

Night Over Water 1991

"WILLIAM MORROW AND COMPANY, INC./NEW YORK" on title page. No date on title
page. Copyright page - 23st and 24th (of 25) lines - "First Edition/1 2 3 4 5 6 7 8 9 10".
DJ price - $23.00/Canada $29.95.
Quarter bound -black cloth with tan sides and no top stain. Maps on pastedowns.

	F/F	F/NF	NF/VG+	VG+/VG	VG/VG-	Good	w/o dj
1st ed	$15	$12	$10	$8	$6	$4	80%

C.S. Forester   (1899 - 1966)

The Horatio Hornblower Saga

Beat to Quarters 1937 3,000 U.S. copies Published in U.K. as *The Happy Return.*
12,000 U.K. copies The first of the Horatio Hornblower novels to be written, covering the period from June to October, 1808, but chronologically in Hornblower's career, this covers the sixth time period.

		F/F	F/NF	NF/VG+	VG+/VG	VG/VG-	Good	w/o dj
1st ed	U.S.	$400	$350	$250	$175	$125	$75	20%
1st ed	U.K.	$200	$175	$125	$75	$50	$25	20%

A Ship of the Line 1938 6,000 U.S. copies Published in U.K. as *Ship of the Line.*
15,000 U.K. copies The second of the Horatio Hornblower novels to be written, covering the period from May to October, 1810, but chronologically in Hornblower's career, this covers the seventh time period.

		F/F	F/NF	NF/VG+	VG+/VG	VG/VG-	Good	w/o dj
1st ed	U.S.	$300	$250	$200	$150	$100	$60	20%
1st ed	U.K.	$250	$200	$150	$100	$75	$35	20%

Flying Colours and A Ship of the Line 1938 7,400 U.K. copies Combined volume issued one day before separate edition. *Flying Colours* is the third of the Horatio Hornblower novels to be written, covering the period from November, 1810, to June, 1811, but chronologically in Hornblower's career, this covers the eighth time period.

		F/F	F/NF	NF/VG+	VG+/VG	VG/VG-	Good	w/o dj
1st ed		$500	$425	$300	$225	$175	$80	20%

Flying Colours 1938 5,000 U.S. copies 12,000 U.K. copies The third of the Horatio Hornblower novels to be written, covering the period from November, 1810, to June, 1811, but chronologically in Hornblower's career, this covers the eighth time period.

		F/F	F/NF	NF/VG+	VG+/VG	VG/VG-	Good	w/o dj
1st ed	U.S.	$300	$250	$200	$150	$100	$60	20%
1st ed	U.K.	$250	$200	$150	$100	$75	$35	20%

Commodore Hornblower 1945 34,500 U.S. copies Published in U.K. as *The Commodore.* 50,000 U.K. copies The fourth of the Horatio Hornblower novels to be written, covering the period from May to October, 1812, but chronologically in Hornblower's career, this covers the ninth time period.

"BOSTON/LITTLE, BROWN AND COMPANY/1945" on title page. Copyright page - 6th and 7th (of 8) lines - "FIRST EDITION/*Published May 1945*". 8th line - "PRINTED IN THE UNITED STATES OF AMERICA". DJ price - $2.50.
Full bound - blue-green with no top stain and white pastedowns.

"MICHAEL JOSEPH LTD/26, *Bloomsburg St., London, W.C.1*" on title page. No date on title page. Copyright page - 1st four lines - "FIRST PUBLISHED 1945/{lion on book symbol with BOOK/PRODUCTION/WAR ECONOMY/STANDARD on pages of book}/THIS BOOK IS PRODUCED IN/COMPLETE CONFORMITY WITH THE/AUTHORIZED ECONOMY STANDARD". Last two lines at bottom of page - "MADE AND PRINTED IN GREAT BRITAIN BY PURNELL AND SONS, LTD./PAULTON (SOMERSET) AND LONDON".
Full bound - gold cloth with no top stain and white pastedowns. DJ price - 9/6. Rear panel of dj contains *"New Novels for 1945"* with 23 novels listed.

		F/F	F/NF	NF/VG+	VG+/VG	VG/VG-	Good	w/o dj
1st ed	U.S.	$100	$85	$60	$40	$30	$15	33%
1st ed	U.K.	$125	$100	$75	$50	$35	$15	33%

Lord Hornblower 1946 40,000 U.S. copies 50,000 U.K. copies The fifth of the Horatio
Hornblower novels to be written, covering the period from October, 1813, to May, 1814, but chronologically in
Hornblower's career, this covers the tenth time period.

"BOSTON/LITTLE, BROWN AND COMPANY/1946" on title page. Copyright page - 6th
and 7th (of 8) lines - "FIRST EDITION/*Published June 1946*". 8th line - "PRINTED IN THE
UNITED STATES OF AMERICA". DJ price $2.50.
Full bound - blue-green with no top stain and white pastedowns.
Note: An edition identical to above except with a 9th line on the copyright page reading "AMERICAN BOOK -
STRATFORD PRESS, INC., NEW YORK" exists. Although "FIRST EDITION" appears, this is not a true first
edition.

		F/F	F/NF	NF/VG+	VG+/VG	VG/VG-	Good	w/odj
1st ed	U.S.	$80	$70	$50	$35	$25	$12	25%
1st ed	U.K.	$100	$90	$65	$50	$35	$20	25%

Mr. Midshipman Hornblower 1950 20,000 U.S. copies 25,000 U.K. copies The
sixth of the Horatio Hornblower novels to be written, covering the period from June, 1794, to March, 1798, but
chronologically in Hornblower's career, this covers the first time period.

		F/F	F/NF	NF/VG+	VG+/VG	VG/VG-	Good	w/odj
1st ed	U.S.	$100	$85	$60	$45	$35	$20	25%
1st ed	U.K.	$125	$100	$75	$60	$40	$25	25%

Lieutenant Hornblower 1952 15,000 U.S. copies 50,000 U.K. copies The seventh of
the Horatio Hornblower novels to be written, covering the period from May, 1800, to March 1803, but
chronologically in Hornblower's career, this covers the second time period.

"*London* /MICHAEL JOSEPH" on title page. No date on title page. Copyright page - seven
lines -"*First published by*/ MICHAEL JOSEPH LTD/ *26 Bloomsburg Street/London, W.C.1*/
1952" at top of page. Bottom two lines - "MADE AND PRINTED IN GREAT BRITAIN BY
FURNELL AND SONS, LTD./PAULTON (SOMERSET) AND LONDON". DJ price - 12s 6d.
Rear panel of dj contains nearly full page photo of author. Full bound - blue cloth with no
top stain and white pastedowns.

		F/F	F/NF	NF/VG+	VG+/VG	VG/VG-	Good	w/odj
1st ed	U.S.	$100	$85	$60	$45	$35	$20	25%
1st ed	U.K.	$100	$85	$60	$45	$35	$20	25%

Hornblower and the Atropos 1953 15,000 U.S. copies 50,000 U.K. copies The
eighth of the Horatio Hornblower novels to be written, covering the period from October, 1805, to January, 1808,
but chronologically in Hornblower's career, this covers the fifth time period.

"Little, Brown and Company *Boston*" on title page. No date on title page. Copyright page -
7th (of 8) line - "FIRST EDITION". DJ price - $3.50.
Full bound - blue-green cloth with gold print and no top stain. White pastedowns.

"*London*/MICHAEL JOSEPH"on title page. No date on title page. Copyright page - 1st (of 9)
line - "*First published by*". DJ price - 12s 6d.
Full bound - brown cloth with no top stain and white pastedowns.

		F/F	F/NF	NF/VG+	VG+/VG	VG/VG-	Good	w/odj
1st ed	U.S.	$80	$70	$50	$35	$25	$12	33%
1st ed	U.K.	$80	$70	$50	$35	$25	$12	33%

Admiral Hornblower in the West Indies 1958 15,000 U.S. copies Published in U.K.
as *Hornblower in the West Indies*. 40,000 U.K. copies The ninth of the Horatio Hornblower

novels to be written, covering the period from May, 1821 to October 1823, but chronologically in Hornblower's career, this covers the eleventh and last time period.

"LITTLE, BROWN AND COMPANY/*Boston   Toronto*" on title page. No date on title page. Copyright page - 8th (of 9) line - "FIRST EDITION". DJ price - $4.00 Full bound - blue-green cloth with gold print and no top stain. White pastedowns.

"London/MICHAEL JOSEPH" on title page. No date on title page. Copyright page - 1st and 2nd (of 10) lines - *"First published by*/MICHAEL JOSEPH LTD". Full bound - blue cloth with gold print and no top stain. White pastedowns.

		F/F	F/NF	NF/VG+	VG+/VG	VG/VG-	Good	w/o dj
1st ed	U.S.	$80	$70	$50	$35	$25	$12	33%
1st ed	U.K.	$90	$80	$60	$40	$30	$15	33%

Hornblower and the Hotspur 1962   20,000 U.S. copies   40,000 U.K. copies   The

tenth of the Horatio Hornblower novels to be written, covering the period from April, 1803, to July, 1805, but chronologically in Hornblower's career, this covers the third time period.

"Little, Brown and Company Boston Toronto" on title page. No date on title page. Copyright page - 7th (of 8) line - "FIRST EDITION". DJ price - $4.95. Full bound - blue-green cloth with gold print and no top stain. White pastedowns.

		F/F	F/NF	NF/VG+	VG+/VG	VG/VG-	Good	w/o dj
1st ed	U.S.	$80	$70	$50	$35	$25	$12	50%
1st ed	U.K.	$80	$70	$50	$35	$25	$12	50%

The Hornblower Companion 1964   8,000 U.S. copies   10,000 U.K. copies   Forester's

eleventh works about Hornblower. This non-fiction account presents maps and charts depicting the locales for each of the Hornblower novels. The book also presents the author's recollections of events and ideas leading to the various Hornblower adventures.

"LITTLE, BROWN AND COMPANY/BOSTON   TORONTO" on title page. No date on title page. Copyright page - 7th (of 10) line - "FIRST EDITION". DJ price - $8.50. Full bound - maroon cloth with light blue top stain and white pastedowns.

		F/F	F/NF	NF/VG+	VG+/VG	VG/VG-	Good	w/o dj
1st ed	U.S.	$150	$125	$80	$55	$40	$15	66%
1st ed	U.K.	$175	$150	$100	$70	$50	$20	66%

Hornblower During the Crisis 1967   15,000 U.S. copies   Published in U.K. as

Hornblower and the Crisis. 25,000 U.K. copies   The twelfth of the Horatio Hornblower novels to be written, covering the period of late 1805, but chronologically in Hornblower's career, this covers the ninth time period. This novel was published after Forestoer's death.

"Little, Brown and Company Boston Toronto" on title page. No date on title page. Copyright page - 10th (of 13) line - "FIRST EDITION". Last line - "PRINTED IN THE UNITED STATES OF AMERICA". DJ price - $4.95. Full bound - blue-green cloth with gold print and no top stain. White pastedowns.

		F/F	F/NF	NF/VG+	VG+/VG	VG/VG-	Good	w/o dj
1st ed	U.S.	$80	$70	$50	$35	$25	$12	66%
1st ed	U.K.	$80	$70	$50	$35	$25	$12	66%

Captain Horatio Hornblower 1939   5,000 U.S. copies   10,000 U.K. copies   One

volumne edition containing *Beat to Quarters*, *Ship of the Line*, and *Flying Colours*.

		F/F	F/NF	NF/VG+	VG+/VG	VG/VG-	Good	w/o dj
1st ed	U.S.	$200	$175	$125	$90	$70	$40	25%
1st ed	U.K.	$300	$250	$175	$125	$100	$50	25%

The Young Hornblower 1960 3,500 U.S. copies   1964 15,000 U.K. copies One volumne edition containing *Mr. Midshipman Hornblower* , *Lieutenant Hornblower*, and *Hornblower and the Atropos.*

		F/F	F/NF	NF/VG+	VG+/VG	VG/VG-	Good	w/o dj
1st ed	U.S.	$100	$85	$60	$45	$35	$20	50%
1st ed	U.K.	$100	$85	$60	$45	$35	$20	50%

The Indomitable Hornblower 1963 5,000 U.S. copies   One volumne edition containing *Commodore Hornblower*, *Lord Hornblower*, and *Admiral Hornblower in the West Indies.*

	F/F	F/NF	NF/VG+	VG+/VG	VG/VG-	Good	w/o dj
1st ed	$100	$85	$60	$45	$35	$20	50%

Note: For a related Hornblower novel, see listing under C. Northcote Parkinson *The Life and Times of Horatio Hornblower.* This biography of Hornblower was reconstructed from documents that Parkinson "uncovered in a London solicitor's attic two dusty deedboxes containing original Hornblower papers, 'a haphazard collection, grouped neither by chronology or subject, but nevertheless a mine of information to which Mr. Forester never had access."

Other Fiction

To the Indies 1940 12,000 U.S. copies Published in U.K. as *The Earthly Paradise.* 15,000 U.K. copies

"BOSTON: LITTLE, BROWN AND COMPANY/1940" on title page. Copyright page - 5th and 6th (of 7) lines - "FIRST EDITION/*Published July 1940*".
Full bound - green with gold letters and red-orange top stain. Map on pastedowns.

	F/F	F/NF	NF/VG+	VG+/VG	VG/VG-	Good	w/o dj
1st ed	$150	$125	$100	$75	$60	$20	20%

The Captain from Connecticut 1941 25,000 U.S. copies 15,000 U.K. copies

"LITTLE, BROWN AND COMPANY BOSTON/1941" on title page. Copyright page - 5th and 6th (of 7) lines - "FIRST EDITION/*Published June 1941*". 7th line - "PRINTED IN THE UNITED STATES OF AMERICA". DJ price $2.50. Full bound - cream with blue top stain and white pastedowns.

	F/F	F/NF	NF/VG+	VG+/VG	VG/VG-	Good	w/o dj
1st ed	$110	$100	$75	$50	$40	$20	25%

Payment Deferred 1942

"*BOSTON* /LITTLE, BROWN AND COMPANY/1942" on title page. Copyright page - 6th (of 7) lines - "*Published June 1942*". 7th line - "PRINTED IN THE UNITED STATES OF AMERICA". DJ price $2.50. Full bound - gray with red ink and no blue top stain. White pastedowns.

	F/F	F/NF	NF/VG+	VG+/VG	VG/VG-	Good	w/o dj

1st ed		$300	$250	$175	$125	$90	$30	25%

The Sky and the Forest   1948   25,000 U.S. copies   40,000 U.K. copies

"LITTLE, BROWN AND COMPANY BOSTON/1948" on title page. Copyright page - 5th and 6th (of 7) lines - "FIRST EDITION/*Published August 1948*". DJ price $2.75. Full bound - burnt orange with no top stain and white pastedowns.

		F/F	F/NF	NF/VG+	VG+/VG	VG/VG-	Good	w/o dj
1st ed		$60	$50	$40	$30	$25	$12	33%

The Barbary Pirates   1953

"RANDOM HOUSE NEW YORK" on title page. No date on title page. Copyright page - 9 lines with no mention of edition or printing number. 9th line - "MANUFACTURED IN THE U.S.A." Page 188 (unnumbered) contains ad for Landmark Books 1-40 and World Landmarks 1-10 (same books as in ad on rear panel of dj). DJ price - "150/150". Book club dj contains words "Young Readers of America" and no price. Full bound - red cloth with yellow top stain and tan pastedowns with figures in blue.

		F/F	F/NF	NF/VG+	VG+/VG	VG/VG-	Good	w/o dj
1st ed		$150	$125	$90	$70	$55	$25	33%

The Good Shepherd   1955   20,000 U.S. copies   40,000 U.K. copies

"London/MICHAEL JOSEPH" on title page. No date on title page. Copyright page - 1st and 2nd (of 9) lines - "*First published by*/MICHAEL JOSEPH LTD". Full bound - black cloth with no top stain and ships at sea in a storm (same as dj front panel) on pastedowns.

"Little, Brown and Company/*BOSTON TORONTO*" on title page. No date on title page. Copyright page - 6th and 7th (of 7) lines - "FIRST EDITION/PRINTED IN THE UNITED STATES OF AMERICA". DJ price - $3.95. Full bound- red cloth with no top stain and white pastedowns.

		F/F	F/NF	NF/VG+	VG+/VG	VG/VG-	Good	w/o dj
1st ed	U.S.	$50	$40	$30	$25	$20	$8	70%
1st ed	U.K.	$60	$50	$40	$30	$20	$8	70%

The Man in the Yellow Raft   1969   Eight Short Stories of World War II

"*Little, Brown and Company/Boston   Toronto*" on title page. Copyright page - 9th and 10th (of 10) lines - "FIRST AMERICAN EDITION/PRINTED IN THE UNITED STATES OF AMERICA". DJ price $5.95.
Quarter bound - green cloth with light blue sides and no top stain. Light blue pastedowns.

		F/F	F/NF	NF/VG+	VG+/VG	VG/VG-	Good	w/o dj
1st ed		$60	$50	$40	$30	$25	$12	70%

Frederick Forsyth (1938-)

The Day of the Jackal   1971

"*New York* / THE VIKING PRESS" on title page. No date on title page. Copyright page - seven lines with no mention of printing number. DJ price - $7.95

Quarter bound - gray cloth with red paper and red top stain.

		F/F	F/NF	NF/VG+	VG+/VG	VG/VG-	Good	w/o dj
1st ed	U.S.	$50	$40	$35	$30	$25	$15	60%
1st ed	U.K.	$75	$60	$50	$40	$30	$20	60%

The Odessa File 1972

"The Viking Press / New York" on title page. No date on title page.
Copyright page - seven lines with no mention of printing number. DJ price $7.95
Quarter bound - black cloth with red paper and red top stain.

"HUTCHINSON OF LONDON" on title page. No date on title page.
Copyright page - 6th (of 11) line - "First published 1972". DJ price - £2.00.
Full bound - black cloth with no top stain and light gray pastedowns.

		F/F	F/NF	NF/VG+	VG+/VG	VG/VG-	Good	w/o dj
1st ed	U.S.	$25	$20	$18	$15	$12	$8	70%
1st ed	U.K.	$45	$40	$35	$25	$20	$15	70%

The Dogs of War 1974

"THE VIKING PRESS NEW YORK" on title page. No date on title page.
Copyright page - eleven lines, no reference to edition number. DJ price - $7.95.
Quarter bound - dark blue cloth with orange sides and no top stain. Black pastedowns.

"*Hutchinson of London*" on title page. No date on title page.
Copyright page - 6th (of 12) line - "First published 1974". DJ price - £2.50.
Full bound - black cloth with no top stain and light gray pastedowns.

		F/F	F/NF	NF/VG+	VG+/VG	VG/VG-	Good	w/o dj
1st ed	U.S.	$20	$18	$15	$12	$10	$7	80%
1st ed	U.K.	$40	$35	$30	$25	$18	$12	70%

The Shepherd 1975

"THE VIKING PRESS NEW YORK" on title page. No date on title page.
Copyright page - thirteen lines, no reference to edition number. DJ price - $4.95.
Quarter bound - dark blue cloth with blue sides and blue top stain. White pastedowns.

		F/F	F/NF	NF/VG+	VG+/VG	VG/VG-	Good	w/o dj
1st ed	U.S.	$18	$15	$12	$10	$8	$6	70%
1st ed	U.K.	$35	$30	$25	$20	$15	$10	70%

The Devil's Alternative 1979

"The Viking Press New York" on title page. No date on title page.
Copyright page - last (of 9) line "1 2 3 4 5 6 7 8 9 10". DJ price - $12.95.
Quarter bound - black cloth with red paper and no top stain.

		F/F	F/NF	NF/VG+	VG+/VG	VG/VG-	Good	w/o dj
1st ed	U.S.	$15	$12	$10	$8	$6	$4	80%
1st ed	U.K.	$20	$15	$12	$10	$8	$5	80%

No Comebacks 1982

"THE VIKING PRESS NEW YORK" on title page. No date on title page.
Copyright page - fourteen lines - no mention of edition number. Later editions have
"Second Impression", etc. as added line at bottom. DJ price - $13.95.
Quarter bound - maroon cloth with white paper and no top stain. Black pastedowns.

		F/F	F/NF	NF/VG+	VG+/VG	VG/VG-	Good	w/o dj
1st ed	U.S.	$15	$12	$10	$8	$6	$4	80%
1st ed	U.K.	$20	$15	$12	$10	$8	$5	80%

The Fourth Protocol 1984

"VIKING" on title page. No date on title page. Copyright page - 5th (of 16) line - "First
Published in 1984". DJ price - $17.95. Quarter bound - gold cloth with gray paper and no top
stain. White pastedowns.

"Hutchinson/London Melbourne Sydney Auckland Johannesburg" on title page. No date
on title page. Copyright page - 11th (of 19) line - "First published 1984". DJ price - £9.95.
Full bound - black cloth with no top stain and tan pastedowns.

		F/F	F/NF	NF/VG+	VG+/VG	VG/VG-	Good	w/o dj
1st ed	U.S.	$15	$12	$10	$8	$6	$4	80%
1st ed	U.K.	$20	$15	$12	$10	$8	$5	80%

The Negotiator 1989

"THE BANTAM BOOKS/NEW YORK TORONTO LONDON SYDNEY AUCKLAND"
No date on title page. Copyright page - last (of 23) line "DC 0 9 8 7 6 5 4 3 2 1".
DJ price - IN U.S./$19.95/IN CANADA/$26.95.
Quarter bound - black cloth with black paper and no top stain. Black pastedowns.

	F/F	F/NF	NF/VG+	VG+/VG	VG/VG-	Good	w/o dj
1st ed	$12	$10	$8	$7	$6	$4	75%

John Fowles

The Collector 1963

"LITTLE, BROWN AND COMPANY BOSTON TORONTO" on title page. No date on
title page. Copyright page - 7th (of 8) line - "FIRST AMERICAN EDITION". DJ price $4.95.
Full bound - burnt orange cloth with no top stain and yellow pastedowns.

	F/F	F/NF	NF/VG+	VG+/VG	VG/VG-	Good	w/o dj
1st ed	$125	$100	$75	$50	$40	$20	60%

The Aristos 1964

"LITTLE, BROWN AND COMPANY BOSTON TORONTO" on title page. No date on
title page. Copyright page - 7th (of 10) line - "FIRST EDITION". DJ price $5.00.
Full bound - brown cloth with olive green top stain and white pastedowns.

	F/F	F/NF	NF/VG+	VG+/VG	VG/VG-	Good	w/o dj

1st ed		$100	$85	$70	$50	$40	$20	60%

The Magus 1965

"LITTLE, BROWN AND COMPANY BOSTON TORONTO" on title page. No date on title page. Copyright page - 7th (of 24) line - "FIRST EDITION". DJ price $7.95. DJ colorful wrap around sketch with ram's head/candle on front panel and masks on rear panel. Matte paper. Full bound - green-yellow cloth with red top stain and white pastedowns.

		F/F	F/NF	NF/VG+	VG+/VG	VG/VG-	Good	w/o dj
1st ed		$80	$65	$50	$40	$30	$20	70%

The French Lieutenant's Woman 1969

"LITTLE, BROWN AND COMPANY BOSTON TORONTO" on title page. No date on title page. Copyright page - 9th (of 12) line - "FIRST EDITION". DJ price - $7.95. Full bound - gray cloth with no top stain. Gray pastedowns.

		F/F	F/NF	NF/VG+	VG+/VG	VG/VG-	Good	w/o dj
1st ed		$80	$65	$50	$40	$30	$20	70%

Dick Francis

The Sport of Queens 1957 U.K. 1969 U.S.

"London/MICHAEL JOSEPH" on title page. No date on title page. Copyright page - first (of 10) line - "First published by" and no later printing indicated. DJ price - 21s. Full bound - bright blue cloth with no top stain and white pastedowns.

"HARPER & ROW, PUBLISHERS/New York and Evanston" on title page. No date on title page. Copyright page - 8th (of 19) line - "FIRST U.S. EDITION 1969". DJ price - $5.95. Quarter bound - black cloth with forest green sides and no top stain. White pastedowns.

		F/F	F/NF	NF/VG+	VG+/VG	VG/VG-	Good	w/o dj
1st ed	U.S.	$125	$100	$80	$65	$50	$30	66%
1st ed	U.K.	$1,000	$800	$650	$500	$400	$200	25%

Dead Cert 1962 U.K. 1962 U.S.

First U.S. edition published by Holt. Copyright page identifies first edition.

		F/F	F/NF	NF/VG+	VG+/VG	VG/VG-	Good	w/o dj
1st ed	U.S.	$1,000	$800	$650	$500	$400	$200	50%
1st ed	U.K.	$2,200	$1,800	$1,500	$1,200	$900	$450	25%

Nerve 1964 U.K. & U.S.

"HARPER & ROW, PUBLISHERS/NEW YORK AND EVANSTON" on title page. No date on title page. Copyright page - 7th (of 9) line "FIRST EDITION". Last line "B-O". DJ with red spine and white backgrounds on front and rear panels. DJ price - $3.95 with "0364" on front DJ flap. Quarter bound - cream cloth with black sides and no top stain. White letters on brown background on pastedown.

		F/F	F/NF	NF/VG+	VG+/VG	VG/VG-	Good	w/o dj
1st ed	U.S.	$400	$325	$250	$175	$125	$60	50%
1st ed	U.K.	$1,000	$850	$700	$500	$400	$200	50%

For Kicks 1965 U.K. & U.S.

"Harper & Row, Publishers/New York and Evanston" on title page. No date on title page. Copyright page - 6th (of 8) line - "FIRST EDITION". DJ price - $3.95. Quarter bound - orange cloth with black sides and no top stain. Black background with white letters on pastedowns.

		F/F	F/NF	NF/VG+	VG+/VG	VG/VG-	Good	w/o dj
1st ed	U.S.	$250	$225	$175	$100	$75	$40	50%
1st ed	U.K.	$500	$450	$350	$250	$200	$100	50%

Odds Against 1965 U.K. 1966 U.S.

"LONDON/MICHAEL JOSEPH" on title page. No date on title page. Copyright page - first four (of 10) lines - *"First published in Great Britain by /MICHAEL JOSEPH LTD/44 Bedford Square/London, W.C.1. "* DJ price - 18s. Reviews of <u>Dead Cert</u>, <u>Nerve</u>, and <u>For Kicks</u> on rear dj panel. Second printing has a line added in the middle of the page stating "SECOND IMPRESSION JANUARY 1966". Later printings are similarly indicated by added lines. Full bound - dark brown cloth with no top stain and white pastedowns.

"Harper & Row, Publishers, New York" on title page. No date on title page. Copyright page - 7th (of 9) line - "FIRST EDITION". Last line - "B-Q". First printing dj is without the three reviews on front flap that appears on later dj. DJ price - $4.95. Quarter bound - pink cloth with black sides and no top stain. Gray background with white letters on pastedowns.

		F/F	F/NF	NF/VG+	VG+/VG	VG/VG-	Good	w/o dj
1st ed	U.S.	$200	$175	$150	$90	$70	$35	50%
1st ed	U.K.	$400	$350	$275	$200	$250	$75	50%

Flying Finish 1966 U.K. 1967 U.S.

*"Harper & Row, Publishers/*NEW YORK AND EVANSTON" on title page. No date on title page. Copyright page - 7th (of 9) line - "FIRST U.S. EDITION". Last line - "E-R". DJ price - $4.95. Quarter bound - maroon cloth with blue sides and no top stain. Blue background with white letters on pastedowns.

"LONDON/MICHAEL JOSEPH" on title page. No date on title page. Copyright page - 1st (of 10) line - "First published in Great Britain by". DJ price - 21s. Full bound - red cloth with no top stain and white pastedowns.

		F/F	F/NF	NF/VG+	VG+/VG	VG/VG-	Good	w/o dj
1st ed	U.S.	$150	$125	$100	$75	$60	$30	50%
1st ed	U.K.	$300	$250	$200	$150	$125	$50	50%

Blood Sport 1967 U.K. 1967 U.S.

"Harper & Row, Publishers New York and Evanston" on title page, No date on title page. Copyright page - 7th (of 9) lines - "FIRST U.S. EDITION". Last line "A-S". DJ price - $4.95. Quarter bound - black cloth with red-orange sides and no top stain. "A HARPER NOVEL OF SUSPENSE" in white on brown background on pastedowns.

"LONDON/MICHAEL JOSEPH" on title page. No date on title page. Copyright page - 1st (of 10) line - *"First published in Great Britain by"*. DJ price - 25s.
Full bound - light blue cloth with no top stain and white pastedowns.

		F/F	F/NF	NF/VG+	VG+/VG	VG/VG-	Good	w/o dj
1st ed	U.S.	$100	$80	$60	$45	$35	$25	60%
1st ed	U.K.	$250	$200	$160	$125	$100	$45	60%

Forfeit 1968 U.K. 1969 U.S.

"LONDON/MICHAEL JOSEPH" on title page. No date on title page. Copyright page - 1st (of 11) line - *"First published in Great Britain by"*. DJ price - 25s net.
Full bound - burnt orange cloth with no top stain and white pastedowns.

"HARPER & ROW, PUBLISHERS/NEW YORK AND EVANSTON" on title page. No date on title page. Copyright page - 8th (of 10) line - "FIRST U.S. EDITION". Last line - "A-T".
DJ price - $4.95.   Quarter bound - green cloth with orange sides and no top stain. Black pastedowns.

		F/F	F/NF	NF/VG+	VG+/VG	VG/VG-	Good	w/o dj
1st ed	U.S.	$90	$75	$60	$50	$40	$20	66%
1st ed	U.K.	$200	$175	$140	$100	$80	$30	66%

Enquiry 1969

"HARPER & ROW, PUBLISHERS NEW YORK AND EVANSTON" on title page. No date on title page. Copyright page - 8th (of 9) line - "FIRST U.S. EDITION". DJ price - $4.95.
Quarter bound - purple cloth with gray sides and no top stain. Purple background with white letters on pastedowns.

"LONDON/MICHAEL JOSEPH" on title page. No date on title page. Copyright page - first (of 18) line - *"First published in Great Britain by"*. DJ price - 25s net/£1.25.
Full bound - red cloth with no top stain and white pastedowns.

		F/F	F/NF	NF/VG+	VG+/VG	VG/VG-	Good	w/o dj
1st ed	U.S.	$80	$65	$50	$40	$30	$15	66%
1st ed	U.K.	$175	$150	$125	$90	$70	$30	66%

Rat Race 1970 U.K. 1971 U.S.

"Harper & Row Publishers/New York Evanston San Francisco London" on title page.
Copyright page - 8th (of 9) line - "FIRST US EDITION". DJ price - $5.95.
Quarter bound - red cloth with black sides and no top stain. White letters on red background on pastedowns. Bottom of last page (blank page) "71 72 73 74 10 9 8 7 6 5 4 3 2 1".

"LONDON/MICHAEL JOSEPH" on title page. No date on title page. Copyright page - 1st (of 19) line - "First published in Great Britain by". DJ price - 30s net/£1.50.
Full bound - blue-green cloth with no top stain and white pastedowns.

		F/F	F/NF	NF/VG+	VG+/VG	VG/VG-	Good	w/o dj
1st ed	U.S.	$80	$65	$50	$40	$30	$15	66%
1st ed	U.K.	$150	$125	$100	$75	$60	$30	66%

Bonecrack 1971 U.K. 1972 U.S.

"LONDON/MICHAEL JOSEPH" on title page. No date on title page. Copyright page - 1st (of 19) line - *"First published in Great Britain by"*. DJ price - £1.75. Full bound - black cloth with no top stain and map against orange background on pastedowns.

Harper & Row U.S. edition. Bottom of last page (blank page) "72 73 10 9 8 7 6 5 4 3 2 1". DJ price - $5.95. "0572" on DJ flap.

		F/F	F/NF	NF/VG+	VG+/VG	VG/VG-	Good	w/odj
1st ed	U.S.	$50	$40	$30	$25	$20	$15	66%
1st ed	U.K.	$100	$80	$60	$50	$40	$30	66%

Smoke Screen 1972 U.K. 1973 U.S.

"HARPER & ROW, PUBLISHERS/New York Evanston San Francisco London" on title page. No date on title page. Copyright page - 8th (of 11) line - "FIRST U.S. EDITION". Bottom of last page (blank page) "73 74 75 10 9 8 7 6 5 4 3 2 1". DJ price - $5.95. Quarter bound - black cloth with orange sides and no top stain. Black background with white letters on pastedowns.

"LONDON/MICHAEL JOSEPH" on title page. No date on title page. Copyright page - 1st (of 15) line - "First published in Great Britain by Michael Joseph". DJ price - £1.95. Full bound - red cloth with no top stain white pastedowns.

		F/F	F/NF	NF/VG+	VG+/VG	VG/VG-	Good	w/odj
1st ed	U.S.	$45	$38	$30	$25	$20	$15	66%
1st ed	U.K.	$90	$80	$60	$50	$40	$30	66%

Slayride 1973 U.K. 1974 U.S.

"MICHAEL JOSEPH/LONDON" on title page. No date on title page. Copyright page - 1st (of 16) line - "First published in Great Britain by MICHAEL JOSEPH LTD". Bottom of last page (blank page) "76 77 10 9 8 7 6 5 4 3 2 1". Full bound - tan-purple cloth with no top stain and white pastedowns.

"HARPER & ROW, PUBLISHERS/*New York, Evanston, San Francisco, London*" on title page. No date on title page. Copyright page - 8th (of 15) line - "FIRST U.S. EDITION". Last page of book, bottom "74 75 77 10 9 8 7 6 5 4 3 2 1". DJ price - $5.95. "0274" on bottom front flap of dj. Quarter bound - light green cloth with blue sides and no top stain. Blue background with white letters on pastedowns.

		F/F	F/NF	NF/VG+	VG+/VG	VG/VG-	Good	w/odj
1st ed	U.S.	$40	$35	$30	$25	$20	$15	66%
1st ed	U.K.	$80	$70	$60	$50	$40	$30	66%

Knockdown 1974 U.K. 1975 U.S.

"LONDON/MICHAEL JOSEPH" on title page. No date on title page. Copyright page - 1st (of 16) line - "First published in Great Britain by MICHAEL JOSEPH, LTD.". DJ price - £2.50. Full bound - purple cloth with no top stain and white pastedowns.

"HARPER & ROW, PUBLISHERS/New York Evanston/San Francisco London" on title page. No date on title page. Copyright page - 8th (of 16) line - "FIRST U.S. EDITION". Last line "75 77 78 79 10 9 8 7 6 5 4 3 2 1". DJ price - $6.95. "0475" on bottom front flap of dj. Quarter bound - black cloth with orange sides and no top stain. Black background with white letters on pastedowns.

		F/F	F/NF	NF/VG+	VG+/VG	VG/VG-	Good	w/o dj
1st ed	U.S.	$35	$30	$25	$20	$15	$10	70%
1st ed	U.K.	$70	$60	$50	$40	$30	$15	70%

High Stakes 1975 U.K. 1976 U.S.

"HARPER & ROW, PUBLISHERS/New York Hagerstown San Francisco London" on title page. No date on title page. Copyright page - 7th (of 15) line - "FIRST U.S. EDITION". Last line "76 77 78 79 10 9 8 7 6 5 4 3 2 1". DJ price - $7.95 with "0576" on fr flap. Quarter bound - black cloth with black sides and no top stain. Red or blue pastedowns (two versions).

"LONDON/MICHAEL JOSEPH" on title page. No date on title page. Copyright page - 1st (of 16) line - "First published in Great Britain by MICHAEL JOSEPH, LTD.". DJ price - £2.95. Full bound - black cloth with no top stain and white pastedowns.

		F/F	F/NF	NF/VG+	VG+/VG	VG/VG-	Good	w/o dj
1st ed	U.S.	$35	$30	$25	$20	$15	$10	70%
1st ed	U.K.	$70	$60	$50	$40	$30	$15	70%

In The Frame 1976 U.K. 1976 U.S.

"Harper & Row, Publishers/New York Hagerstown San Francisco London" on title page. No date on title page. Copyright page - 7th (of 15) line - "FIRST U.S. EDITION". Last line "77 78 79 80 10 9 8 7 6 5 4 3 2 1". DJ price - $8.95. Quarter bound - brown cloth with tan sides and no top stain. Tan pastedowns.

"LONDON/MICHAEL JOSEPH" on title page. No date on title page. Copyright page - 1st (of 16) line - "First published in Great Britain by MICHAEL JOSEPH, LTD.". DJ price - £3.25. Full bound - black cloth with no top stain and white pastedowns.

		F/F	F/NF	NF/VG+	VG+/VG	VG/VG-	Good	w/o dj
1st ed	U.S.	$35	$30	$25	$20	$15	$10	70%
1st ed	U.K.	$70	$60	$50	$40	$30	$15	70%

Risk 1977 U.K. 1978 U.S.

"HARPER & ROW, PUBLISHERS/New York, Hagerstown, San Francisco, London" on title page. No date on title page. Copyright page - 6th (of 15) line - "FIRST U.S. EDITION". Last line "78 79 80 81 82 10 9 8 7 6 5 4 3 2 1". DJ price $8.95. Quarter bound - black cloth with light gray sides and no top stain. Green pastedowns.

"LONDON/MICHAEL JOSEPH" on title page. No date on title page. Copyright page - 1st (of 15) line - "First published in Great Britain by". DJ price - £3.95. Full bound - black cloth with no top stain white pastedowns.

		F/F	F/NF	NF/VG+	VG+/VG	VG/VG-	Good	w/o dj
1st ed	U.S.	$35	$30	$25	$20	$15	$10	70%
1st ed	U.K.	$70	$60	$50	$40	$30	$15	70%

Trial Run 1978 U.K. 1979 U.S.

"HARPER & ROW, PUBLISHERS/New York, Hagerstown,/San Francisco, London" on title page. No date on title page. Copyright page - 6th (of 16) line "FIRST U.S. EDITION". Last line "79 80 81 82 83 84 10 9 8 7 6 5 4 3 2 1". DJ price - $8.95. Quarter bound - black cloth with gray sides and no top stain. Map on pastedowns.

"LONDON/MICHAEL JOSEPH" on title page. No date on title page. Copyright page - 1st (of 12) line - "First published in Great Britain by Michael Joseph, Ltd". DJ price - £4.50. Full bound - black cloth with no top stain and map of Moscow on pastedowns.

		F/F	F/NF	NF/VG+	VG+/VG	VG/VG-	Good	w/odj
1st ed	U.S.	$35	$30	$25	$20	$15	$10	70%
1st ed	U.K.	$65	$55	$45	$35	$25	$15	70%

Whip Hand 1979 U.K. 1980 U.S.

"HARPER & ROW, PUBLISHERS/NEW YORK/Cambridge   London/Hagerstown Mexico City/Philadelphia   Sao Paulo/San Francisco   Sydney" on page opposite title page. No date on title page. Copyright page - 8th (of 19) line - "FIRST U.S. EDITION". Last line "80 81 82 83 84   10 9 8 7 6 5 4 3 2 1". DJ price - $9.95. Quarter bound - black cloth with tan sides and no top stain. Tan pastedowns.

"LONDON/MICHAEL JOSEPH" on title page. No date on title page. Copyright page - 1st (of 11) line - "First published in Great Britain by Michael Joseph". Full bound - red cloth with no top stain white pastedowns.

		F/F	F/NF	NF/VG+	VG+/VG	VG/VG-	Good	w/odj
1st ed	U.S.	$30	$25	$20	$15	$10	$8	75%
1st ed	U.K.	$55	$45	$35	$25	$20	$15	75%

Reflex U.K. 1980   U.S. 1981   50,000 U.S. copies

"G.P. Putnam's Sons/New York" on title page.   Copyright page - ten lines, no mention of edition number.   Tenth line "PRINTED IN THE UNITED STATES OF AMERICA".   Later editions have an eleventh line such as "Second Impression".   DJ price - $11.95. Quarter bound - black spine with black paper and no top stain. Cream pastedowns.

"LONDON/MICHAEL JOSEPH" on title page. No date on title page. Copyright page - 1st (of 12) line - "First published in Great Britain by Michael Joseph Limited". DJ price - £5.95. Full bound - black cloth with no top stain and white pastedowns.

		F/F	F/NF	NF/VG+	VG+/VG	VG/VG-	Good	w/odj
1st ed	U.S.	$25	$20	$15	$10	$8	$6	75%
1st ed	U.K.	$50	$40	$30	$20	$15	$10	75%

Twice Shy 1981 U.K. 1982 U.S. 60,000 U.S. copies

"G.P. PUTNAM'S SONS   NEW YORK" on title page. No date on title page. Copyright page - ten lines with no mention of printing number. DJ price - $13.95. Quarter bound - black spine with black paper and purple pastedowns. No top stain.

"LONDON/MICHAEL JOSEPH" on title page. No date on title page. Copyright page - 1st (of 17) line - "First published in Great Britain by Michael Joseph". DJ price - £6.95. Full bound - black cloth with no top stain white pastedowns.

		F/F	F/NF	NF/VG+	VG+/VG	VG/VG-	Good	w/odj
1st ed	U.S.	$25	$20	$15	$10	$8	$6	75%

1st ed	U.K.	$50	$40	$30	$20	$15	$10	75%

Banker 1982 U.K. 1983 U.S. 75,000 U.S. copies

"G.P. PUTNAM'S SONS NEW YORK" on title page. No date on title page. Copyright page - 1st (of 11) line - "First American Edition". DJ price - $14.95.
Quarter bound - dark blue spine with blue paper and pastedowns. No top stain.

		F/F	F/NF	NF/VG+	VG+/VG	VG/VG-	Good	w/o dj
1st ed	U.S.	$25	$20	$15	$10	$8	$6	75%
1st ed	U.K.	$50	$40	$30	$20	$15	$10	75%

The Danger 1983 U.K. 1984 U.S. 100,000 U.S. copies

"G.P. Putnam's Sons | New York" on title page. No date on title page. Copyright page - eleven lines, no mention of edition number. Tenth line "PRINTED IN THE UNITED STATES OF AMERICA". Later editions have an extra line such as "Second Impression". DJ price - $15.95.
Quarter bound - gold spine with light gold paper and no top stain. Gold pastedowns.

"LONDON/MICHAEL JOSEPH" on title page. No date on title page. Copyright page - 1st (of 16) line - "First published in Great Britain by". DJ price - £7.95.
Full bound - black cloth with no top stain and white pastedowns.

		F/F	F/NF	NF/VG+	VG+/VG	VG/VG-	Good	w/o dj
1st ed	U.S.	$20	$15	$10	$8	$6	$4	75%
1st ed	U.K.	$40	$30	$20	$15	$10	$6	75%

Proof 1984 U.K. 1985 U.S. 110,000 U.S. copies

"G.P. Putnam's Sons New York" on title page. No date on title page. Copyright page - th last (of 15) line - "1 2 3 4 5 6 7 8 9 10". No use of the word "edition". DJ price - $16.95.
Quarter bound - dark blue spine with blue paper and pastedowns. No top stain.

		F/F	F/NF	NF/VG+	VG+/VG	VG/VG-	Good	w/o dj
1st ed	U.S.	$20	$15	$10	$8	$6	$4	75%
1st ed	U.K.	$40	$30	$20	$15	$10	$6	75%

Break In 1985 U.K. 1986 U.S.

"G.P. PUTNAM'S SONS/NEW YORK" on title page. No date on title page. Copyright page - last (of 17) line - "1 2 3 4 5 6 7 8 9 10". No use of the word "edition". DJ price - $17.95.
Quarter bound - brown spine with burnt orange paper and pastedowns. No top stain.

"MICHAEL JOSEPH/LONDON" on title page. No date on title page. Copyright page - 1st (of 21) line - "First Published in Great Britain by". Full bound - black cloth with no top stain and white pastedowns.

		F/F	F/NF	NF/VG+	VG+/VG	VG/VG-	Good	w/o dj
1st ed	U.S.	$20	$15	$10	$8	$6	$4	75%
1st ed	U.K.	$40	$30	$20	$15	$10	$6	75%

A Jockey's Life: The Biography of Lester Piggott 1986 U.S. Also **Lester The**

Official Biography 1986 U.K.

		F/F	F/NF	NF/VG+	VG+/VG	VG/VG-	Good	w/o dj
1st ed	U.S.	$40	$35	$30	$25	$20	$10	75%
1st ed	U.K.	$45	$40	$35	$30	$25	$12	75%

Bolt 1986 U.K. 1987 U.S. 140,000 U.S. copies

"G.P. PUTNAM'S SONS/NEW YORK" on title page. No date on title page. Copyright page -
last (of 18) line - "1 2 3 4 5 6 7 8 9 10". No use of the word "edition". DJ price - $17.95.
Quarter bound - gray spine with gray paper and pastedowns. No top stain.

"MICHAEL JOSEPH/LONDON" on title page. No date on title page. Copyright page - 1st (of
21) line - "First Published in Great Britain by" DJ price - £9.95.
Full bound - black cloth with no top stain and white pastedowns.

		F/F	F/NF	NF/VG+	VG+/VG	VG/VG-	Good	w/o dj
1st ed	U.S.	$20	$15	$10	$8	$6	$4	75%
1st ed	U.K.	$40	$30	$20	$15	$10	$6	75%

Hot Money 1987 U.K. 1988 U.S. 155,000 U.S. copies

"G.P. PUTNAM'S SONS/NEW YORK" on title page. No date on title page. Copyright page -
last (of 18) line - "1 2 3 4 5 6 7 8 9 10". 5th line - "First American Edition 1988". DJ price -
$17.95. Quarter bound - black spine with black paper and gray pastedowns. No top stain.

"MICHAEL JOSEPH/LONDON" on title page. No date on title page. Copyright page - 1st (of
18) line - "First Published in Great Britain by Michael Joseph, Ltd" DJ price - £10.95.
Full bound - blackj cloth with no top stain and white pastedowns.

		F/F	F/NF	NF/VG+	VG+/VG	VG/VG-	Good	w/o dj
1st ed	U.S.	$20	$15	$10	$8	$6	$4	75%
1st ed	U.K.	$40	$30	$20	$15	$10	$6	75%

The Edge 1988 U.K. 1989 U.S. 60,000 U.S. copies

"G.P. PUTNAM'S SONS/*New York*" on title page. No date on title page. Copyright page -
4th (of 20) line - "*First American Edition 1989*" and last line - "1 2 3 4 5 6 7 8 9 10". No use of
the word "edition". DJ price - $18.95.
Quarter bound - brown spine with tan paper and no top stain. Tan pastedowns.

"MICHAEL JOSEPH/LONDON" on title page. No date on title page. Copyright page - 9th (of
26) line - "First Published 1988". Full bound - blue cloth with no top stain and white
pastedowns.

		F/F	F/NF	NF/VG+	VG+/VG	VG/VG-	Good	w/o dj
1st ed	U.S.	$20	$15	$10	$8	$6	$4	75%
1st ed	U.K.	$40	$30	$20	$15	$10	$6	75%

Straight 1989 U.K. 1989 U.S. 225,000 U.S. copies

"G.P. PUTNAM'S SONS/*New York*" on title page. No date on title page. Copyright page -
last (of 17) line - "1 2 3 4 5 6 7 8 9 10". No use of the word "edition". DJ price - $18.95.
Quarter bound - black spine with gray paper and no top stain. Blue pastedowns.

"MICHAEL JOSEPH/London" on title page. No date on title page. Copyright page - 9th (of 24) line - "First published 1989.". DJ price - Canada $24.95 £12.95. Full bound - blue cloth with no top stain and white pastedowns.

		F/F	F/NF	NF/VG +	VG +/VG	VG/VG -	Good	w/o dj
1st ed	U.S.	$20	$15	$10	$8	$6	$4	75%
1st ed	U.K.	$40	$30	$20	$15	$10	$6	75%

Longshot 1990 U.K.   1990 U.S.

"G.P. PUTNAM'S SONS/New York" on title page. No date on title page. Copyright page - 17th (of 19) line - "1 2 3 4 5 6 7 8 9 10". No use of the word "edition". DJ price - $19.95. Quarter bound - blue-green spine with green paper and no top stain. Green pastedowns.

"MICHAEL JOSEPH/London" on title page. No date on title page. Copyright page - 9th (of 24) line - "First published 1990.". DJ price - Canada $24.95   £13.99. Full bound - black cloth with no top stain and white pastedowns.

		F/F	F/NF	NF/VG +	VG +/VG	VG/VG -	Good	w/o dj
1st ed	U.S.	$20	$15	$10	$8	$6	$4	75%
1st ed	U.K.	$40	$30	$20	$15	$10	$6	75%

Comeback 1991

"G.P. PUTNAM'S SONS/New York" on title page. No date on title page. Copyright page - 17th (of 19) line - "1 2 3 4 5 6 7 8 9 10". No use of the word "edition". DJ price - $21.95. Quarter bound - blue-green spine with gray paper and no top stain. Gray pastedowns.

		F/F	F/NF	NF/VG +	VG +/VG	VG/VG -	Good	w/o dj
1st ed	U.S.	$20	$15	$10	$8	$6	$4	75%
1st ed	U.K.	$40	$30	$20	$15	$10	$6	75%

Driving Force 1992

"G.P. PUTNAM'S SONS   NEW YORK" on title page. No date on title page. Copyright page - 17th (of 19) line - "1 2 3 4 5 6 7 8 9 10". No use of the word "edition". DJ price - $21.95. Quarter bound - orange spine with tan paper and no top stain. Tan pastedowns.

"MICHAEL JOSEPH/LONDON" on title page. No date on title page. Copyright page - 9th (of 25) line - "First published in Great Britain 1992". DJ price - Canada $25.99   £14.99. Full bound - black cloth with no top stain and white pastedowns.

		F/F	F/NF	NF/VG +	VG +/VG	VG/VG -	Good	w/o dj
1st ed	U.S.	$20	$15	$10	$8	$6	$4	75%
1st ed	U.K.	$40	$30	$20	$15	$10	$6	75%

John Gardner

The Derek Torry Books

A Complete State of Death 1969

"Jonathan Cape Thirty Bedford Square London" on title page. No date on title page. Copyright page - 1st (of 9) line "First published 1969". DJ price - 25s. Full bound - brown cloth with black top stain and white pastedowns.

	F/F	F/NF	NF/VG+	VG+/VG	VG/VG-	Good	w/odj
1st US ed	$40	$35	$30	$25	$20	$10	70%
1st UK ed	$60	$55	$50	$40	$30	$10	70%

The Corner Men   1974

"DOUBLEDAY & COMPANY, INC./Garden City, New York/1976" on title page. Copyright page - 11th (of 11) line "First Edition in the United States of America". DJ price - $7.95. Quarter bound - maroon cloth with red sides and no top stain. White pastedowns.

"*London/* MICHAEL JOSEPH" on title page. No date on title page. Copyright page - 1st (of 19) line "*First published in Great Britain by*". DJ price - L3.00. Full bound - blue cloth with no top stain and white pastedowns.

	F/F	F/NF	NF/VG+	VG+/VG	VG/VG-	Good	w/odj
1st US ed	$30	$25	$20	$15	$10	$7	80%
1st UK ed	$50	$45	$40	$40	$30	$10	80%

The Boysie Oakes Books

The Liquidator   1964   1st Boysie Oakes book

"*New York   The Viking Press*" on title page. No date on title page. Copyright page - 3rd (of 8) line "Published in 1964 by The Viking Press, Inc." 6th line "Printed in U.S.A. by The Colonial Press, Inc." Full bound - blue cloth with black top stain and white pastedowns.
Note: The most common book club edition has no book club impression on the rear board but is distinguished from a true first edition by the 6th line on the copyright page which indicates the printer as Mahony & Roese, Inc.

	F/F	F/NF	NF/VG+	VG+/VG	VG/VG-	Good	w/odj
1st US ed	$50	$45	$40	$30	$20	$10	70%
1st UK ed	$75	$70	$60	$50	$30	$10	70%

Understrike   1965   2nd Boysie Oakes book

"NEW YORK THE VIKING PRESS" on title page. No date on title page. Copyright page - 3rd (of 6) line "Published in 1965 by The Viking Press, Inc.". 6th line "Printed in U.S.A. by Vail-Ballou Press, Inc., Binghamton, N.Y."
Quarter bound - orange cloth with black sides and orange top stain. White pastedowns.

	F/F	F/NF	NF/VG+	VG+/VG	VG/VG-	Good	w/odj
1st US ed	$45	$40	$35	$30	$20	$10	70%
1st UK ed	$70	$65	$55	$45	$30	$10	70%

Amber Nine   1966   3rd Boysie Oakes book

"New York THE VIKING PRESS" on title page. No date on title page. Copyright page - 3rd (of 20) line "Published in 1966 by The Viking Press, Inc,". 6th line "Printed in U.S.A. by The Colonial Press Inc." DJ price - $3.95.
Quarter bound - orange cloth with black sides and orange top stain. White pastedowns.

	F/F	F/NF	NF/VG+	VG+/VG	VG/VG-	Good	w/odj

		F/F	F/NF	NF/VG+	VG+/VG	VG/VG-	Good	w/odj
1st US ed		$40	$35	$30	$25	$20	$10	70%
1st UK ed		$60	$55	$50	$40	$30	$10	70%

Madrigal 1967   4th Boysie Oakes book

"NEW YORK / THE VIKING PRESS"on title page. No date on title page. Copyright page - 3rd (of 8) line "First published in 1968 by The Viking Press, Inc." 6th line "Printed in U.S.A." DJ price - $4.95.
Quarter bound - black cloth with forest green sides and black top stain. Black pastedowns.

		F/F	F/NF	NF/VG+	VG+/VG	VG/VG-	Good	w/odj
1st US ed		$40	$35	$30	$25	$20	$10	70%
1st UK ed		$60	$55	$50	$40	$30	$10	70%

Founder Member 1969   5th Boysie Oakes book

"FREDERICK MULLER" on title page. No date on title page. Copyright page - 1st (of 8) line *First published in Great Britain 1969 by*". DJ price - 25s/L1.25p. Full bound - blue cloth with no top stain and white pastedowns.

		F/F	F/NF	NF/VG+	VG+/VG	VG/VG-	Good	w/odj
1st US ed		$40	$35	$30	$25	$20	$10	70%
1st UK ed		$60	$55	$50	$40	$30	$10	70%

Traitor's Exit 1970   6th Boysie Oakes book

"FREDERICK MULLER" on title page. No date on title page. Copyright page - 1st (of 13) line *First published in Great Britain 1970"*. DJ price - 25/-net/L1.25 Rear dj flap is blank.
Full bound - brown cloth with no top stain and white pastedowns.

		F/F	F/NF	NF/VG+	VG+/VG	VG/VG-	Good	w/odj
1st US ed		$35	$30	$25	$20	$15	$8	70%
1st UK ed		$55	$50	$45	$40	$30	$10	70%

Air Apparent US 1971   The Airline Pirates UK   7th Boysie Oakes book

"G.P. Putnam's Sons New York" on title page. No date on title page. Copyright page - 1st (of 9) line *"FIRST AMERICAN EDITION 1971"*. DJ price - $5.95. Full bound - red cloth with no top stain and white pastedowns.

		F/F	F/NF	NF/VG+	VG+/VG	VG/VG-	Good	w/odj
1st US ed		$30	$25	$20	$15	$10	$7	80%
1st UK ed		$50	$45	$40	$40	$30	$10	80%

A Killer for a Song 1975   8th Boysie Oakes book

"HODDER AND STOUGHTON/LONDON SYDNEY AUCKLAND TORONTO" on title page. No date on title page. Copyright page - 3rd (of 11) line "..... First printed 1975. ...." DJ price - L2.50. Full bound - blue-green cloth with no top stain and white pastedowns.

		F/F	F/NF	NF/VG+	VG+/VG	VG/VG-	Good	w/odj
1st US ed		$30	$25	$20	$15	$10	$7	80%

1st UK ed		$50	$45	$40	$40	$30	$10	80%

The Return of Moriarty 1974

"*G.P. Putnam's Sons/New York*" on title page. No date on title page. Copyright page - seven lines with no mention of printing or edition number. DJ price - $8.95. Full bound - black cloth with no top stain and white pastedowns.

		F/F	F/NF	NF/VG+	VG+/VG	VG/VG-	Good	w/o dj
1st US ed		$45	$40	$35	$25	$20	$10	70%
1st UK ed		$90	$75	$60	$50	$40	$15	70%

The Revenge of Moriarty 1975

"*G.P. Putnam's Sons/New York*" on title page. No date on title page. Copyright page - 1st (of 8) line "First American Edition 1975". DJ price - $8.95. Full bound - black cloth with no top stain and white pastedowns.

"*Weidenfeld and Nicolson London*" on title page. No date on title page. Copyright page - 14 lines with no mention of printing or edition number. DJ price - L3.65. Full bound - red cloth with no top stain and white pastedowns.

		F/F	F/NF	NF/VG+	VG+/VG	VG/VG-	Good	w/o dj
1st US ed		$40	$35	$30	$25	$20	$10	70%
1st UK ed		$80	$65	$50	$40	$30	$10	70%

Other Novels

The Werewolf Trace 1977

"*Doubleday & Company, Inc./Garden City, New York/1977*" on title page. Copyright page - 6th (of 6) line "First Edition in the United States of America". DJ price - $7.95. Quarter bound - black cloth with brown sides and no top stain. White pastedowns.

		F/F	F/NF	NF/VG+	VG+/VG	VG/VG-	Good	w/o dj
1st US ed		$25	$20	$15	$10	$8	$6	80%
1st UK ed		$40	$30	$25	$20	$12	$6	80%

The Nostradamus Traitor 1979

"DOUBLEDAY & COMPANY, INC./GARDEN CITY, NEW YORK 1979" on title page. Copyright page - last (of 11) line "First Edition". DJ price - $8.95. Quarter bound - red cloth with black sides and no top stain. White pastedowns.

		F/F	F/NF	NF/VG+	VG+/VG	VG/VG-	Good	w/o dj
1st ed		$25	$20	$15	$10	$8	$6	80%

Sue Grafton

A is for Alibi 1982 First of the Kinsey Millhone mysteries.

"HOLT, RINEHART AND WINSTON 1982/New York" on title page.
Copyright page - 16th (of 19) line -*"First Edition"*. Last line - *"1 3 5 7 9 10 8 6 4 2"*.
DJ price - $12.95. Full bound - gray with no top stain and white pastedowns.

	F/F	F/NF	NF/VG+	VG+/VG	VG/VG-	Good	w/o dj
1st ed		$600	$500	$400	$250	$200	$125	75%

B is for Burglar 1985

"HOLT, RINEHART AND WINSTON/New York" on title page. No date on title page.
Copyright page - 15th (of 19) line -*"First Edition"*. 18th line - *"1 3 5 7 9 10 8 6 4 2"*.
DJ price - $14.95. Quarter bound - red cloth with gray sides and no top stain. White pastedowns.

	F/F	F/NF	NF/VG+	VG+/VG	VG/VG-	Good	w/o dj
1st ed		$500	$350	$250	$175	$150	$100	75%

C is for Corpse 1986

"HENRY HOLT AND COMPANY/New York" on title page. No date on title page.
Copyright page - 24th (of 25) line - *"1 3 5 7 9 10 8 6 4 2"*.
DJ price - $14.95. Full bound - light gray with no top stain and white pastedowns.

	F/F	F/NF	NF/VG+	VG+/VG	VG/VG-	Good	w/o dj
1st ed		$300	$250	$200	$150	$125	$50	75%

D is for Deadbeat 1987

"HENRY HOLT AND COMPANY/New York" on title page. No date on title page.
Copyright page - 15th (of 18) line -*"First Edition"*, 17th line - *"1 3 5 7 9 10 8 6 4 2"*.
DJ price - $15.95. Full bound - black with no top stain and white pastedowns.

	F/F	F/NF	NF/VG+	VG+/VG	VG/VG-	Good	w/o dj
1st ed		$150	$120	$90	$75	$50	$25	75%

E is for Evidence 1988

"HENRY HOLT AND COMPANY/New York" on title page. No date on title page.
Copyright page - 17th (of 20) line - "First Edition", 19th line - "1 3 5 7 9 10 8 6 4 2".
DJ price - $15.95. Quarter bound - black cloth with gray sides and no top stain. White pastedowns.

	F/F	F/NF	NF/VG+	VG+/VG	VG/VG-	Good	w/o dj
1st ed		$60	$50	$40	$30	$20	$10	75%

F is for Fugitive 1989

"HENRY HOLT AND COMPANY/New York" on title page. No date on title page.
Copyright page - 26th (of 28) line - "First Edition", 28th line - "1 3 5 7 9 10 8 6 4 2".
DJ price - $15.95.

	F/F	F/NF	NF/VG+	VG+/VG	VG/VG-	Good	w/o dj
1st ed		$35	$30	$25	$20	$15	$10	75%

G is for Gumshoe 1990

"HENRY HOLT AND COMPANY New York" on page opposite title page. No date on title page. Copyright page - 27th (of 33) line - "First Edition", last line "10 9 8 7 6 5 4 3 2 1". DJ price - $16.95. Quarter bound - black cloth with gray sides and no top stain. White pastedowns.

	F/F	F/NF	NF/VG+	VG+/VG	VG/VG-	Good	w/o dj
1st ed	$25	$20	$15	$12	$10	$8	80%

H is for Homicide 1991

"Henry Holt and Company/New York" on title page. No date on title page. Copyright page - 24th (of 30) line - "First Edition", last line "1 2 3 4 5 6 7 8 9 10" DJ price- $17.95. Quarter bound - black cloth with gray sides and no top stain. White pastedowns.

	F/F	F/NF	NF/VG+	VG+/VG	VG/VG-	Good	w/o dj
1st ed	$15	$12	$10	$8	$6	$4	80%

I is for Innocent 1992

"Henry Holt and Company New York" on page opposite title page. No date on title page. Copyright page - 23th (of 29) line - "First Edition - 1992", last line - "10 9 8 7 6 5 4 3 2 1". DJ price - $18.95. Quarter bound - black cloth with red sides and no top stain. White pastedowns.

	F/F	F/NF	NF/VG+	VG+/VG	VG/VG-	Good	w/o dj
1st ed	$15	$12	$10	$8	$6	$4	80%

J is for Judgement 1993

"Henry Holt and Company/New York" on title page. No date on title page. Copyright page - 19th (of 23) line - "First Edition - 1993", last line - "1 3 5 7 9 10 8 6 4 2" DJ price - $21.95. Quarter bound - black cloth with blue sides and no top stain. White pastedowns.

	F/F	F/NF	NF/VG+	VG+/VG	VG/VG-	Good	w/o dj
1st ed	$15	$12	$10	$8	$6	$4	80%

Martha Grimes

The Man with a Load of Mischief 1981

"LITTLE, BROWN AND COMPANY/Boston Toronto" on title page. No date on title page. Copyright page - 8th (of 19) line - "FIRST EDITION". DJ price - $12.95. Full bound - burnt-orange cloth with no top stain and white pastedowns.

	F/F	F/NF	NF/VG+	VG+/VG	VG/VG-	Good	w/o dj
1st ed	$200	$150	$125	$75	$50	$20	70%

The Old Fox Deceiv'd 1982

"Little, Brown and Company/Boston Toronto" on title page. No date on title page. Copyright page - 7th (of 18) line - "FIRST EDITION". Quarter bound - blue cloth with orange sides and no top stain. White pastedowns.

	F/F	F/NF	NF/VG+	VG+/VG	VG/VG-	Good	w/o dj
1st ed	$125	$100	$75	$60	$45	$20	70%

The Anodyne Necklace 1983

"Little, Brown and Company/BOSTON TORONTO" on title page. No date on title page.
Copyright page - 8th (of 20) line - "FIRST EDITION". DJ price - $14.95. Quarter bound -
green cloth with tan sides and no top stain. White pastedowns.

	F/F	F/NF	NF/VG+	VG+/VG	VG/VG-	Good	w/o dj
1st ed	$100	$80	$60	$40	$30	$15	80%

The Dirty Duck 1984

"LITTLE, BROWN AND COMPANY BOSTON TORONTO" on title page. No date on title
page. Copyright page - 8th (of 19) line - "FIRST EDITION". DJ price - $14.95. Quarter bound
- gray cloth with light blue-green sides and no top stain. White pastedowns.

	F/F	F/NF	NF/VG+	VG+/VG	VG/VG-	Good	w/o dj
1st ed	$35	$30	$25	$15	$10	$6	80%

Jerusalem Inn 1984

"LITTLE, BROWN AND COMPANY/BOSTON TORONTO" on title page. No date on title
page. Copyright page - 7th (of 21) line - "FIRST EDITION". DJ price - $15.95. Quarter bound
- gray cloth with blue sides and no top stain. White pastedowns.

	F/F	F/NF	NF/VG+	VG+/VG	VG/VG-	Good	w/o dj
1st ed	$35	$30	$25	$15	$10	$6	80%

Help the Poor Struggler 1985

"Little, Brown and Company/BOSTON TORONTO" on title page. No date on title page.
Copyright page - 7th (of 23) line - "FIRST EDITION". DJ price - $15.95. Quarter bound - red
cloth with light gray sides and no top stain. White pastedowns.

	F/F	F/NF	NF/VG+	VG+/VG	VG/VG-	Good	w/o dj
1st ed	$30	$25	$20	$13	$10	$6	80%

The Deer Leap 1985

"LITTLE, BROWN AND COMPANY/BOSTON TORONTO" on title page. No date on title
page. Copyright page - 7th (of 19) line - "FIRST EDITION". DJ price - $15.95. Quarter bound
- blue cloth with gray sides and no top stain. White pastedowns.

	F/F	F/NF	NF/VG+	VG+/VG	VG/VG-	Good	w/o dj
1st ed	$25	$20	$15	$10	$8	$5	80%

I Am the Only Running Footman 1986

"LITTLE, BROWN AND COMPANY/BOSTON TORONTO" on title page. No date on title
page. Copyright page - 7th (of 31) line - "FIRST EDITION". DJ price - $15.95. Quarter bound
- blue cloth with light gold sides and no top stain. White pastedowns.

	F/F	F/NF	NF/VG+	VG+/VG	VG/VG-	Good	w/o dj
1st ed	$25	$20	$15	$10	$8	$5	80%

The Five Bells and Bladebone 1987

"LITTLE, BROWN AND COMPANY/Boston Toronto" on title page. No date on title page. Copyright page - 8th (of 19) line - "FIRST EDITION". DJ price - $15.95.
Quarter bound - brown cloth with gray sides and no top stain. White pastedowns.

	F/F	F/NF	NF/VG+	VG+/VG	VG/VG-	Good	w/o dj
1st ed	$20	$15	$12	$9	$7	$4	80%

The Old Silent 1989

"LITTLE, BROWN AND COMPANY/BOSTON TORONTO LONDON" on title page. No date on title page. Copyright page - 6th (of 35) line - "FIRST EDITION". 30th line - "10 9 8 7 6 5 4 3 2 1". DJ price - $18.95/$22.95 in Canada. Quarter bound - steel-blue cloth with cream sides and no top stain. Lavender pastedowns.

	F/F	F/NF	NF/VG+	VG+/VG	VG/VG-	Good	w/o dj
1st ed	$20	$15	$12	$9	$7	$4	80%

John Grisham

A Time To Kill 1989 5,000 copies

First edition, published by Wynwood Press in 1989, is extremely rare. True first edition makes no mention of The Firm on either the dj or in the foreward to the book. The book was reprinted in 1993 by Doubleday. First issues of the Doubleday edition contain the words "First Edition" on the copyright page. These are not true firsts.

	F/F	F/NF	NF/VG+	VG+/VG	VG/VG-	Good	w/o dj
1st ed	$2,500	$2,200	$1,800	$1,300	$1,100	$600	70%

The Firm 1991

"DOUBLEDAY/_____/NEW YORK LONDON TORONTO SYDNEY AUCKLAND" on page opposite title page. No date on title page. Copyright page - 25th and 26th (of 26) lines - "First Edition/1 3 5 7 9 10 8 6 4 2". DJ price - U.S. $19.95/CANADA $24.95. No different for later editions.
Quarter bound - black cloth with gray sides and no top stain. Gold pastedowns.

	F/F	F/NF	NF/VG+	VG+/VG	VG/VG-	Good	w/o dj
1st ed	$175	$135	$100	$80	$60	$40	95%

The Pelican Brief 1992

"DOUBLEDAY/NEW YORK LONDON TORONTO SYDNEY AUCKLAND" on title page. No date on title page. Copyright page - 22nd, 23rd, and 24th (of 24) lines - "March 1992/First Edition/1 3 5 7 9 10 8 6 4 2". DJ price U.S. - $22.50/Canada $27.50.
First issue dj has no bar code at the bottom of the front dj flap. Later issues have bar code.
Quarter bound - black cloth with brown sides and no top stain. Burnt orange pastedowns.

	F/F	F/NF	NF/VG+	VG+/VG	VG/VG-	Good	w/o dj
1st ed	$40	$35	$30	$25	$20	$10	70%

The Client 1993

"DOUBLEDAY/New York London Toronto Sydney Auckland" on title page. No date on title page. Copyright page - 23rd and 24th (of 24) lines - "First Edition/1 3 5 7 9 10 8 6 4 2".
DJ price U.S. - $23.50/CANADA $27.50.
Quarter bound - black cloth with gray sides and no top stain. Black pastedowns.

	F/F	F/NF	NF/VG+	VG+/VG	VG/VG-	Good	w/o dj
1st ed	$25	$20	$15	$12	$10	$7	90%

The Chamber 1994

"DOUBLEDAY/New York London Toronto Sydney Auckland" on title page. No date on title page. Copyright page - 25th and 26th (of 26) lines - "First Edition/1 3 5 7 9 10 8 6 4 2".
DJ price - U.S. $24.95/CANADA $29.95.
Quarter bound - purple cloth with gray sides and no top stain. Purple pastedowns.

	F/F	F/NF	NF/VG+	VG+/VG	VG/VG-	Good	w/o dj
1st ed	$20	$15	$12	$9	$6	$4	90%

Alex Haley

Roots 1976   Made into popular television miniseries.

"DOUBLEDAY & COMPANY, INC./GARDEN CITY, NEW YORK/1976 " on title page.
Copyright page - last (of 17) line - "First Edition". DJ price - $12.50.
Quarter bound - black cloth with tan sides and no top stain. White pastedowns.
First edition DJ contains a photo of author on entire rear panel. Photo shows the standing author to below the knees. Author is wearing a dark tie with white stripped pattern. Later DJ shows author holding a chair.

	F/F	F/NF	NF/VG+	VG+/VG	VG/VG-	Good	w/o dj
1st ed	$60	$50	$40	$30	$25	$10	70%

Thomas Harris

Black Sunday 1975

G.P. Putnam's Sons New York" on title page. No date on title page. Copyright page - nine lines - no mention of printing number. DJ price $7.95.
Full bound - red cloth with no top stain and white pastedowns.

	F/F	F/NF	NF/VG+	VG+/VG	VG/VG-	Good	w/o dj
1st ed	$100	$80	$50	$35	$25	$10	60%

The Silence of the Lamb 1988

"ST. MARTIN'S PRESS NEW YORK" on title page. No date on title page. Copyright page - 19th and 20th (of 20) lines - "First Edition/10 9 8 7 6 5 4 3 2 1". DJ price - $18.95.

Quarter bound - maroon cloth with gray sides and no top stain. White pastedowns.

		F/F	F/NF	NF/VG+	VG+/VG	VG/VG-	Good	w/o dj
1st ed		$40	$30	$20	$15	$10	$8	70%

Ben Hecht

Mircle in the Rain 1943   Made into popular film starring Van Johnson. 52 pages.

"1943/NEW YORK: ALFRED A. KNOPF " on title page. Copyright page - 8th (of 11) line - "FIRST EDITION". DJ price - $1.00.
Full bound - mauve cloth no top stain and white pastedowns.

		F/F	F/NF	NF/VG+	VG+/VG	VG/VG-	Good	w/o dj
1st ed		$40	$35	$25	$18	$12	$8	50%

Joseph Heller

Catch-22   1961

"SIMON AND SCHUSTER NEW YORK 1961"on title page. Copyright page - 8th (of 11) line - "FIRST PRINTING". DJ price - $5.95. Full page photo on rear panel.
Full bound - blue cloth with orange top stain and white pastedowns.
Note: True 1st edition has the Simon & Schuster logo on the very first page of the book. First trade editions have two blank pages preceding page with logo. Both editions are indicated as First Edition. First issue dj does not have reviews on rear panel. Second issue dj contains reviews on rear panel.

		F/F	F/NF	NF/VG+	VG+/VG	VG/VG-	Good	w/o dj
1st ed	1st iss dj	$1,200	$950	$650	$450	$350	$150	40%
1st tr ed	1st iss dj	$900	$750	$500	$350	$275	$125	25%
1st tr ed	2nd dj	$350	$300	$225	$175	$125	$75	50%

Ernest Hemingway (1899-61)

U.S. novelist, born in Oak Park, Ill. In WWI he served as an ambulance driver in France, then he joined the Italian infantry and was wounded. After the war, he became a correcpondent in Paris where he met and was strongly influenced by Gertrude Stein. He published *Three Stories and Ten Poems* (1923), the short stories *In Our Time* (1924), and the novel *The Torrents of Spring* (1926), but it was the novel *The Sun Also Rises* (1926) that established his reputation as a writer. This novel about expatrites also established Hemingway as the spokesman for the Lost Generation. He continued his reputation with *A Farewell to Arms* (1929) and such short stories as *The Killers* and *The Snows of Kilimanjaro*. *To Have and Have Not* (1937) was not as well received as his two previous novels, but *For Whom the Bell Tolls* (1940), which drew on his experience as a correspondent in the Spanish Civil War, was a critical and popular success. His non-fiction also concerned itself with people leading dangerous or especially virile lives and facing the consequences with stoic courage. *Death in the Afternoon* (1932) is about bullfighting while *Green Hills of Africa* (1935) is about big game hunting. The novel *The Old Man and the Sea* appeared in 1952. Hemingway received the Nobel Prize for Literature in 1954. He committed suicide in 1954. Several works were published after his death; *A Moveable Feast* (1964), memoirs of Paris in the 1920's; *Islands in the Stream* (1970); *The Nick Adams Stories* (1972).

The Torrents of Spring 1926

		F/F	F/NF	NF/VG+	VG+/VG	VG/VG-	Good	w/o dj
1st ed		$4,000	$3,000	$2,500	$2,000	$1,500	$750	10%

The Sun Also Rises 1926   5,090 copies in 1st issue. 1st issue has 3 letter p's in the word stopped on page 181, line 26.

		F/F	F/NF	NF/VG+	VG+/VG	VG/VG-	Good	w/o dj
1st ed		$8,000	$6,000	$5,000	$4,000	$3,000	$1,500	10%

Men Without Women 1927

		F/F	F/NF	NF/VG+	VG+/VG	VG/VG-	Good	w/o dj
1st ed		$850	$750	$650	$500	$400	$250	15%

A Farewell to Arms 1929   1st trade edition is without notice about characters.

		F/F	F/NF	NF/VG+	VG+/VG	VG/VG-	Good	w/o dj
1st ed		$850	$750	$650	$500	$400	$250	15%

Death in the Afternoon 1932   10,300 copies

		F/F	F/NF	NF/VG+	VG+/VG	VG/VG-	Good	w/o dj
1st ed		$900	$800	$700	$550	$400	$250	10%

Winner Take Nothing 1933   1st ed "A"

		F/F	F/NF	NF/VG+	VG+/VG	VG/VG-	Good	w/o dj
1st ed		$800	$700	$600	$500	$400	$250	20%

Green Hill of Africa 1935

		F/F	F/NF	NF/VG+	VG+/VG	VG/VG-	Good	w/o dj
1st ed		$800	$700	$600	$500	$400	$250	20%

To Have and Have Not 1937   1st ed "A"

		F/F	F/NF	NF/VG+	VG+/VG	VG/VG-	Good	w/o dj
1st ed		$750	$650	$550	$450	$375	$200	20%

For Whom the Bell Tolls 1940   1st state dj is without photographer's name.

"NEW YORK/CHARLES SCRIBNER'S SONS/1940" on title page. Copyright page - last (of 7) line - "A". DJ price - $2.75. Full page photo of author with *"Ernest Hemingway"* below. Full bound - tan speckled cloth with no top stain. White pastedowns.

		F/F	F/NF	NF/VG+	VG+/VG	VG/VG-	Good	w/o dj
1st ed	1st st	$400	$350	$275	$200	$150	$100	25%
1st ed	2nd st	$150	$100	$80	$60	$50	$30	33%

Across the River and Into the Trees 1950   1st issue dj has yellow letters on spine. 2nd issue dj has orange letters.

		F/F	F/NF	NF/VG+	VG+/VG	VG/VG-	Good	w/o dj
1st ed	1st dj	$150	$125	$75	$50	$35	$15	20%

1st ed	2nd dj	$50	$40	$30	$25	$20	$10	50%

The Old Man and the Sea 1952 First appeared in Sept. 1, 1952 Life Magazine. (NF $25)

		F/F	F/NF	NF/VG+	VG+/VG	VG/VG-	Good	w/o dj
1st ed		$350	$275	$225	$200	$175	$100	20%

Tony Hillerman

The Blessing Way 1970

"HARPER & ROW, PUBLISHERS/NEW YORK, EVANSTON, AND LONDON" on title page. No date on title page. Copyright page - 9th (of 10) line - "FIRST EDITION".
Page 202 - "70 71 72 73 10 9 8 7 6 5 4 3 2 1". DJ price $4.95. Quarter bound - purple cloth with blue sides and no top stain. Black background with white letters on pastedowns.
Note: The words "FIRST EDITION" on the copyright page are NOT sufficient for identifying a true first edition. The sequence on the bottom of the last page of the book (a blank page) must be as shown.

		F/F	F/NF	NF/VG+	VG+/VG	VG/VG-	Good	w/o dj
1st ed		$1,200	$1,100	$800	$500	$300	$100	60%

The Fly on the Wall 1971

"HARPER & ROW, PUBLISHERS/New York, Evanston, San Francisco, London" on title page. No date on title page. Copyright page - 8th (of 10) line - "FIRST EDITION". Last line on page 212 "71 72 73 10 9 8 7 6 5 4 3 2 1". DJ price $5.95. Quarter bound - light blue cloth with light blue sides and no top stain. Light blue background with white letters on pastedowns.

		F/F	F/NF	NF/VG+	VG+/VG	VG/VG-	Good	w/o dj
1st ed		$900	$800	$600	$350	$250	$75	60%

The Boy Who Made Dragonfly 1972

"Harper & Row, Publishers/*New York, Evanston, San Francisco, London*" on title page. No date on title page. Copyright page 14th (of 14) line - "FIRST EDITION". 1st issue dj is machine-clipped at bottom, leaving $4.50 as the issue price. Illustrated front board showing boy in corn field with dragonfly. Tan rear board and pastedowns.
Note: A library version of the 1st issue dj is machine-clipped at the top, leaving $4.11 as the issue price. The library version of the book has a "Harpercrest" stamp on the bottom of the rear board.

		F/F	F/NF	NF/VG+	VG+/VG	VG/VG-	Good	w/o dj
1st ed		$450	$350	$300	$200	$125	$50	65%

The Great Taos Bank Robbery 1973

Alburquerque: U of NM Press. Copyright page states "FIRST EDITION". 1st issue - yellowish gray cloth with a single illustration on the rear panel of the dj. 2nd issue - grayish yellow cloth with two illustrations on rear panel of dj.

		F/F	F/NF	NF/VG+	VG+/VG	VG/VG-	Good	w/o dj
1st iss dj		$450	$350	$300	$200	$125	$50	60%
2nd dj		$400	$300	$275	$175	$100	$40	70%

Dance Hall of the Dead 1973 Winner of Edgar Allan Poe Award

"harper & row, publishers/new york evanston san francisco london" on title page. No date on title page. Copyright page - 9th (of 17) line - "FIRST EDITION". "73 74 75 76 77 10 9 8 7 6 5 4 3 2 1" on page 168.
DJ price $5.95. Quarter bound - burnt orange cloth with light blue sides and no top stain. Blue background with white letters on pastedowns.

		F/F	F/NF	NF/VG+	VG+/VG	VG/VG-	Good	w/odj
1st ed		$800	$700	$500	$350	$250	$100	60%

Listening Woman 1978

"HARPER & ROW, PUBLISHERS/New York, Hagerstown, San Francisco, London" on page opposite title page. No date on title page. Copyright page - 7th (of 16) line - "FIRST EDITION". Last line "78 79 80 81 82 10 9 8 7 6 5 4 3 2 1". DJ price $7.95. Quarter bound - light tan cloth with dark tan sides and no top stain. Black background with white letters on pastedowns.
Note: A BOMC edition with above wording exists. These are distinguished by djs without a price and an BOMC indent in the bottom of the rear board.

		F/F	F/NF	NF/VG+	VG+/VG	VG/VG-	Good	w/odj
1st ed		$400	$300	$225	$175	$125	$50	70%

People of Darkness 1980

"HARPER & ROW, PUBLISHERS/New York/Cambridge London/Hagerstown Mexico City/Philadelphia Sao Paulo/San Francisco Sydney" on page opposite title page. No date on title page. Copyright page - 7th (of 17) line - "FIRST EDITION". Last line "80 81 82 83 84 10 9 8 7 6 5 4 3 2 1". DJ price $9.95. Quarter bound - red cloth with light gray sides and no top stain. Black background with white letters on pastedowns.

		F/F	F/NF	NF/VG+	VG+/VG	VG/VG-	Good	w/odj
1st ed		$400	$300	$225	$175	$125	$50	70%

The Dark Wind 1982

"HARPER & ROW, PUBLISHERS, New York/Cambridge, Philadelphia, San Francisco/London, Mexico City, Sao Paulo, Sydney" on title page. No date on title page. Copyright page - 8th (of 16) line - "FIRST EDITION". Last line "82 83 84 85 86 10 9 8 7 6 5 4 3 2 1". DJ price $12.50. Quarter bound - blue cloth with blue sides and no top stain. White pastedowns.

		F/F	F/NF	NF/VG+	VG+/VG	VG/VG-	Good	w/odj
1st ed		$175	$150	$110	$90	$75	$30	70%

The Ghostway 1985

"HARPER & ROW, PUBLISHERS, New York/Cambridge, Philadelphia, San Francisco, London/Mexico City, Sao Paulo, Singapore, Sydney" on title page. No date on title page. Copyright page - 11th (of 20) line - "FIRST HARPER & ROW EDITION 1985". Last line - "85 86 87 88 89 10 9 8 7 6 5 4 3 2 1". DJ price $13.95. Quarter bound - blue cloth with burnt orange sides and no top stain. White pastedowns.

	F/F	F/NF	NF/VG+	VG+/VG	VG/VG-	Good	w/odj

1st ed		$125	$100	$75	$50	$35	$15	70%

Skinwalkers 1987

"HARPER & ROW, PUBLISHERS, New York/Cambridge, Philadelphia, San Francisco, Washington/London, Mexico City, Sao Paulo, Singapore, Sydney" on title page. No date on title page. Copyright page - 9th (of 18) line - "FIRST EDITION". Last line "86 87 88 89 90 HC 10 9 8 7 6 5 4 3 2 1". DJ price $15.95. Quarter bound - red cloth with white sides and no top stain. Cream pastedowns.

		F/F	F/NF	NF/VG+	VG+/VG	VG/VG-	Good	w/o dj
1st ed		$25	$20	$15	$12	$10	$8	80%

A Thief of Time 1988

"HARPER & ROW, PUBLISHERS/NEW YORK, CAMBRIDGE, PHILADELPHIA/SAN FRANCISCO, WASHINGTON, LONDON, MEXICO CITY/SAO PAULO, SINGAPORE, SYDNEY" on title page. No date on title page. Copyright page - 9th (of 19) line - "FIRST EDITION". Last line - "88 89 90 91 92 HC 10 9 8 7 6 5 4 3 2 1". DJ price $15.95 Full bound - white cloth with no top stain and maps on pastedowns.

		F/F	F/NF	NF/VG+	VG+/VG	VG/VG-	Good	w/o dj
1st ed		$25	$20	$15	$10	$8	$5	85%

Talking God 1989

"HARPER & ROW, PUBLISHERS, New York/Grand Rapids, Philadelphia, St. Louis, San Francisco/London, Singapore, Sydney, Tokyo, Toronto" on title page. No date on title page. Copyright page - 8th (of 12) line "FIRST EDITION". Last line "89 90 91 92 93 CC/HC 10 9 8 7 6 5 4 3 2 1". DJ price $17.95. Quarter bound - navy blue cloth with tan sides and no top stain. Navy blue pastedowns.

		F/F	F/NF	NF/VG+	VG+/VG	VG/VG-	Good	w/o dj
1st ed		$20	$15	$12	$9	$7	$4	85%

Coyote Waits 1990

"HARPER & ROW, PUBLISHERS, New York/Grand Rapids, Philadelphia, St. Louis, San Francisco/London, Singapore, Sydney, Tokyo, Toronto" on title page. No date on title page. Copyright page - 8th (of 18) line - "FIRST EDITION". Last line - "90 91 92 93 94 HC 10 9 8 7 6 5 4 3 2 1". DJ price U.S. $19.95/CANADA $24.95". Quarter bound - maroon cloth with gold sides and no top stain. Purple pastedowns.

		F/F	F/NF	NF/VG+	VG+/VG	VG/VG-	Good	w/o dj
1st ed		$20	$15	$12	$9	$7	$4	85%

Sacred Clowns 1993

"Harper Collins *Publishers*" on title page. No date on title page. Copyright page - 12th (of 23) line - "FIRST EDITION". Last line - "93 94 95 96 97 /RRD 10 9 8 7 6 5 4 3 2 1". DJ price $23.00. Quarter bound - cream cloth with burnt orange sides and no top stain. Burnt orange pastedowns.

	F/F	F/NF	NF/VG+	VG+/VG	VG/VG-	Good	w/o dj

1st ed		$15	$12	$10	$8	$6	$3	85%

The Joe Leaphorn Mysteries 1989

		F/F	F/NF	NF/VG+	VG+/VG	VG/VG-	Good	w/o dj
1st ed		$45	$40	$25	$15	$10	$6	80%

The Jim Chee Mysteries 1990

"Harper Collins *Publishers*" on title page. No date on title page. Copyright page - 12th (of 16) line - "FIRST EDITION". 16th line - "90 91 92 93 94 CC/HC 10 9 8 7 6 5 4 3 2 1". DJ price USA $15.95/CANADA $21.50. Quarter bound - blue cloth with speckled tan sides and no top stain. Speckled tan pastedowns.

		F/F	F/NF	NF/VG+	VG+/VG	VG/VG-	Good	w/o dj
1st ed		$30	$25	$20	$12	$9	$6	80%

Leaphorn & Chee 1992

"Harper Collins *Publishers*" on title page. No date on title page. Copyright page - 18th (of 32) line - "FIRST EDITION". 32nd line - "92 93 94 95 96 CC/RRD 10 9 8 7 6 5 4 3 2 1". DJ price USA $19.00/CANADA $25.50. Quarter bound - red cloth with speckled tan sides and no top stain. White pastedowns.

		F/F	F/NF	NF/VG+	VG+/VG	VG/VG-	Good	w/o dj
1st ed		$25	$20	$17	$12	$9	$6	80%

P.D. James

Cover Her Face 1962

		F/F	F/NF	NF/VG+	VG+/VG	VG/VG-	Good	w/o dj
1st ed		$400	$350	$250	$175	$125	$40	60%

A Mind To Murder 1963

		F/F	F/NF	NF/VG+	VG+/VG	VG/VG-	Good	w/o dj
1st ed		$325	$250	$175	$125	$100	$35	60%

Unnatural Causes 1967

"New York/CHARLES SCRIBNER'S SONS on title page. No date on title page. Copyright page - 8 lines with no mention of printing number. DJ price $3.95. Full bound - blue cloth with no top stain and white pastedowns.

		F/F	F/NF	NF/VG+	VG+/VG	VG/VG-	Good	w/o dj
1st ed		$200	$175	$125	$100	$75	$30	60%

The Maul and the Pear Tree   U.K. 1971   U.S. 1986   written with T.A. Critchley

"THE MYSTERIOUS PRESS New York" on title page. No date on title page. Copyright page - 7th and 8th (of 19) lines - "First Printing: March 1986/10 9 8 7 6 5 4 3 2 1". DJ price - $17.95.

Quarter bound - blue cloth with orange sides and no top stain. City map on pastedowns.

	F/F	F/NF	NF/VG+	VG+/VG	VG/VG-	Good	w/o dj
1st UK	$150	$125	$90	$75	$60	$30	60%
1st US	$20	$18	$14	$10	$8	$5	80%

Shroud for a Nightingale 1971

"CHARLES SCRIBNER'S SONS/New York" on title page. No date on title page. Copyright page - 10 lines with no mention of edition or printing number. DJ price $4.95. Quarter bound - red cloth with gray sides and no top stain and white pastedowns.

	F/F	F/NF	NF/VG+	VG+/VG	VG/VG-	Good	w/o dj
1st ed	$150	$125	$90	$75	$50	$20	60%

An Unsuitable Job for a Woman 1972

"CHARLES SCRIBNER'S SONS/New York" on title page. No date on title page. Copyright page - 9 lines with no mention of edition or printing number; 6th (of 9) line - "A.2.73[c]". DJ price $5.95. Full bound - rose cloth with no top stain and white pastedowns.

	F/F	F/NF	NF/VG+	VG+/VG	VG/VG-	Good	w/o dj
1st ed	$150	$125	$85	$70	$40	$15	70%

The Black Tower 1975   An Adam Dalgliesh Mystery

"CHARLES SCRIBNER'S SONS/NEW YORK" on title page. No date on title page. Copyright page - 6th (of 9) line "1 3 5 7 9 11 13 15 17 19 C/C 20 18 16 14 12 10 8 6 4 2". DJ price $6.95. Full bound - black cloth with no top stain and white pastedowns.

	F/F	F/NF	NF/VG+	VG+/VG	VG/VG-	Good	w/o dj
1st ed	$45	$40	$30	$20	$15	$8	70%

Death of an Expert Witness 1977

"Charles Scribner's Sons/New York" on title page. No date on title page. Copyright page - 8th (of 11) line "1 3 5 7 9 11 13 15 17 19 v/c 20 18 16 14 12 10 8 6 4 2". DJ price $8.95

	F/F	F/NF	NF/VG+	VG+/VG	VG/VG-	Good	w/o dj
1st ed	$30	$25	$20	$15	$10	$6	70%

Innocent Blood 1980

"Charles Scribner's Sons, New York" on title page. No date on title page. Copyright page - 11th (of 12) line "1 3 5 7 9 11 13 15 17 19 F/C 20 18 16 14 12 10 8 6 4 2". DJ price $10.95. Quarter bound - black cloth with red sides and no top stain. Red pastedowns.

	F/F	F/NF	NF/VG+	VG+/VG	VG/VG-	Good	w/o dj
1st ed	$25	$20	$16	$12	$10	$6	80%

The Skull Beneath the Skin 1982

"CHARLES SCRIBNER'S SONS/New York" on title page. No date on title page. Copyright page - 16th (of 21) line "1 3 5 7 9 11 13 15 17 19 F/C 20 18 16 14 12 10 8 6 4 2". DJ price $13.95.

Quarter bound - black cloth with black sides and no top stain. White pastedowns.

	F/F	F/NF	NF/VG +	VG +/VG	VG/VG -	Good	w/o dj
1st ed	$25	$20	$16	$12	$10	$6	80%

James Joyce

Finnagan's Wake 1939

"New York: The Viking Press/1939" on title page. Copyright page - 1st (of 7) line "First published May 1939". DJ price $5.00. Full bound - black cloth with blue-green top stain and white pastedowns. Note: First U.K. edition prices are double those shown below. Errata entitled "Corrections of Misprints in Finnegan's Wake" was issued by Viking in 1945.

	F/F	F/NF	NF/VG +	VG +/VG	VG/VG -	Good	w/o dj
1st ed	$500	$450	$350	$250	$175	$75	60%

Garrison Keillor

Lake Wobegon Days 1985

"VIKING" on title page. No date on title page. Copyright page - 14th (of 36) line "First published in 1985 by Viking Penguin Inc." No other mention of printing number. Later printings have a 37th line indicating the printing number. DJ price $17.95. Writeup on rear dj flap of 1st issue dj refers to National Public Radio. 1st issue dj has a sticker, added to rear flap, stating "CORRECTION: Our radio/show is broadcast by/American Public Radio,/not CBS, NPR, CPR, or/any of the other guys. G.K." Later issue dj have reference corrected to American Public Radio. Quarter bound - red cloth with tan sides and no top stain. Speckled tan pastedowns.

	F/F	F/NF	NF/VG +	VG +/VG	VG/VG -	Good	w/o dj
1st ed	$50	$45	$35	$25	$15	$8	70%

Stephen King (1947 -)

Many of King's books were first released in signed and numbered limited editions. This guide catalogs only the first trade editions of King's full length hardcover books.

Carrie 1974   30,000 copies

Doubleday, Garden City with "1974" on the title page. Copyright page states "First Edition". Inner margin of page 199 contains a date code of "P6". DJ price - $5.95. Purple cloth with gold lettering on spine.

	F/F	F/NF	NF/VG +	VG +/VG	VG/VG -	Good	w/o dj
1st ed	$500	$400	$300	$200	$150	$75	50%

'Salem's Lot 1975   20,000 copies

Doubleday, Garden City with "1975" on the title page. Copyright page states "First Edition". Inner margin of page 439 contains a date code of "Q37". Quarter bound - black cloth with red sides. Issued in three dust jackets. First state, first issue dj refers to Father "Cody" in the writeup on the front flap and carries a retail price of $8.95. First state, second issue dj still refers to Father "Cody" but the $8.95 price is clipped and new price of $7.95 has been added. Second state dj has an unclipped price of $7.95 and "Cody" changed to "Callahan".

		F/F	F/NF	NF/VG+	VG+/VG	VG/VG-	Good	w/o dj
1st ed	1st state, 1st issue dj	$1,100	$900	$700	$500	$400	$200	10%
1st ed	1st st, 2nd issue dj	$850	$725	$550	$400	$325	$150	15%
1st ed	2nd st dj	$600	$500	$350	$250	$190	$80	20%

The Shining 1977 25,000 copies

"DOUBLEDAY & COMPANY, INC./GARDEN CITY, NEW YORK 1977" on title page. DJ price - $8.95. Copyright page - last (of 20) line - "FIRST EDITION". Inner margin of page 447 contains a date code of "R49". Quarter bound - black cloth with tan sides and no top stain. White pastedowns.

		F/F	F/NF	NF/VG+	VG+/VG	VG/VG-	Good	w/o dj
1st ed		$250	$200	$175	$125	$100	$50	50%

Night Shift 1978 12,000 copies

"*Doubleday & Company, Inc.*/GARDEN CITY, NEW YORK/1978" on title page. Copyright page - last (of 29) line - "FIRST EDITION". Inner margin of page 336 contains a date code of "S52". DJ price - $8.95. DJ with banner upper left corner of DJ front panel "Excursions/into horror/by the author of/CARRIE and THE SHINING/Introduction by: John D. MacDonald". Quarter bound - black cloth with red sides and no top stain. White pastedowns.

		F/F	F/NF	NF/VG+	VG+/VG	VG/VG-	Good	w/o dj
1st ed		$500	$400	$300	$250	$200	$75	50%

The Stand 1978 70,000 copies

"DOUBLEDAY & COMPANY, INC., GARDEN CITY, NEW YORK/1978" on title page. Copyright page - last (of 37) line - "*First Edition*". Inner margin of page 823 contains a date code of "T39". DJ price - $12.95. Quarter bound - black cloth with gold sides and no top stain. White pastedowns.

		F/F	F/NF	NF/VG+	VG+/VG	VG/VG-	Good	w/o dj
1st ed		$250	$200	$150	$125	$75	$40	50%

The Dead Zone 1979 50,000 copies

"THE VIKING PRESS NEW YORK" on title page. No date on title page. Copyright page - 3rd (of 20) line - "First published in 1979 by The Viking Press". DJ price - $11.95. Quarter bound - black cloth with black sides and no top stain. White pastedowns.

		F/F	F/NF	NF/VG+	VG+/VG	VG/VG-	Good	w/o dj
1st ed		$65	$50	$40	$30	$25	$15	70%

Firestarter 1980 100,000

"THE VIKING PRESS NEW YORK" on title page. No date on title page. Copyright page - 14th and 15th (of 15) lines - "A limited first edition of this book has/been published by

Phantasia Press". On later printings, a 16th line - "10 9 8 7 6 5 4 3 2" is added. DJ price - $13.95. Quarter bound - orange cloth with black sides and no top stain. White pastedowns.

	F/F	F/NF	NF/VG+	VG+/VG	VG/VG-	Good	w/o dj
1st ed	$40	$35	$30	$25	$20	$10	80%

Danse Macabre 1981

"New York EVEREST HOUSE *Publishers"* on title page. No date on title page. Copyright page - 6th (of 13) line - "RRD281". DJ price - $13.95. Second printing indicated as "2RRD481" Quarter bound - maroon cloth with red sides and no top stain. White pastedowns.

	F/F	F/NF	NF/VG+	VG+/VG	VG/VG-	Good	w/o dj
1st ed	$75	$60	$50	$35	$25	$15	80%

Cujo 1981 150,000 copies

"THE VIKING PRESS/NEW YORK" on title page. No date on title page. Copyright page - 3rd (of 20) line - "First published in 1981 by The Viking Press". No other reference to printing number. On later printings, several more lines are added with the bottom line becoming a print number line such as "2 3 4 5 6 7 8 9". DJ price - $13.95. Quarter bound - black cloth with tan sides and no top stain. White pastedowns.

	F/F	F/NF	NF/VG+	VG+/VG	VG/VG-	Good	w/o dj
1st ed	$45	$35	$25	$20	$15	$8	80%

Different Seasons 1982 200,000 copies

"THE VIKING PRESS NEW YORK" on page opposite the title page. No date on title page. Copyright page - 3rd (of 30) line - "First published in 1982 by The Viking Press" . Later printings have a 31st line add at the bottom such as "2 3 4 5 6 7 8 9 10". DJ price - $16.95. Quarter bound - dark blue cloth with blue sides and no top stain. White pastedowns.

	F/F	F/NF	NF/VG+	VG+/VG	VG/VG-	Good	w/o dj
1st ed	$50	$40	$30	$25	$20	$8	80%

Fear Itself: The Horror Fiction of Stephen King 1982 Tim Underwood and Chuck Miller, Editors.

"Underwood-Miller/San Francisco, California/Columbia, Pennsylvania/1982" on title page. Copyright page - 14th (of 30) line - "FIRST EDITION". DJ price - $13.95. Quarter bound - black cloth with red sides and no top stain. Speckled tan pastedowns.

	F/F	F/NF	NF/VG+	VG+/VG	VG/VG-	Good	w/o dj
1st ed	$35	$30	$20	$15	$10	$6	80%

The Dark Tower: The Gunslinger 1982 10,000 copies of first printing and 10,000 copies of second printing. "DONALD M. GRANT PUBLISHER, INC." on title page. No date on title page. Copyright page - 4th (of 23) line - "First Edition". DJ price - Trade $20.00/Limited $60.00. Full bound - brown with no top stain and pastedowns with water color picture viewed through fence. Second printing indicated as such on copyright page. First issue dj shows price for both Trade Edition and Deluxe Edition. Second issue dj has price for Trade Edition only.

	F/F	F/NF	NF/VG+	VG+/VG	VG/VG-	Good	w/o dj

1st ed	1st iss	$550	$500	$450	$375	$325	$250	20%
1st ed	2nd iss	$175	$150	$125	$90	$75	$40	25%

Christine 1983 270,000 copies

"The Viking Press New York" on title page. No date on title page.
Copyright page - 3rd (of 38) line - "First published in 1983 by The Viking Press".   Later
printings have a 39th line add at the bottom such as "2 3 4 5 6 7 8 9 10".   DJ price - $16.95.
Quarter bound - black cloth with red sides and no top stain. White pastedowns.

		F/F	F/NF	NF/VG+	VG+/VG	VG/VG-	Good	w/o dj
1st ed		$35	$30	$25	$20	$15	$8	80%

Pet Sematary 1983 250,000 copies

"DOUBLEDAY AND COMPANY, INC./GARDEN CITY, NEW YORK/1983" on title page.
Copyright page - last (of 19) line - "FIRST EDITION". DJ price $15.95.
Full bound - black cloth with red pastedowns and no top stain.

		F/F	F/NF	NF/VG+	VG+/VG	VG/VG-	Good	w/o dj
1st ed		$35	$30	$25	$20	$15	$8	80%

The Talisman 1984 Written with Peter Straub

"VIKING/G.P. PUTNAM'S SONS" on title page. No date on title page.
Last line on page opposite the copyright page - "Designed by Ann Gold". This line is
replaced by "Second Printing, November, 1984" on second printing. DJ price - $18.95.
Quarter bound - red cloth with black sides and no top stain. White pastedowns.

		F/F	F/NF	NF/VG+	VG+/VG	VG/VG-	Good	w/o dj
1st ed		$25	$20	$17	$12	$10	$7	80%

Skelton Crew 1985

"G.P. PUTNAM'S SONS/NEW YORK" on title page. No date on title page.
Last line on page opposite the copyright page - "1 2 3 4 5 6 7 8 9 10". DJ price - $18.95.
Quarter bound - black cloth with black sides and no top stain. Tan pastedowns.

		F/F	F/NF	NF/VG+	VG+/VG	VG/VG-	Good	w/o dj
1st ed		$30	$25	$20	$15	$10	$7	75%

It! 1986 800,000 copies

"VIKING" on title page. No date on title page.
Copyright page - 1/2 inch blank space after line 27 (of 35) - "Set in Garamond No. 3." is used
on later printings to add printing information such as "Second Printing". DJ price - $22.95.
Quarter bound - black cloth with black sides and no top stain. Gray pastedowns.

		F/F	F/NF	NF/VG+	VG+/VG	VG/VG-	Good	w/o dj
1st ed		$22	$18	$15	$12	$8	$5	80%

The Dark Tower II: The Drawing of the Three 1987 30,000 copies

"DONALD M. GRANT, PUBLISHER, INC." on title page. Copyright page - 11 (of 13) line - "FIRST EDITION". DJ price - Trade Edition $35.00/Deluxe Edition $100.00. Full bound - black cloth with no top stain. Gray pastedowns with drawing of man and birds in flight.

		F/F	F/NF	NF/VG+	VG+/VG	VG/VG-	Good	w/o dj
1st ed		$75	$60	$45	$30	$25	$15	25%

Misery 1987 1,000,000 copies

"VIKING" on title page. No date on title page. Copyright page - line 9 (of 50) - "First published in 1987 by Viking Penguin, Inc.". No reference to printing number. Later printings indicated by 51st line such as "Second Printing June 1987". DJ price - $18.95. Quarter bound - black cloth with gray sides and no top stain. Red pastedowns.

		F/F	F/NF	NF/VG+	VG+/VG	VG/VG-	Good	w/o dj
1st ed		$22	$18	$15	$12	$8	$5	80%

Tommyknockers 1987

"G.P. PUTNAM'S SONS/New York" on title page. No date on title page. Copyright page - 35th and 36th (of 36) lines - "1 2 3 4 5 6 7 8 9 10/Permission to Come". DJ price - $19.95. U.S./$27.95 CAN. Quarter bound - black cloth with green sides and no top stain. Green pastedowns. First issue dj has "Stephen King" in red. The second issue dj has the "Stephen King" in gold.

		F/F	F/NF	NF/VG+	VG+/VG	VG/VG-	Good	w/o dj
1st ed	1st iss	$25	$20	$16	$12	$9	$5	60%
1st ed	2nd iss	$20	$17	$13	$10	$7	$4	80%

The Eyes of the Dragon 1987 400,000 copies

"VIKING" on the title page. No date on title page. Copyright page - No reference to edition or printing number. Line 17 (of 40) - "First published in 1987 by Viking Penguin, Inc." Lines 28, 29, and 30 - "Printed in the United States of America by/Arcata Graphics Fairfield, Pennsylvania/Composition by NK Graphics, Keene, New Hampshire". Space after line 32 "Designed by Amy Hill". DJ price - $18.95. Quarter bound - cream cloth with green sides and no top stain. Green pastedowns.

		F/F	F/NF	NF/VG+	VG+/VG	VG/VG-	Good	w/o dj
1st ed		$30	$25	$20	$15	$10	$6	80%

NightVisions 5 1988 A collection of three original short stories by Stephen King (The Reploids, Sneakers, and Dedication) plus six others by Dan Simmons, and George R.R. Martin.

"DARK HARVEST/Arlington Hts., Illinois 1988" on title page. Copyright page - 15th (of 16) line - "FIRST EDITION". DJ price - $22.00 Full bound - tan cloth with no top stain and speckled light tan pastedowns.

		F/F	F/NF	NF/VG+	VG+/VG	VG/VG-	Good	w/o dj
1st ed		$40	$35	$27	$20	$15	$8	60%

The Dark Half 1989 1,500,000 U.S. copies 55,000 U.K. copies

"Viking" on page opposite the title page. No date on title page. Copyright page - 12th (of 41) line - "1 3 5 7 9 10 8 6 4 2". DJ price - $21.95 U.S./$27.95 CAN.

Quarter bound - black cloth with black sides and no top stain. Violet pastedowns.
Note: U.K. edition, which is the true first, is worth 50% than the U.S. edition.

		F/F	F/NF	NF/VG+	VG+/VG	VG/VG-	Good	w/o dj
1st ed		$20	$17	$13	$10	$7	$4	80%

Feast of Fear: Conversations with Stephen King 1989 Tim Underwood and Chuck Miller, Editors.

"Carroll & Graf Publishers, Inc./New York" on title page. No date on title page.
Copyright page - 6th (of 15) line - "First Carroll & Graf edition". DJ price - $18.95.
Quarter bound - red cloth with black sides and no top stain. White pastedowns.

		F/F	F/NF	NF/VG+	VG+/VG	VG/VG-	Good	w/o dj
1st ed		$20	$17	$13	$10	$7	$4	80%

Four Past Midnight 1990

"VIKING" on title page. No date on title page. Copyright page - 17th (of 45) line - "10 9 8 7 6 5 4 3 2 1". DJ price - U.S. $22.95/CANADA $29.95. Quarter bound - black cloth with black sides and no top stain. Gold pastedowns.

		F/F	F/NF	NF/VG+	VG+/VG	VG/VG-	Good	w/o dj
1st ed		$20	$17	$13	$10	$7	$4	80%

Needful Things 1991

"VIKING" on title page. No date on title page. Copyright page - 11th (of 51) line - "1 3 5 7 9 10 8 6 4 2". DJ price - U.S. $24.95/Canada $29.99.
Quarter bound - black cloth with gray sides and no top stain. Red pastedowns.

		F/F	F/NF	NF/VG+	VG+/VG	VG/VG-	Good	w/o dj
1st ed		$20	$17	$13	$10	$7	$4	80%

The Dark Tower III: The Wastelands 1991

"DONALD M. GRANT, PUBLISHER, INC./HAMPTON FALLS, NEW HAMPSHIRE" on title page. Copyright page - 27th (of 29) line - "FIRST EDITION". DJ price - Trade Edition $38.00. Full bound - red cloth with no top stain. Pink background pastedowns with drawing of boy and animal.

		F/F	F/NF	NF/VG+	VG+/VG	VG/VG-	Good	w/o dj
1st ed		$50	$40	$30	$20	$15	$10	25%

Gerald's Game 1992

"Viking" on title page. No date on title page. Copyright page - 13th (of 45) line - "1 3 5 7 9 10 8 6 4 2". DJ price - $23.50.
Quarter bound - black cloth with black sides and no top stain. Black pastedowns.

		F/F	F/NF	NF/VG+	VG+/VG	VG/VG-	Good	w/o dj
1st ed		$20	$17	$13	$10	$7	$4	80%

Dolores Claiborne 1993

"Viking" on title page. No date on title page. Copyright page - 16th (of 44) line - "1 3 5 7 9 10 8 6 4 2". DJ price - $23.50/Canada $28.99.
Quarter bound - black cloth with black sides and no top stain. White or gold pastedowns.

		F/F	F/NF	NF/VG+	VG+/VG	VG/VG-	Good	w/o dj
1st ed		$20	$17	$13	$10	$7	$4	80%

John LeCarre´ (1931-)

Pseudonym of David Cornwell, English novelist known for well-crafted thrillers. His best known book is _The Spy Who Came in from the Cold_ (1963), a realistic treatment of spies and their world that drew on his own experience in the British Intellience. Later novels include _The Looking-Glass War_ (1965), _A Small Town in Germany_ (1968), and his famous Karla trilogy - _Tinker, Tailor, Solder, Spy_ (1974), _The Honourable Schoolboy_ (1977), and _Smiley's People_ (1980).

Call for the Dead 1961 U.K.   1962 U.S. George Smiley's first appearance in a LeCarre mystery.

		F/F	F/NF	NF/VG+	VG+/VG	VG/VG-	Good	w/o dj
1st ed	U.S.	$750	$600	$500	$450	$400	$250	20%
1st ed	U.K.	$3,500	$3,000	$2,500	$2,000	$1,700	$1,000	20%

A Murder of Quality 1962 U.K.   1963 U.S.

		F/F	F/NF	NF/VG+	VG+/VG	VG/VG-	Good	w/o dj
1st ed	U.S.	$600	$500	$400	$350	$300	$175	20%
1st ed	U.K.	$3,000	$2,500	$2,000	$1,500	$1,200	$700	20%

The Spy Who Came in from the Cold 1963

"LONDON/VICTOR GOLLANCZ LTD/1963" on title page. Copyright page - 1st (of 3) line - "Victor Gollancz Limited 1963". DJ red background on front panel and spine; rest plain white; DJ price - 18/- net.
Full bound - light blue cloth with no top stain and white pastedowns.

"Coward-McCann, Inc./New York" on title page. No date on title page. Copyright page - 2nd (of 9) line -"FIRST AMERICAN EDITION 1964". No mention of impression number or letter indicating print run exists on true first. DJ price - $4.50. Rear panel of dj contains only three reveiews (as opposed to four and then five on later printings).
Quarter bound - red cloth with brown sides and no top stain. Light gold pastedowns.

		F/F	F/NF	NF/VG+	VG+/VG	VG/VG-	Good	w/o dj
1st ed	U.S.	$125	$100	$75	$50	$40	$20	33%
1st ed	U.K.	$600	$500	$400	$300	$250	$125	33%

The Looking-Glass War 1965

"Coward-McCann, Inc. New York" on title page. No date on title page.
Copyright page - 2nd (of 7) line "First American Edition 1965" No mention of the number of the "impression". DJ price - $4.95 (no difference for later editions).
Full bound - black cloth with light green top stain and olive green pastedowns.
Note: Later editions with "First American Edition 1965" were also produced. These books are distinguished by an impression number in the space between "Number: 65-20401" and "MANUFACTURED IN THE UNITED STATES OF AMERICA". These are not true First Editions.

		F/F	F/NF	NF/VG +	VG + /VG	VG/VG -	Good	w/o dj
1st ed	U.S.	$50	$45	$35	$25	$20	$10	70%
1st ed	U.K.	$80	$70	$55	$45	$35	$20	70%

A Small Town in Germany 1968

"Coward-McCann, Inc. New York" on title page. No date on title page.
Copyright page - 2nd (of 6) line - "First American Edition 1968". No mention of the number of the "impression". DJ price - $6.95 (no difference for later editions).
Full bound - red cloth with red top stain. White pastedowns.
Note: Later editions with "First American Edition 1968" were also produced. These books are distinguished by an extra line containing the impression number in the space between "Library of Congress Catalog Card Number: 67-15283" and "PRINTED IN THE UNITED STATES OF AMERICA". These are not true First Editions.

"HEINEMANN:LONDON" on title page. No date on title page.
Copyright page - 4th (of 9) line - "First Published 1968". DJ price - 30s.
Full bound - maroon cloth with no top stain and white pastedowns.

		F/F	F/NF	NF/VG +	VG + /VG	VG/VG -	Good	w/o dj
1st ed	U.S.	$50	$45	$35	$25	$20	$10	70%
1st ed	U.K.	$80	$70	$55	$45	$35	$20	70%

The Naive and Sentimental Lover 1971

"Alfred A. Knopf   New York   1972" on title page. Copyright page - last (of 12) line - "FIRST AMERICAN EDITION". DJ price - $7.95 (no different for later editions).
Full bound - gold cloth with red top stain and white pastedowns.
Note: A Book Club edition with "FIRST EDITION" was also produced. This book is distinguished by small square indentation on rear board below and to the right of the much larger Knopf logo impression. DJ on the Book Club edition has no price. The Book Club edition is slightly narrower than the true first. This is not a true First Edition.

HODDER AND STOUGHTON/LONDON SYDNEY AUCKLAND TORONTO"on title page. No date on title page. Copyright page - 1st (of 9) line - "........... First published in 1977". Full bound - black cloth with no top stain and gray pastedowns.

		F/F	F/NF	NF/VG +	VG + /VG	VG/VG -	Good	w/o dj
1st ed	U.S.	$20	$15	$12	$10	$8	$5	85%
1st ed	U.K.	$50	$40	$30	$20	$15	$8	70%

Tinker, Tailor, Soldier, Spy 1974   George Smiley begins his pursuit of Karla. First book in the trilogy.

"ALFRED A. KNOPF: New York/1974" on title page.
Copyright page - 19th and 20th (of 20) lines - "Manufactured in the United States of America/FIRST EDITION". DJ price - $7.95 (no difference for later editions).
Full bound - black cloth with maroon top stain and white pastedowns.
Note: A Book Club edition with "First American Edition" was also produced. This book is distinguished by small square indentation on rear board below below and to the right of the much larger Knopf logo impression. DJ on the Book Club edition has no price. The Book Club edition is slightly narrower and has a brighter red top stain than does the true first. This is not a true First Edition.

"HODDER AND STOUGHTON/LONDON SYDNEY AUCKLAND TORONTO" on title page. No date on title page. Copyright page - 1st (of 7) line "Copyright © 1974 by LeCarre Productions. First printed 1974. ISBN 0 340" DJ price - £2.95.
Full bound - black cloth with no purple stain and beige pastedowns.

		F/F	F/NF	NF/VG +	VG + /VG	VG/VG -	Good	w/o dj

1st ed	U.S.	$35	$30	$25	$20	$15	$10	85%
1st ed	U.K.	$70	$60	$50	$40	$30	$20	70%

The Honourable Schoolboy 1977   Second book in the Karla trilogy.

"Alfred A. Knopf   New York/1977" on title page.
Copyright page - 20th and 21st (of 21) lines - "Manufactured in the United States of America/First Trade Edition". DJ price - $7.95 (no difference for later editions).
Full bound - black cloth with gray top stain and white pastedowns.

"HODDER AND STOUGHTON/LONDON SYDNEY AUCKLAND TORONTO" on title page. No date on title page. Copyright page - 4th (of 12) line *"Copyright © 1977 by Authors Workshop AG. First printed 1977."*
Full bound - dark blue cloth with no top stain. Pastedowns maps.

		F/F	F/NF	NF/VG+	VG+/VG	VG/VG-	Good	w/o dj
1st ed	U.S.	$25	$20	$15	$10	$8	$6	85%
1st ed	U.K.	$60	$50	$40	$25	$15	$10	70%

Smiley's People 1980   Last book in the Karla trilogy.

"Alfred A. Knopf   New York/1980" on title page. Copyright page - last three (of 18) lines - "A limited edition of this book has been privately printed./Manufactured in the United States of America/First Trade Edition".   DJ price - $10.95 (no difference for later editions).
Full bound - black cloth no top stain and white pastedowns.

"HODDER AND STOUGHTON/LONDON SYDNEY AUCKLAND TORONTO" on title page. No date on title page. Copyright page - 7th and 8th (of 15) line - "Copyright © 1979 by Authors Workshop AG. First printed in Great/Britain 1980. ,,,,,,,,,,,"
DJ price - £5.95. Full bound - dark blue cloth with no top stain. White pastedowns.

		F/F	F/NF	NF/VG+	VG+/VG	VG/VG-	Good	w/o dj
1st ed	U.S.	$25	$20	$15	$10	$8	$6	85%
1st ed	U.K.	$60	$50	$40	$25	$15	$10	70%

Little Drummer Girl 1983

"ALFRED A. KNOPF   NEW YORK 1983" on title page.   Copyright page - last (of 13) line - "FIRST EDITION". DJ price - $15.95 (no difference for later editions).
Full bound - maroon cloth no top stain and white pastedowns.

		F/F	F/NF	NF/VG+	VG+/VG	VG/VG-	Good	w/o dj
1st ed	U.S.	$15	$13	$10	$8	$6	$3	80%
1st ed	U.K.	$25	$20	$17	$12	$10	$6	80%

A Perfect Spy 1986

"ALFRED A. KNOPF   NEW YORK 1986" on title page. Copyright page - last (of 13) line - "FIRST EDITION". DJ price - $18.95 (no difference for later editions).
Full bound - black cloth no top stain and white pastedowns.

		F/F	F/NF	NF/VG+	VG+/VG	VG/VG-	Good	w/o dj
1st ed	U.S.	$15	$13	$10	$8	$6	$3	80%

1st ed	U.K.	$22	$19	$16	$12	$10	$6	80%

Russia House 1989

"Alfred A. Knopf   New York 1989" on title page. Copyright page - last (of 28) line - "First Edition".   DJ price - $19.95 (no difference for later editions).
Full bound - black cloth no top stain and white pastedowns.

		F/F	F/NF	NF/VG+	VG+/VG	VG/VG-	Good	w/o dj
1st ed	U.S.	$15	$13	$10	$8	$6	$3	80%
1st ed	U.K.	$22	$19	$16	$12	$10	$6	80%

The Secret Pilgrim 1991

"1991/ALFRED A. KNOPF   NEW YORK" on title page. Copyright page - last (of 10) line - "First Edition".   DJ price - $21.95 (no difference for later editions).
Full bound - black cloth no top stain and white pastedowns.

		F/F	F/NF	NF/VG+	VG+/VG	VG/VG-	Good	w/o dj
1st ed	U.S.	$12	$10	$8	$6	$5	$3	80%
1st ed	U.K.	$20	$17	$12	$9	$7	$4	80%

The Night Manager 1993

"ALFRED A. KNOPF/NEW YORK/1993" on title page. Copyright page - last (of 17) line - "First Edition".   DJ price - $24.00 (no difference for later editions).
Full bound -purple-gray cloth no top stain and white pastedowns.

		F/F	F/NF	NF/VG+	VG+/VG	VG/VG-	Good	w/o dj
1st ed	U.S.	$12	$10	$8	$6	$5	$3	80%
1st ed	U.K.	$20	$17	$12	$9	$7	$4	80%

Elmore Leonard

Fifty-Two Pickup 1974 Delacorte

		F/F	F/NF	NF/VG+	VG+/VG	VG/VG-	Good	w/o dj
1st ed		$300	$250	$150	$100	$75	$30	50%

Swag 1976

"DELACORTE PRESS/NEW YORK" on title page. No date on title page. Copyright page - 9th (of 15) line - "First Printing".

		F/F	F/NF	NF/VG+	VG+/VG	VG/VG-	Good	w/o dj
1st ed		$250	$200	$150	$75	$50	$15	60%

Unknown Man No. 89 1977

"DELACORTE PRESS/NEW YORK" on title page. No date on title page. Copyright page - 7th (of 14) line - "First Printing". DJ price - $8.95. Quarter bound - black cloth with blue sides and no top stain. Light gold pastedowns.

	F/F	F/NF	NF/VG+	VG+/VG	VG/VG-	Good	w/o dj
1st ed	$250	$200	$150	$75	$50	$15	60%

City Primeval 1980

"ARBOR HOUSE/NEW YORK" on title page. No date on title page. Copyright page - 13th (of 13) line - "10 9 8 7 6 5 4 3 2 1". DJ price - $10.95. Quarter bound - gray cloth with blue sides and no top stain. White pastedowns.

	F/F	F/NF	NF/VG+	VG+/VG	VG/VG-	Good	w/o dj
1st ed	$40	$35	$25	$15	$10	$6	70%

Split Images 1981

"ARBOR HOUSE/New York" on title page. No date on title page. Copyright page - 10th (of 10) line - "10 9 8 7 6 5 4 3 2 1". DJ price - $12.50. Quarter bound - red cloth with black sides and no top stain. White pastedowns.

	F/F	F/NF	NF/VG+	VG+/VG	VG/VG-	Good	w/o dj
1st ed	$35	$30	$20	$15	$10	$6	80%

Cat Chaser 1982

"ARBOR HOUSE/New York" on title page. No date on title page. Copyright page - 14th (of 14) line - "10 9 8 7 6 5 4 3 2 1". DJ price - $13.50. Quarter bound - light gray cloth with blue sides and no top stain. White pastedowns.

	F/F	F/NF	NF/VG+	VG+/VG	VG/VG-	Good	w/o dj
1st ed	$35	$30	$20	$15	$10	$6	80%

Stick 1983

	F/F	F/NF	NF/VG+	VG+/VG	VG/VG-	Good	w/o dj
1st ed	$30	$25	$18	$15	$10	$6	80%

LaBrava 1983

"ARBOR HOUSE/NEW YORK" on title page. No date on title page. Copyright page - 9th (of 12) line - "10 9 8 7 6 5 4 3 2 1". DJ price - $14.95. Quarter bound - black cloth with red sides and no top stain. White pastedowns.

	F/F	F/NF	NF/VG+	VG+/VG	VG/VG-	Good	w/o dj
1st ed	$25	$20	$15	$12	$8	$5	90%

Glitz 1986

"ARBOR HOUSE/New York" on title page. No date on title page. Copyright page - 7th (of 18) line - "10 9 8 7 6 5 4 3 2 1". DJ price - $14.95. "385" on bottom of rear dj flap. Quarter bound - black cloth with black sides and no top stain. White pastedowns.

	F/F	F/NF	NF/VG+	VG+/VG	VG/VG-	Good	w/o dj
1st ed	$35	$30	$20	$15	$10	$6	90%

Bandits 1987   First printing 250,000 copies

"ARBOR HOUSE New York" on title page. No date on title page. Copyright page - 6th (of 19) line - "10 9 8 7 6 5 4 3 2 1". DJ price - $17.95. Quarter bound - blue cloth with blue sides and no top stain. Dark blue pastedowns.

		F/F	F/NF	NF/VG +	VG+/VG	VG/VG-	Good	w/o dj
1st ed		$20	$15	$10	$8	$6	$4	90%

Touch 1987

"Arbor House/New York" on title page. No date on title page. Copyright page - 7th (of 13) line - "10 9 8 7 6 5 4 3 2 1". DJ price - $17.95. Quarter bound - cream cloth with blue sides and no top stain. Blue pastedowns.

		F/F	F/NF	NF/VG +	VG+/VG	VG/VG-	Good	w/o dj
1st ed		$20	$15	$10	$8	$6	$4	90%

Freaky Deaky 1988

"ARBOR HOUSE/WILLIAM MORROW/NEW YORK" on title page. No date on title page. Copyright page - 18th (of 18) lines - "10 9 8 7 6 5 4 3 2 1". DJ price - $18.95. Quarter bound - white cloth with white sides and no top stain. Pale blue pastedowns.

		F/F	F/NF	NF/VG +	VG+/VG	VG/VG-	Good	w/o dj
1st ed		$20	$15	$10	$8	$6	$4	90%

Killshot 1989

"ARBOR HOUSE WILLIAM MORROW/NEW YORK" on title page. No date on title page. Copyright page - 16th and 17th (of 18) lines - "First Edition/1 2 3 4 5 6 7 8 9 10". DJ price - $18.95. Quarter bound - black cloth with black sides and no top stain. Dark gray pastedowns.

		F/F	F/NF	NF/VG +	VG+/VG	VG/VG-	Good	w/o dj
1st ed		$20	$15	$10	$8	$6	$4	90%

Ira Levin

Rosemary's Baby 1967

"RANDON HOUSE NEW YORK" on title page. No date on title page.
Copyright page - 1st (of 10) line - "FIRST PRINTING".
DJ price - $4.95 with 4/67 on front flap of dj. (Unchanged for later printings.)
Quarter bound - navy cloth with lavender sides and gray top stain. White pastedowns.

		F/F	F/NF	NF/VG +	VG+/VG	VG/VG-	Good	w/o dj
1st ed		$75	$60	$40	$30	$20	$10	80%

John D. MacDonald

John D. MacDonald's first novel, _The Brass Cupcake_, was published in 1950. Since then, he has been one of this country's most prolific writers with more than seventy novels published. _The Brass Cupcake_, like most of his early works, was published only in paperback. *The Deep Blue Good-By*, published in 1964, was the first of his Travis McGee adventure novels. Colors in the title are a characteristic of The Travis McGee novels. There are twenty-one novels in the Travis McGee series. Of these, the first fourteen were first published in paperback. These were all later released in hardbound volumes although in very limited quantities. The last seven followed the more typical sequence of hardbound firsts followed by paperback releases. Publishers number paperbacks with a code which normally appears on both the front cover and the spine. The code, which is used for inventory control, is changed each time the book price is changed. The code itself is often not sufficient in identifying a first edition paperback since several printings could be make before the price is changed. Three means are used to distinguish between printings when the book code is unchanged. The first, the End Print Number (EPN), is a code placed on the last page of text and is used to indicate printings after the first printing. An EPN would take the form "69-9-2". This would indicate that the second printing was made in September 1969. The second way to distinguish a printing number is a series of bullets or dots on the copyright page, with each bullet representing a printing so that ". . ." would indicate a third printing. The third means of identifying a first edition involves the mail in ads at the back of the books. The highest numbered book in the advertisement (not always the last one on the list) changes as printing number changes. For example, the first edition of *The Long Lavender Look* is identified as "2325-095 2311 Purple". This indicates that the code 2325-095 is used on more than the first printing. The mail in ad at the back of a first edition will have 2311 *A Purple Place for Dying* as the highest numbered book listed. The second printing of *The Long Lavender Look* is "2325-095 2522 Pink".

The Deep Blue Good-By   1964   First Travis McGee novel.

Paperback. 1st ed k1405 no EPN;   2nd ed k1405 ". ."

	Fine	VG+	VG-	Good
1st ed wrapps	$50	$25	$15	$6

"J.B. LIPPINCOTT COMPANY/*Philadelphia and New York*" on title page. No date on title page. Copyright page - 2nd (of 14) line - "First hardbound edition 1975". No other reference to printing number. DJ price - $6.95.
Quarter bound - blue cloth with blue sides and no top stain. Blue pastedowns.

	F/F	F/NF	NF/VG+	VG+/VG	VG/VG-	Good	w/o dj
1st ed	$250	$200	$150	$125	$100	$50	70%

Nightmare in Pink   1964   Second Travis McGee novel.

Paperback. 1st ed k1406 Copyright page - 2nd line - "#K1406".   2nd ed k1406 has two large dots on the second line of the copyright page.

	Fine	VG+	VG-	Good
1st ed wrapps	$50	$25	$15	$6

"J.B. Lippincott Company/*Philadelphia and New York*" on title page. No date on title page. Copyright page - 2nd (of 14) line - "First hardbound edition 1976". DJ price - $6.95.
Quarter bound - red cloth with pink sides and no top stain. White pastedowns.

	F/F	F/NF	NF/VG+	VG+/VG	VG/VG-	Good	w/o dj
1st ed	$175	$150	$125	$100	$75	$40	70%

A Purple Place for Dying   1964   Third Travis McGee novel.

Paperback. 1st ed k1417 Copyright page - 2nd line - "#K1417".   2nd ed k1417 has two large dots on the second line of the copyright page.

	Fine	VG+	VG-	Good
1st ed wrapps	$45	$25	$15	$6

"J.B. LIPPINCOTT COMPANY/PHILADELPHIA AND NEW YORK" on title page. No date on title page. Copyright page - 8th (of 13) line - "First hardbound edition 1976". DJ price - $7.95. Quarter bound - blue cloth with blue sides and no top stain. White pastedowns. Second printing has "2 3 4 5 6 7 8 9 10" as new 8th line.

		F/F	F/NF	NF/VG +	VG +/VG	VG/VG -	Good	w/o dj
1st ed		$175	$150	$125	$100	$75	$40	70%

The Quick Red Fox   1964   Fourth Travis McGee novel.

Paperback. 1st ed k1464 no EPN;   2nd ed d1610

	Fine	VG+	VG-	Good
1st ed wrapps	$45	$25	$15	$6

"J.B. Lippincott Company/PHILADELPHIA AND NEW YORK" on title page. No date on title page. Copyright page - 12 lines with no mention of printing number. DJ price - $5.95 at bottom of front flap and 374 at top. Full bound - red cloth with no top stain and white pastedowns. Second printing is indicated as "Second Printing". Some later issues have "Second printing" on bottom of front dj flap.

		F/F	F/NF	NF/VG +	VG +/VG	VG/VG -	Good	w/o dj
1st ed		$250	$200	$150	$125	$100	$50	60%

A Deadly Shade of Gold   1965   Fifth Travis McGee novel.

Paperback. 1st ed d1499 no EPN;   2nd ed d1499 "65-6-2"

	Fine	VG+	VG-	Good
1st ed wrapps	$40	$20	$12	$6

"J.B. LIPPINCOTT COMPANY/PHILADELPHIA AND NEW YORK" on title page. No date on title page. Copyright page - 4th (of 13) line - "First hardbound edition 1974". DJ price - $7.50. DJ exists with and without "175" at the bottom of the front flap. Quarter bound - black spine with light blue sides and no top stain. White pastedowns.
Note: A Book Club edition exists with "First hardbound edition 1974" on the copyright page. This volume has the book club square indentation on the rear board and no price on the dj.

		F/F	F/NF	NF/VG +	VG +/VG	VG/VG -	Good	w/o dj
1st ed		$250	$200	$150	$125	$100	$50	60%

Bright Orange for the Shroud   1965   Sixth Travis McGee novel.

Paperback. 1st ed d1573 no EPN;   2nd ed d1573 "66-11-2"

	Fine	VG+	VG-	Good
1st ed wrapps	$40	$20	$12	$6

"J.B. Lippincott Company /PHILADELPHIA & NEW YORK/1972" on title page. Copyright page - 15 lines with no reference to edition or printing number. DJ price - $5.95 with "1072" on front dj flap. Full bound - black-orange cloth with no top stains and white pastedowns. Second (the only other printing) printing indicated as "Second Printing", 2nd dj price - $7.95.

		F/F	F/NF	NF/VG +	VG +/VG	VG/VG -	Good	w/o dj
1st ed		$300	$250	$175	$125	$100	$50	60%

Darker Than Amber 1966   Seventh Travis McGee novel.

Paperback. 1st ed d1674 no EPN;   2nd ed d1674 "67-9-2"

	Fine	VG+	VG-	Good
1st ed wrapps	$40	$20	$12	$6

First hardbound edition published April 1970 by Lippincott. No reference to printing number. DJ price - $4.95 with "470" on front dj flap. Second (the only other printing) printing indicated as "Second Printing" and "HB 5E" in gutter, pg 207 verso; 2nd dj price - $5.95. 2nd dj has two versions - one w/ "470" and one w/o "470" or "$5.95"

		F/F	F/NF	NF/VG +	VG+/VG	VG/VG-	Good	w/o dj
1st ed		$325	$275	$200	$150	$125	$60	60%

One Fearful Yellow Eye 1967   Eighth Travis McGee novel.

Paperback. 1st ed d1750;   2nd ed 1848-050

	Fine	VG+	VG-	Good
1st ed wrapps	$40	$20	$12	$6

"J.B. Lippincott Company/Philadelphia and New York" (all on one line) on title page. Copyright page - 5th (of 18) line - "First hardbound edition 1977". Last line - "2 4 6 8 9 7 5 3 1". DJ price - $8.95. No reference to printing number on either the second or the third printings. Quarter bound - black cloth with red sides and no top stains. White pastedowns.

		F/F	F/NF	NF/VG +	VG+/VG	VG/VG-	Good	w/o dj
1st ed		$150	$125	$110	$100	$75	$40	80%

Pale Gray for Guilt 1968   Ninth Travis McGee novel.

Paperback. 1st ed 1893-050 no EPN;   2nd ed 1893-050 "68-4-2"

	Fine	VG+	VG-	Good
1st ed wrapps	$35	$18	$12	$6

"J.B. Lippincott Company/Philadelphia & New York/1971" on title page. Copyright page - 7 lines with no mention of printing number. Front DJ flap "971" at top and $5.50 at bottom. Full bound - green cloth with no top stain and white pastedowns.

		F/F	F/NF	NF/VG +	VG+/VG	VG/VG-	Good	w/o dj
1st ed		$300	$250	$175	$125	$100	$50	50%

The Girl in the Plain Brown Paper Wrapper 1969   Tenth Travis McGee novel.

Paperback. 1st ed 2023-075 no EPN;   2nd thru 6th ed 2023-075 all with a EPN

	Fine	VG+	VG-	Good
1st ed wrapps	$40	$20	$12	$6

"J.B. Lippincott Company/PHILADELPHIA NEW YORK/1973" on title page. Two printings were made. Some 1st editions have "First hardbound edition" on the copyright page; some have eleven lines with no mention of printing number. On all firsts, and only on firsts, the

gutter on page 276 in blank. DJ price - "373" at top and "$5.95" at bottom of front flap. Full
bound - gold cloth with no top stain and white pastedowns.
Second printings are distinguished by "Second printing" on some and by "HB6E" in gutter
on page 276 on others. Some 2nd dj have "373".

		F/F	F/NF	NF/VG+	VG+/VG	VG/VG-	Good	w/o dj
1st ed		$275	$225	$200	$150	$110	$60	70%

Dress Her in Indigo 1969   Eleventh Travis McGee novel.

Paperback. 1st ed 2127-075 no EPN;   2nd ed 2127-075 "69-12-2"

	Fine	VG+	VG-	Good
1st ed wrapps	$35	$18	$12	$6

"J.B. Lippincott Company/Philadelphia and New York/1971" on title page.
Copyright page - 8 lines with no mention of printing number. Front flap on 1st dj has "271"
at the top and "$5.50" at the bottom. Full bound - blue-black swirls with no top stain and
white pastedowns. A total of four printings were made. Nothing on the book itself
distinguishes between the four. All have dj prices of $5.50. Only the first dj has "271".

		F/F	F/NF	NF/VG+	VG+/VG	VG/VG-	Good	w/o dj
1st ed		$275	$225	$200	$150	$110	$60	80%

The Long Lavender Look 1970   Twelfth Travis McGee novel.

Paperback. 1st ed 2325-095 2311 Purple;   2nd ed 2325-095 2522 Pink

	Fine	VG+	VG-	Good
1st ed wrapps	$30	$15	$10	$5

"J.P. Lippincott Company/PHILADELPHIA AND NEW YORK/1972" on title page.
Copyright page - 13 lines with no mention of printing number.
DJ price $5.50.   DJ displays B&W photos. "372" on front flap. Full bound - black with
purple speckles and no top stain. White pastedowns. Only one printing was made.

		F/F	F/NF	NF/VG+	VG+/VG	VG/VG-	Good	w/o dj
1st ed		$300	$250	$175	$125	$100	$50	50%

A Tan and Sandy Silence 1972   Thirteenth Travis McGee novel.

Paperback. 1st ed 2513-095 "January 1972" and no mail ad; 2nd ed 2513-095 2522 Pink

	Fine	VG+	VG-	Good
1st ed wrapps	$30	$15	$10	$5

COMPANY/Philadelphia and New York" on title page. No date on title page. Copyright
page - 2nd and 3rd (of 17) lines - "First hardbound edition 1979/2 4 6 8 9 7 5 3 1". Front flap
on 1st dj has "$8.95" at the bottom. Quarter bound - brown cloth with tan sides and no top
stain. White pastedowns. Only one printing was made.

		F/F	F/NF	NF/VG+	VG+/VG	VG/VG-	Good	w/o dj
1st ed		$150	$125	$110	$100	$75	$40	50%

The Scarlet Ruse 1973 Fourteenth Travis McGee novel.

Paperback. 1st ed 2744-125 2513 Tan;   2nd ed 2744-125 2828 Red

	Fine	VG+	VG-	Good
1st ed wrapps	$30	$15	$10	$5

"Lippincott & Crowell, Publishers New York" on title page. Copyright page - 11th (of 19) line - "FIRST EDITION" and last line - "80 81 82 83 84 10 9 8 7 6 5 4 3 2 1". DJ price - $9.95. Quarter bound - red cloth with red sides and no top stain. White pastedowns. Only one printing was made.

	F/F	F/NF	NF/VG+	VG+/VG	VG/VG-	Good	w/o dj
1st ed	$125	$90	$75	$50	$40	$25	70%

The Turquoise Lament 1973 Fifteenth Travis McGee novel.

"*J.P. LIPPINCOTT COMPANY/Philadelphia and New York*" on title page. No date on title page. Copyright page - 3rd (of 14) line "FIRST EDITION". 2nd printing and 4th printing are indicated as such while the 3rd printing contains no reference to printing number. DJ price - $6.95. Full bound - black with no top stain and gold pastedowns. Four printings were made by Lippincott.

	F/F	F/NF	NF/VG+	VG+/VG	VG/VG-	Good	w/o dj
1st ed	$60	$50	$40	$30	$20	$10	70%

The Dreadful Lemon Sky 1975 Sixteenth Travis McGee novel.

"J.B. Lippincott Company/*Philadelphia and New York*" on title page. No date on title page. Five printings were made. Three variations of the first printing exist. Most common - Copyright page - 13 lines & no mention of printing (later printings are all designated as such and have a 14th line such as "Second Printing") and no gutter marks. Two other versions of the first printing exist. One has a printing key of "1" and the gutter marks (these marks identify the printer) "HB2E on page 228 . The other has no printing key and the gutter mark- "HB8E". DJ price - $6.95. ("Second Printing appears at the bottom of the front dj flap for some later printings). Quarter bound - black cloth and black sides with no top stain and yellow pastedowns.

	F/F	F/NF	NF/VG+	VG+/VG	VG/VG-	Good	w/o dj
1st ed	$30	$25	$20	$15	$10	$6	60%

The Empty Copper Sea 1978 Seventeenth Travis McGee novel.

"J.B. LIPPINCOTT COMPANY/Philadelphia and New York" on title page. No date on title page. Five printings were made. Two variations of the first printing exist. Most common - Copyright page - 3rd (of 14) line "First edition". 4th line "2 4 6 8 9 7 5 3 1". No gutter marks. DJ price - $8.95.   Same for all printings. The other version of the first printing is the same except it has gutter marks on page 239 verso - "HB 10H".
Quarter bound - brown cloth and gold sides with no top stain and gold pastedowns.

	F/F	F/NF	NF/VG+	VG+/VG	VG/VG-	Good	w/o dj
1st ed	$20	$15	$12	$10	$8	$6	80%

The Green Ripper 1979 Eighteenth Travis McGee novel.

"J.B. LIPPINCOTT COMPANY/*New York*" on title page. No date on title page. Copyright page - 6th and 7th (of 14) lines "First edition/2 4 6 8 9 7 5 3 1". DJ price - $9.95

Quarter bound - gray cloth and lime green sides with no top stain and lime pastedowns.

		F/F	F/NF	NF/VG+	VG+/VG	VG/VG-	Good	w/o dj
1st ed		$20	$15	$12	$10	$8	$6	80%

Free Fall in Crimson 1981 Nineteenth Travis McGee novel.

"HARPER & ROW, PUBLISHERS, New York/Cambridge, Hagerstown, Philadelphia, San Francisco,/London, Mexico City, Sao Paulo, Sydney" on title page. No date on title page.
Copyright page - 11th (of 19) lines - "FIRST EDITION". Last line "81 82 83 84 85 10 9 8 7 6 5 4 3 2 1". DJ price - $10.95. Quarter bound - black cloth and red sides with no top stain and white pastedowns.

		F/F	F/NF	NF/VG+	VG+/VG	VG/VG-	Good	w/o dj
1st ed		$25	$20	$17	$12	$8	$6	80%

Cinnamon Skin 1982 Twentieth Travis McGee novel.

"HARPER & ROW, PUBLISHERS, New York/Cambridge, Philadelphia, San Francisco, London/Mexico City, Sao Paulo, Sydney" on title page. No date on title page.
Copyright page - 10th (of 18) lines - "FIRST EDITION". Last line - "82 83 84 85 10 9 8 7 6 5 4 3 2 1". DJ price - $10.95. Quarter bound - tan cloth and cinnamon sides with no top stain and white pastedowns.

		F/F	F/NF	NF/VG+	VG+/VG	VG/VG-	Good	w/o dj
1st ed		$15	$12	$10	$8	$6	$4	80%

The Lonely Silver Rain 1985 Twenty-first Travis McGee novel.

"ALFRED A. KNOPF/New York 1985" on title page.
Copyright page - last (of 18) lines -"First Edition". DJ price - $15.95
Quarter bound - red cloth and white sides with no top stain and white pastedowns.

		F/F	F/NF	NF/VG+	VG+/VG	VG/VG-	Good	w/o dj
1st ed		$15	$12	$10	$8	$6	$4	80%

The Brass Cupcake 1950 Cover price 25¢

Paperback. 1st ed Gold Medal #124. Only one printing of #124 was made.

	Fine	VG+	VG-	Good
1st ed wrapps	$60	$40	$20	$10

Murder for the Bride 1951 Cover price 25¢

Paperback. 1st ed Gold Medal #164. Only one printing of #164 was made.

	Fine	VG+	VG-	Good
1st ed wrapps	$50	$35	$20	$10

Judge Me Not 1951 Cover price not shown.

Paperback. 1st ed Gold Medal #186. Two printings of #186 were made. Second printing is indicated on the copyright page. First printing has no indication.

Fine	VG+	VG-	Good

1st ed wrapps	$50	$35	$20	$10

Weep for Me 1951   Cover price 25¢

Paperback. 1st ed Gold Medal #200. One printing of #200 was made. Only two printings of any kind were made at all (second printing is #884) then the author requested that no more printings be made.

	Fine	VG+	VG-	Good
1st ed wrapps	$75	$50	$30	$15

The Damned 1952   Cover price not shown.

Paperback. 1st ed Gold Medal #240. Four printings of #240 were made. Copyright page of first printing - "First Printing, May 1952".

	Fine	VG+	VG-	Good
1st ed wrapps	$25	$15	$10	$5

Dead Low Tide 1953   Cover price not shown.

Paperback. 1st ed Gold Medal #298. Only one printing of #298 was made.

	Fine	VG+	VG-	Good
1st ed wrapps	$25	$15	$10	$5

The Neon Jungle 1953   Cover price not shown.

Paperback. 1st ed Gold Medal #323. Only one printing of #323 was made.

	Fine	VG+	VG-	Good
1st ed wrapps	$50	$35	$20	$10

All These Condemned 1954   Cover price 25¢

Paperback. 1st ed Gold Medal #420. Two printings of #420 were made. Copyright page of first printing - "First Printing, August 1954".

	Fine	VG+	VG-	Good
1st ed wrapps	$20	$15	$10	$5

Area of Suspicion 1954   Cover price 25¢

Paperback. 1st ed Dell #12. Only one printing of #12 was made. "FIRST/EDITION/12" on upper left corner of front cover.

	Fine	VG+	VG-	Good
1st ed wrapps	$20	$15	$10	$5

A Bullet For Cinderella 1955   Cover price 25¢

Paperback. 1st ed Dell #62. Only one printing of #62 was made. "FIRST/EDITION/62" on upper left corner of front cover. This book was retitled On The Make for one paperback print run only - the second printing of the book - 35¢ 1960 "DELL/FIRST EDITION/B134" on upper left corner of front cover. B134 is NOT a first edition.

	Fine	VG+	VG-	Good
1st ed wrapps	$20	$15	$10	$5

Cry Hard, Cry Fast 1955   Cover price 25¢

Paperback. 1st ed Popular Library #675. Only one printing of #675 was made.

	Fine	VG+	VG-	Good
1st ed wrapps	$25	$15	$10	$5

You Live Once 1956   Cover price 25¢

Paperback. 1st ed Popular Library #737. Only one printing of #737 was made. This book was retitled You Kill Me for one paperback print run only - the second printing of the book - 35¢ 1961 Popular Library #G507. G507 is NOT a first edition.

	Fine	VG+	VG-	Good
1st ed wrapps	$25	$15	$10	$5

April Evil 1956   Cover price 25¢

Paperback. 1st ed Dell #85. Two printings of #85 were made with do difference between the two. "FIRST/EDITION/85" appears on upper left corner of front cover of both.

	Fine	VG+	VG-	Good
1st ed wrapps	$25	$15	$10	$5

Border Town Girl 1956   Cover price 25¢

Paperback. 1st ed Popular Library #750. Only one printing of #759 was made.

	Fine	VG+	VG-	Good
1st ed wrapps	$25	$15	$10	$5

Murder In The Wind 1956   Cover price 25¢

Paperback. 1st ed Dell #A113. Only one printing of #A113 was made.

	Fine	VG+	VG-	Good
1st ed wrapps	$25	$15	$10	$5

Death Trap 1957   Cover price 25¢

Paperback. 1st ed Dell #A130. Only one printing of #A130 was made.

	Fine	VG+	VG-	Good
1st ed wrapps	$20	$14	$9	$4

The Price of Murder 1957   Cover price 25¢

Paperback. 1st ed Dell #A152. Two printings of #A152 were made. "First printing - October, 1957" on copyright page of first printing.

	Fine	VG+	VG-	Good
1st ed wrapps	$20	$14	$9	$4

The Empty Trap 1957   Cover price 25¢

Paperback. 1st ed Popular Library #830. Only one printing of #830 was made.

	Fine	VG+	VG-	Good
1st ed wrapps	$20	$14	$9	$4

A Man of Affairs 1957   Cover price 35¢

Paperback. 1st ed Dell #B112. Only one printing of #B112 was made.

	Fine	VG+	VG-	Good
1st ed wrapps	$20	$14	$9	$4

Deceivers 1958   Cover price 35¢

Paperback. 1st ed Dell #B117. Two printings of #B117 were made. "First printing - May, 1958" on copyright page of first printing.

	Fine	VG+	VG-	Good
1st ed wrapps	$20	$14	$9	$4

Clemmie 1958   Cover price 35¢

Paperback. 1st ed Gold Medal #s777. Two printings of #s777 were made. "First printing - June, 1958" on copyright page of first printing.

	Fine	VG+	VG-	Good
1st ed wrapps	$20	$14	$9	$4

Soft Touch 1958   Cover price 35¢

Paperback. 1st ed Dell #B121. Only one printing of #B121 was made.

	Fine	VG+	VG-	Good
1st ed wrapps	$20	$14	$9	$4

Deathly Welcome 1959   Cover price 35¢

Paperback. 1st ed Dell #B127. Only one printing of #B127 was made.

	Fine	VG+	VG-	Good
1st ed wrapps	$20	$14	$9	$4

The Beach Girls 1959   Cover price 35¢

Paperback. 1st ed Gold Medal #s907. Only one printing of #s907 was made.

	Fine	VG+	VG-	Good
1st ed wrapps	$20	$14	$9	$4

Slam The Big Door 1960   Cover price 35¢

Paperback. 1st ed Gold Medal #s907. Only one printing of #s907 was made.

	Fine	VG+	VG-	Good
1st ed wrapps	$15	$10	$7	$3

The Only Girl In The Game 1960   Cover price 35¢

Paperback. 1st ed Gold Medal #s1015. Only one printing of #s1015 was made.

	Fine	VG+	VG-	Good
1st ed wrapps	$15	$10	$7	$3

Where Is Janice Gantry 1961   Cover price 35¢

Paperback. 1st ed Gold Medal #s1076. Only one printing of #s1076 was made.

	Fine	VG+	VG-	Good
1st ed wrapps	$15	$10	$7	$3

On Monday We Killed Them All 1961   Cover price 35¢

Paperback. 1st ed Gold Medal #s1177. Only one printing of #s1177 was made.

	Fine	VG+	VG-	Good
1st ed wrapps	$12	$8	$5	$2

A Key To The Suite 1962   Cover price 35¢

Paperback. 1st ed Gold Medal #s1198. Only one printing of #s1198 was made.

	Fine	VG+	VG-	Good
1st ed wrapps	$12	$8	$5	$2

The Girl, the Gold Watch & Everything 1962   Cover price 35¢

Paperback. 1st ed Gold Medal #s1259. Only one printing of #s1259 was made.

	Fine	VG+	VG-	Good
1st ed wrapps	$12	$8	$5	$2

I Could Go On Singing 1963   Cover price 40¢

Paperback. 1st ed Gold Medal #k1291. Only one printing of #k1291 was made.

	Fine	VG+	VG-	Good
1st ed wrapps	$12	$8	$5	$2

On The Run 1963   Cover price 40¢

Paperback. 1st ed Gold Medal #k1292. Only one printing of #k1292 was made.

	Fine	VG+	VG-	Good

1st ed wrapps	$12	$8	$5	$2

The Drowner 1963   Cover price 40¢

Paperback. 1st ed Gold Medal #k1302. Only one printing of #k1302 was made.

	Fine	VG+	VG-	Good
1st ed wrapps	$12	$8	$5	$2

End of The Tiger and other stories 1966   Cover price 50¢

Paperback. 1st ed Gold Medal #d1690. Only one printing of #d1690 was made.

	Fine	VG+	VG-	Good
1st ed wrapps	$8	$5	$3	$1

S*E*V*E*N 1971   Cover price 75¢

Paperback. 1st ed Gold Medal #T2412. Three printings of #T2412 were made. Means for establishing First Edition not fully determined. Check mail-in ad.

	Fine	VG+	VG-	Good
1st ed wrapps	$5	$3	$2	$1

Other Times, Other Worlds 1978   Cover price $1.95

Paperback. 1st ed Fawcett #14037. Only one printing @ $1.95 was made. Collection of Sci-Fi short stories.

	Fine	VG+	VG-	Good
1st ed wrapps	$5	$3	$2	$1

Two 1983   Cover price $2.50

Paperback. 1st ed Carroll and Graf Unauthorized Printing. Only one printing. "First Carroll and Graf Edition" on copyright page. 0-88184-011-4 (correct number) shown on back cover. 0-88184-001-4 (incorrect number) shown on title page.

	Fine	VG+	VG-	Good
1st ed wrapps	$20	$14	$9	$4

Alistair MacLean (1893-1960)

H.M.S. Ulysses 1955 U.K.   1956 U.S.

"DOUBLEDAY & COMPANY, INC./Garden City, N.Y., 1956" on title page.   Copyright page - 6th (of 10) line - "First published, 1956, in the United States",   last line - "FIRST EDITION". DJ price - $3.95.   Rear panel - "LOCATE/ENGAGE/DESTROY THESE ARE/THE CLASSIC REQUIREMENTS OF A NAVAL SHIP IN WARTIME/H.M.S. ULYSSES By ALISTAIR MacLEAN" Full bound - gray cloth with no top stain.   Pastedown drawing of HMS Ulysses.

		F/F	F/NF	NF/VG+	VG+/VG	VG/VG-	Good	w/o dj
1st ed		$65	$50	$40	$30	$20	$10	50%

The Guns of Navarone 1957

		F/F	F/NF	NF/VG+	VG+/VG	VG/VG-	Good	w/o dj
1st ed		$90	$75	$60	$45	$35	$20	50%

South by Java Head 1958

"1958/DOUBLEDAY & COMPANY, INC./GARDEN CITY, NEW YORK" on title page. Copyright page - 7th (of 7) line - "FIRST EDITION". DJ price - $3.95. Rear panel - half page photo of author w/ bio. Full bound - gray cloth with yellow top stain and white pastedowns.

		F/F	F/NF	NF/VG+	VG+/VG	VG/VG-	Good	w/o dj
1st ed		$60	$50	$40	$30	$20	$10	50%

Night without End 1960

		F/F	F/NF	NF/VG+	VG+/VG	VG/VG-	Good	w/o dj
1st ed		$55	$45	$35	$25	$20	$10	50%

The Secret Ways 1959 Published as The Last Frontier in U.K.

"Doubleday & Company, Inc., Garden City, New York/1959" on title page. Copyright page - 8th (of 8) line - "First Edition". Rear panel - "The wind blew . . . . was all that mattered."/THE SECRET WAYS/by/ALISTAIR MACLEAN. Full bound - black cloth with no top stain. Pastedown map of Hungary.

		F/F	F/NF	NF/VG+	VG+/VG	VG/VG-	Good	w/o dj
1st ed	U.S.	$50	$40	$30	$25	$20	$10	50%

Fear is the Key 1961

Copyright page - 9th (of 9) line "FIRST EDITION".
Full bound blue cloth with blue-green top stain and white pastedowns.

"Collins/ST JAMES'S PLACE, LONDON/1961" on title page. Copyright page - six lines with no mention of printing number. Lines 3 through 6 - "© Gilach A. G., 1961/Printed in Great Britain/Collins Clear-Type Press/London and Glasgow". DJ price 15s. Full bound - red-orange cloth with no top stain and white pastedowns.

		F/F	F/NF	NF/VG+	VG+/VG	VG/VG-	Good	w/o dj
1st ed		$45	$35	$28	$22	$17	$8	50%

The Dark Crusader (U.K. only) 1961 Written under pseudonym Ian Stuart. Published in the U.S. as The Black Shrike 1970, in paperback only, under Alistair MacLean.

A Fawcett Gold Medal Book. W2340 95¢ Picture of gold medal in upper right corner of front cover. Copyright page - dedication at top of page, then 13 lines on bottom of page. Last two lines "Printed in the United States of America/November 1970". Front cover - "by the author of/PUPPET ON A CHAIN/and THE GUNS OF/NAVARONE". Second printing has "FAWCET/GOLD MEDAL/M2340 95c" in place of the picture of the gold medal and has "by the author of/BEAR ISLAND and/PUPPET ON A CHAIN" on front cover.

Fine	VG+	VG-	Good

1st ed US wrapps	$30	$20	$15	$10

		F/F	F/NF	NF/VG+	VG+/VG	VG/VG-	Good	w/o dj
1st ed	U.K.	$60	$50	$40	$30	$20	$10	50%

The Golden Rendezvous 1962

	F/F	F/NF	NF/VG+	VG+/VG	VG/VG-	Good	w/o dj
1st ed	$40	$30	$20	$15	$10	$8	60%

The Satan Bug 1962

	F/F	F/NF	NF/VG+	VG+/VG	VG/VG-	Good	w/o dj
1st ed	$40	$30	$20	$15	$10	$8	60%

Ice Station Zebra 1963

"Doubleday & Company, Inc./Garden City, New York/1963" on title page. Copyright page - 11th (of 11) line - "First Edition". DJ price - $3.95.
Full bound - light blue cloth with no top stain. Pastedown drawing of U.S.S. Dolphin.

	F/F	F/NF	NF/VG+	VG+/VG	VG/VG-	Good	w/o dj
1st ed	$40	$30	$20	$15	$10	$8	60%

When Eight Bells Toll 1966

"DOUBLEDAY & COMPANY, INC., GARDEN CITY, NEW YORK/1966" on title page.
Copyright page - 9th (of 9) line - "FIRST EDITION". DJ price $4.95. Rear panel - 2/3 page portrait of Alistair MacLean. Full bound - black cloth with no top stain. Pastedowns blue.

	F/F	F/NF	NF/VG+	VG+/VG	VG/VG-	Good	w/o dj
1st ed	$30	$25	$20	$15	$10	$7	70%

Where Eagles Dare 1967

"1967/Doubleday & Company, Inc., Garden City, New York" on title page. Copyright page - 5th (of 5) line -"First Edition". DJ price - $4.95. Rear panel - full page portrait of Alistair MacLean. Full bound - black cloth with no top stain. Pastedowns orange.

	F/F	F/NF	NF/VG+	VG+/VG	VG/VG-	Good	w/o dj
1st ed	$25	$20	$15	$12	$9	$6	80%

Force 10 From Navarone 1968

"1968/Doubleday & Company, Inc., Garden City, New York" on title page.
Copyright page - 5th (of 5) line - "First Edition in the United States of America".
DJ price - $4.95. Full bound - black cloth with no top stain. Red pastedowns.

	F/F	F/NF	NF/VG+	VG+/VG	VG/VG-	Good	w/o dj
1st ed	$25	$20	$15	$12	$9	$6	80%

Puppet on a Chain 1969

111

"GARDEN CITY, NEW YORK/DOUBLEDAY & COMPANY, INC./1969" on title page.
Copyright page - 5th (of 5) line - "First Edition in the United States of America".
DJ price - $5.95. Rear panel - "As one of Interpol's . . . . drug ring./Puppet on a Chain/Alistair MacLean". Full bound - blue cloth with no top stain.

		F/F	F/NF	NF/VG+	VG+/VG	VG/VG-	Good	w/o dj
1st ed		$20	$15	$12	$10	$8	$5	80%

Caravan to Vaccares 1970

"DOUBLEDAY & COMPANY, INC./GARDEN CITY, NEW YORK/1970" on title page.
Copyright page - 5th (of 5) line - "FIRST EDITION IN THE UNITED STATES OF AMERICA". DJ price - $5.95. Rear panel - full page portrait of Alistair MacLean.
Full bound - black cloth with no top stain. Pastedowns red.

"COLLINS/*St James's Place, London* 1970" on title page. Copyright page - four lines - "ISBN 0 00 221124 6/c Alistair MacLean, 1970/Collins Clear-Type Press/London and Glasgow".
DJ price £1.50 net/30s. net. Full bound - dark green cloth with no top stain and white pastedowns.

		F/F	F/NF	NF/VG+	VG+/VG	VG/VG-	Good	w/o dj
1st ed		$20	$15	$12	$10	$8	$5	80%

Bear Island 1971

"DOUBLEDAY & COMPANY, INC., GARDEN CITY, NEW YORK/1971" on title page.
Copyright page - 5th (of 5) line - "FIRST EDITION". DJ price - $5.95. Rear panel - "A film to be . . . .accompanied them on the journey to . . . /Bear Island/by Alistair MacLean".
Full bound - green-blue cloth with no top stain. Pastedowns green-blue.

"COLLINS/ST. JAMES'S PLACE, LONDON/1976" on title page.
Copyright page - 4h (of 9) line -"First published 1971".
Rear panel - photo of Alistair MacLean.

		F/F	F/NF	NF/VG+	VG+/VG	VG/VG-	Good	w/o dj
1st ed		$20	$15	$12	$10	$8	$5	80%

Captain Cook   Non-fiction

"Doubleday & Company, Inc./Garden City, New York" on title page. No date on title page.
Copyright page - four lines "Library of Congress Catalog Card No:70-180092/©Alistair MacLean 1972/All Rights Reserved/Printed in Great Britain".
Full bound - dark green cloth with no top stain and maps on pastedowns.

		F/F	F/NF	NF/VG+	VG+/VG	VG/VG-	Good	w/o dj
1st ed		$20	$15	$12	$10	$8	$5	80%

The Way to Dusty Death 1973

"Doubleday & Company, Inc./Garden City, New York 1973" on title page.
Copyright page - 6th (of 6) line - "First Edition in the United States of America".
DJ price - $5.95. Rear panel - continuation on picture on front panel.
Full bound - black cloth with no top stain. Pastedowns gold.

		F/F	F/NF	NF/VG+	VG+/VG	VG/VG-	Good	w/o dj
1st ed		$20	$15	$12	$10	$8	$5	80%

Breakheart Pass 1974

"1974/Doubleday & Company, Inc., Garden City, New York" on title page.
Copyright page - 6th (of 6) line - "First Edition in the United States of America".
DJ price - $5.95. Rear panel - full page portrait of Alistair MacLean.
Quarter bound - orange-brown cloth with blue paper and no top stain. Pastedowns blue.

		F/F	F/NF	NF/VG+	VG+/VG	VG/VG-	Good	w/o dj
1st ed		$20	$15	$12	$10	$8	$5	80%

Circus 1975

"1975/Doubleday & Company, Inc., Garden City, New York" on title page.
Copyright page - 6th (of 6) line - "First Edition in the United States of America".
DJ price - $6.95. Rear panel - "Bruno Wildermann was used to . . . have time to be afraid. . ./
Alistair MacLean/CIRCUS". Quarter bound - orange-brown cloth with gold paper and no
top stain. Pastedowns drawing of prison and laboratory.

		F/F	F/NF	NF/VG+	VG+/VG	VG/VG-	Good	w/o dj
1st ed		$20	$15	$12	$10	$8	$5	80%

The Golden Gate 1976

"Doubleday & Company, Inc./Garden City, New York 1976" on title page.
Copyright page - 11th (of 11) line - "First Edition in the United States of America".
DJ price - $7.95 (no difference for later editions).
Quarter bound - navy blue cloth with red paper and no top stain. White pastedowns.

"COLLINS/St. James's Place, London, 1976" on title page. Copyright page - 4th (of 9) line -
"First Published 1976". Rear panel - photo of Alistair MacLean.

		F/F	F/NF	NF/VG+	VG+/VG	VG/VG-	Good	w/o dj
1st ed		$20	$15	$12	$10	$8	$5	80%

Seawitch 1977

"1977/Doubleday & Company, Inc., Garden City, New York" on title page. Copyright page -
11th (of 11) line - "First Edition in the United States of America". DJ price - $7.95. Rear
panel - "Lord Worth was used . . . . time was running out for all of them . . . ./Alister
MacLean/SEAWITCH". Quarter bound - black cloth with brown paper and no top stain.

"COLLINS/St James's Place, London/1977" on title page. Copyright page - 4th (of 9) line -
"First published 1977". DJ price £3.50 NET. Full bound - steel gray cloth with no top stain
and white pastedowns.

		F/F	F/NF	NF/VG+	VG+/VG	VG/VG-	Good	w/o dj
1st ed		$20	$15	$12	$10	$8	$5	80%

Goodbye California 1978

"Doubleday & Company, Inc./Garden City, New York/1978" on title page. Copyright page -
11th (of 11) line - "FIRST EDITION IN THE UNITED STATES OF AMERICA".
DJ price - $8.95. Rear panel - "The seismologist . . . . If tomorrow comes./from Goodbye/
California/Alistair/MacLean". Quarter bound - blue cloth with blue paper and no top stain.

	F/F	F/NF	NF/VG+	VG+/VG	VG/VG-	Good	w/o dj

1st ed		$20	$15	$12	$10	$8	$5	80%

Athabasca 1980

"DOUBLEDAY & COMPANY, INC./GARDEN CITY, NEW YORK/1980" on title page.
Copyright page -16th (of 16) line - "First Edition". DJ price - $11.95. Rear panel - "Two
excellent . . . will find it in/ATHABASCA/Alistair MacLean/ISBN: 0-385-17204-4".
Quarter bound - maroon cloth with black paper and no top stain. Gray map pastedowns.

	F/F	F/NF	NF/VG+	VG+/VG	VG/VG-	Good	w/o dj
1st ed	$20	$15	$12	$10	$8	$5	80%

River of Death 1981

"COLLINS/St James's Place, London /1981" on title page. Copyright page - 11th (of 15) line -
"First published 1981". DJ price £7.50 NET. Full bound - dark green cloth with no top stain
and white pastedowns.

	F/F	F/NF	NF/VG+	VG+/VG	VG/VG-	Good	w/o dj
1st ed	$20	$15	$12	$10	$8	$5	80%

Partisans 1983

"1983/DOUBLEDAY & COMPANY, INC., GARDEN CITY, NEW YORK" on title page.
Copyright page -11th (of 11) line - "First Edition".
DJ price - $14.95. Rear panel - full page portrait of Alistair MacLean ISBN: 0-385-18262-7.
Quarter bound - black cloth with red paper and no top stain. Pastedowns blue.

	F/F	F/NF	NF/VG+	VG+/VG	VG/VG-	Good	w/o dj
1st ed	$20	$15	$12	$10	$8	$5	80%

Floodgate 1983

"DOUBLEDAY & COMPANY, INC.,/GARDEN CITY, NEW YORK/1984" on title page.
Copyright page -11th (of 11) line - "FIRST EDITION".
DJ price - $15.95. Rear panel - 2/3 page portrait of Alistair MacLean.
Quarter bound - black cloth with red paper and no top stain. Pastedowns white.

	F/F	F/NF	NF/VG+	VG+/VG	VG/VG-	Good	w/o dj
1st ed	$20	$15	$12	$10	$8	$5	80%

San Andreas 1985

"DOUBLEDAY & COMPANY, INC., GARDEN CITY, NEW YORK/1985" on title page.
Copyright page -11th (of 11) line - "First Edition".
DJ price - $16.95. Rear panel - continuation of picture on front panel ISBN: 0-385-23152-0.
Quarter bound - black cloth with dark blue paper and no top stain.

	F/F	F/NF	NF/VG+	VG+/VG	VG/VG-	Good	w/o dj
1st ed	$20	$15	$12	$10	$8	$5	80%

Santorini 1987

"DOUBLEDAY & COMPANY, Inc., Garden City, New York/1987" on title page. Copyright
page -10th (of 10) line - "First Edition in the United States of America". DJ price - $16.95.

Quarter bound - dark blue cloth with blue paper and no top stain. White pastedowns.

	F/F	F/NF	NF/VG+	VG+/VG	VG/VG-	Good	w/o dj
1st ed		$20	$15	$12	$10	$8	$5	80%

Death Trains 1989

	F/F	F/NF	NF/VG+	VG+/VG	VG/VG-	Good	w/o dj
1st ed		$20	$15	$12	$10	$8	$5	80%

Bernard Malamud

The Natural 1952

"Harcourt, Brace and Company New York" on title page. Copyright page - fifth (of 7) line - "first edition". DJ price - $3.00. Three binding exist (blue, red, and grey). All are full bound with no top stain and white pastedowns. No price differences exist between the different bindings.

	F/F	F/NF	NF/VG+	VG+/VG	VG/VG-	Good	w/o dj
1st ed		$900	$700	$550	$450	$350	$150	50%

John Phillips Marquand (1893-1960)

U.S. novelist, born in Wilmington, Delaware, who is know for his novels about wealthy New Englanders. These include _The Late George Apley_ (1937 - Pulitzer Prize 1938), _Wickford Point_ (1939) and _H.M. Pulham, Esquire_ (1941). He also wrote a number of novels and detective stories about a Japanese detective, Mr. Moto.

The Late George Apley 1937

	F/F	F/NF	NF/VG+	VG+/VG	VG/VG-	Good	w/o dj
1st ed		$50	$40	$35	$30	$20	$12	50%

H.M. Pulham, Esquire 1941

Presentation copy. Price double that show for first edition.
"LITTLE, BROWN AND COMPANY BOSTON/PUBLISHERS" on title page.
Copyright page - 8 lines (missing lines 8, 9, and 10 in first edition). Page following copyright page of title page -"This is one of nine hundred/and fifty copies of/ H. M. PULHAM, ESQUIRE/printed and especially bound/for presentation".
DJ - Green background with blank rear panel and inside flaps - no price. Quarter bound with red cloth spine and light green cloth sides and red top stain. White pastedowns.

"LITTLE, BROWN AND COMPANY BOSTON/1941" on title page. Copyright page - lines 8, 9, and 10 (of 11) "First Edition, after the printing/of 950 copies for presentation/Published February, 1941". DJ - BOMC seal inside front flap, no price.
Full bound - tan cloth with maroon top stain. White pastedowns.

	F/F	F/NF	NF/VG+	VG+/VG	VG/VG-	Good	w/o dj
1st ed		$25	$20	$18	$15	$10	$8	60%

So Little Time 1943

"LITTLE, BROWN AND COMPANY BOSTON/1943" on title page.
Copyright page - six lines with no reference to printing number.
Bottom of rear inside dj lap contains the "Men in the Service Need Books" box.
Full bound - tan cloth with red top stain and white pastedowns.

		F/F	F/NF	NF/VG+	VG+/VG	VG/VG-	Good	w/odj
1st ed		$25	$20	$18	$15	$10	$8	70%

Point of No Return 1949

"LITTLE, BROWN AND COMPANY BOSTON/1949" on title page.
Copyright page - 7th (of 25) line - "Published February, 1949".
DJ price - $3.50. Rear panel - half page photo of author with bio underneath.

		F/F	F/NF	NF/VG+	VG+/VG	VG/VG-	Good	w/odj
1st ed		$25	$20	$18	$15	$10	$8	70%

Sincerely, Willis Wayde 1955

"LITTLE, BROWN AND COMPANY/Boston   Toronto" on title page. No date on title
page. Copyright page - 8th (of 11) line - "FIRST EDITION". DJ price - $3.95.
Full bound - tan cloth with yellow top stain and white pastedowns.

		F/F	F/NF	NF/VG+	VG+/VG	VG/VG-	Good	w/odj
1st ed		$20	$15	$12	$10	$8	$5	70%

Stopover: Tokyo 1957

"LITTLE, BROWN AND COMPANY/BOSTON   TORONTO" on title page. No date on
title page. Copyright page - 6th (of 15) line - "FIRST EDITION". DJ price - $3.95.
Full bound - dark pink cloth with no top stain and white pastedowns.

		F/F	F/NF	NF/VG+	VG+/VG	VG/VG-	Good	w/odj
1st ed		$25	$20	$18	$15	$10	$8	50%

Women and Thomas Harrow 1958

"LITTLE, BROWN AND COMPANY/Boston   Toronto" on title page. No date on title
page. Copyright page - 7th (of 10) line - "FIRST EDITION".
Full bound - tan cloth with yellow top stain and white pastedowns.

		F/F	F/NF	NF/VG+	VG+/VG	VG/VG-	Good	w/odj
1st ed		$20	$15	$12	$10	$8	$5	70%

Fr?cis Van Wyck Mason

Popular U.S. novelist, born in Boston, educated at Harvard, known for his historical novels, most notably his
Revolutionary War tetralogy consisting of _Three Harbours_ (1938), _Stars on the Seas_ (1940), _Rivers of Glory_ (1942),
and _Eagle in the Sky_ (1948) and his Civil War series _Proud New Flags_ (1951), _Blue Hurricane_ (1954), and _Our
Valiant Few_ (1956)   Mason also authored the Colonel (originally as Captain, then Major) North adventure
series.

The Revolutionary War tetralogy:

Three Harbours

		F/F	F/NF	NF/VG+	VG+/VG	VG/VG-	Good	w/o dj
1st ed		$75	$60	$45	$30	$20	$8	60%

Stars on the Sea 1940

"J.P. LIPPINCOTT COMPANY/PHILADELPHIA AND NEW YORK" on title page.
Copyright page - 5th (of 5) line -"*First Edition*". DJ price - $2.75.
Full bound - blue cloth with blue top stain and maps on pastedowns.

		F/F	F/NF	NF/VG+	VG+/VG	VG/VG-	Good	w/o dj
1st ed		$75	$60	$45	$30	$20	$8	60%

Rivers of Glory 1942

"J.P. LIPPINCOTT COMPANY/PHILADELPHIA AND NEW YORK/1792-1942" on title page.
Copyright page - 5th (of 5) line - "FIRST EDITION". DJ price - $2.75.
Full bound - blue cloth with blue-gray top stain and maps on pastedowns.

		F/F	F/NF	NF/VG+	VG+/VG	VG/VG-	Good	w/o dj
1st ed		$70	$55	$40	$30	$20	$8	60%

Eagle in the Sky 1948

"J.P. LIPPINCOTT COMPANY/PHILADELPHIA AND NEW YORK" on title page. No date
on title page. Copyright page - 5th (of 5) line - "FIRST EDITION". DJ price - $3.00.
Full bound - blue cloth with no top stain and white pastedowns.

		F/F	F/NF	NF/VG+	VG+/VG	VG/VG-	Good	w/o dj
1st ed		$60	$50	$35	$25	$17	$7	60%

The Civil War tetralogy:
Proud New Flags 1951

		F/F	F/NF	NF/VG+	VG+/VG	VG/VG-	Good	w/o dj
1st ed		$50	$45	$35	$25	$17	$7	60%

Blue Hurricane 1954

"J.P. LIPPINCOTT COMPANY/PHILADELPHIA AND NEW YORK" on title page. No date
on title page. Copyright page - 4th (of 5) line - "FIRST EDITION". DJ price - $3.75.
Full bound - blue cloth with red top stain and maps on pastedowns.

		F/F	F/NF	NF/VG+	VG+/VG	VG/VG-	Good	w/o dj
1st ed		$40	$30	$20	$15	$12	$6	70%

Our Valient Few 1956

"*Boston* Little, Brown and Company *Toronto*" on title page. No date on title page.
Copyright page - 6th (of 9) line - "FIRST EDITION". DJ price - $3.95.
Full bound - light gray cloth with no top stain and white pastedowns.

		F/F	F/NF	NF/VG+	VG+/VG	VG/VG-	Good	w/o dj
1st ed		$40	$30	$20	$15	$12	$6	70%

Cutlass Empire 1949   A novel on life of Henry Morgan.

"DOUBLEDAY & COMPANY, INC. GARDEN CITY, NEW YORK, 1949" on title page.
Copyright page - 8th (of 8) line - "FIRST EDITION". DJ price - $3.00.
Full bound - green cloth with burnt orange top stain and maps on pastedowns.

	F/F	F/NF	NF/VG+	VG+/VG	VG/VG-	Good	w/o dj
1st ed	$50	$40	$30	$20	$15	$10	50%

Golden Admiral 1953   A novel of Sir Francis Drake and the Armada.

"DOUBLEDAY & COMPANY, INC./Garden City, New York, 1953" on title page.
Copyright page - 8th (of 8) line - "FIRST EDITION". DJ price - $3.95.
Full bound - blue cloth with no top stain and maps on pastedowns.

	F/F	F/NF	NF/VG+	VG+/VG	VG/VG-	Good	w/o dj
1st ed	$50	$40	$30	$20	$15	$10	50%

Silver Leopard 1955   A novel of the first crusade.

"DOUBLEDAY & COMPANY, INC., GARDEN CITY, NEW YORK, 1955" on title page.
Copyright page - 9th (of 9) line - "First Edition". DJ price - $3.95. Rear panel - full page photo
of author with three line underneath (no different for later issues).
Full bound - red cloth with no top stain and maps on pastedowns.

	F/F	F/NF	NF/VG+	VG+/VG	VG/VG-	Good	w/o dj
1st ed	$40	$30	$22	$15	$12	$9	70%

The Young Titan 1959   A novel of colonial America and of the siege of Louisburg.

"Doubleday & Company, Inc., Garden City, New York/1959" on title page.
Copyright page - 8th (of 8) line - "First Edition". DJ price - $5.95.
Full bound - blue cloth with no top stain and maps on pastedowns.

	F/F	F/NF	NF/VG+	VG+/VG	VG/VG-	Good	w/o dj
1st ed	$40	$30	$22	$15	$12	$9	70%

The Sea 'Venture 1961   A novel of the settling of the Bermudas.

"GARDEN CITY, N.Y./*Doubleday & Company, Inc./1961*" on title page. Copyright page -
8th (of 8) line -*"First Edition"*. Full bound - dark green with no top stain and maps on
pastedowns.

	F/F	F/NF	NF/VG+	VG+/VG	VG/VG-	Good	w/o dj
1st ed	$40	$30	$22	$15	$12	$9	70%

Manila Galleon 1961

"LITTLE, BROWN AND COMPANY   BOSTON   TORONTO" on title page. No date on title
page. Copyright page - 7th (of 10) line - "FIRST EDITION". DJ price - $5,95.
Full bound - maroon cloth with no top stain and maps on pastedowns.

		F/F	F/NF	NF/VG+	VG+/VG	VG/VG-	Good	w/o dj
1st ed		$35	$27	$20	$15	$12	$9	70%

Wild Horizon 1966

"Little, Brown and Company   Boston   Toronto" on title page. No date on title page.
Copyright page - 7th (of 10) line "FIRST EDITION". DJ price - $6.95.
Full bound - Blue cloth with blue top stain and maps on pastedowns.

		F/F	F/NF	NF/VG+	VG+/VG	VG/VG-	Good	w/o dj
1st ed		$35	$25	$18	$13	$11	$8	70%

Harpoon in Eden 1969

"1969/Doubleday & Company, Inc., Garden City, New York" on title page.
Copyright page -5th (of 5) line - "FIRST EDITION". DJ price - $6.95.
Quarter bound - Gray cloth with light blue sides and no top stain. White pastedowns.

		F/F	F/NF	NF/VG+	VG+/VG	VG/VG-	Good	w/o dj
1st ed		$30	$23	$17	$12	$10	$8	70%

Brimstone Club 1971

"LITTLE, BROWN AND COMPANY   BOSTON   TORONTO" on title page. No date on
title page. Copyright page - 9th (of 12) line - "FIRST EDITION". D price - $7.95.
Full bound - red cloth with blue top stain and map on pastedowns.

		F/F	F/NF	NF/VG+	VG+/VG	VG/VG-	Good	w/o dj
1st ed		$25	$20	$15	$12	$10	$8	70%

Roads to Liberty 1972   A special abridged edition of Three Harbours, Stars on the Sea, Wild Horizons, and Eagle in the Sky.

"LITTLE, BROWN AND COMPANY   BOSTON   TORONTO" on title page.
Copyright page - 10th (of 25) line - "FIRST EDITION". D price - $12.95.
Full bound - green cloth with no top stain and map on pastedowns.

		F/F	F/NF	NF/VG+	VG+/VG	VG/VG-	Good	w/o dj
1st ed		$20	$15	$12	$10	$8	$6	70%

Log Cabin Noble 1973

"DOUBLEDAY & COMPANY, INC./GARDEN CITY, NEW YORK/1973" on title page.
Copyright page - 6th (of 6) line - "FIRST EDITION" . DJ price - $7.95.
Quarter bound - blue cloth with cleam sides and no top stain. Map on pastedowns.

		F/F	F/NF	NF/VG+	VG+/VG	VG/VG-	Good	w/o dj
1st ed		$30	$23	$17	$12	$10	$8	70%

Trumpets Sound No More 1975

"LITTLE, BROWN AND COMPANY   BOSTON   TORONTO/1975" on title page.
Copyright page - 7th (of 18) line - "FIRST EDITION". DJ price - $8.95.
Full bound - red cloth with no top stain and map on pastedowns.

	F/F	F/NF	NF/VG+	VG+/VG	VG/VG-	Good	w/o dj
1st ed	$20	$15	$12	$10	$8	$6	70%

Guns for Rebellion 1977   A novel about the American Revolution.

"DOUBLEDAY & COMPANY, INC./GARDEN CITY, NEW YORK/1977" on title page.
Copyright page - 15th (of 15) line - *"First Edition"*. DJ price - $9.95.
Full bound - red cloth with no top stain and white pastedowns.

	F/F	F/NF	NF/VG+	VG+/VG	VG/VG-	Good	w/o dj
1st ed	$20	$15	$12	$10	$8	$6	70%

Armored Giants 1980   A novel of the Civil War.

"LITTLE, BROWN AND COMPANY BOSTON TORONTO" on title page. No date on title
page. Copyright page - 8th (of 20) line "FIRST EDITION". DJ price - $13.95.
Full bound - green cloth with no top stain and light gold pastedowns.

	F/F	F/NF	NF/VG+	VG+/VG	VG/VG-	Good	w/o dj
1st ed	$20	$15	$12	$10	$8	$6	70%

The Major North Intrigue Stories

Seeds of Murder 1930   A Captain North adventure.

	F/F	F/NF	NF/VG+	VG+/VG	VG/VG-	Good	w/o dj
1st ed	$700	$550	$450	$300	$250	$125	10%

The Vespers Service Murders 1931   A Captain North adventure.

"GARDEN CITY, N.Y. PUBLISHED FOR/THE CRIME CLUB, INC./BY DOUBLEDAY,
DORAN & COMPANY, INC." on title page. No date on title page. Copyright page - 5th (of 5)
line - "FIRST EDITION". Full bound - black cloth with burnt-orange top stain and red
pastedowns. DJ price - $2.00.

	F/F	F/NF	NF/VG+	VG+/VG	VG/VG-	Good	w/o dj
1st ed	$600	$500	$400	$275	$225	$100	10%

The Fort Terror Murders 1931   A Captain North adventure.

"GARDEN CITY, N.Y. PUBLISHED FOR/THE CRIME CLUB, INC./BY DOUBLEDAY,
DORAN & COMPANY, INC." on title page. No date on title page. Copyright page - 5th (of 5)
line - "FIRST EDITION". Full bound - black cloth with yellow top stain and printing on
white pastedowns. DJ price - $2.00.

	F/F	F/NF	NF/VG+	VG+/VG	VG/VG-	Good	w/o dj
1st ed	$600	$500	$400	$275	$225	$100	10%

The Yellow Arrow Murders 1932   A Captain North adventure.

"GARDEN CITY, N.Y. PUBLISHED FOR/THE CRIME CLUB, INC./BY DOUBLEDAY,
DORAN & COMPANY, INC." No date on title page. Copyright page - 5th (of 5)
line - "FIRST EDITION". Full bound - black cloth with yellow top stain and white

pastedowns. DJ price - $2.00.

	F/F	F/NF	NF/VG+	VG+/VG	VG/VG-	Good	w/o dj
1st ed	$550	$475	$375	$250	$200	$100	10%

The Branded Spy Murders 1932   A Captain North adventure.

	F/F	F/NF	NF/VG+	VG+/VG	VG/VG-	Good	w/o dj
1st ed	$550	$475	$375	$250	$200	$100	10%

Spider House 1932   Mystery League

"THE MYSTERY LEAGUE, INC./NEW YORK and LONDON/MCMXXXII" on title page.
Copyright page - 6th (of 6) line - "FIRST EDITION". Full bound - black cloth with maroon
top stain and green and white pastedowns. DJ has no price.

	F/F	F/NF	NF/VG+	VG+/VG	VG/VG-	Good	w/o dj
1st ed	$100	$75	$60	$45	$35	$15	20%

The Shanghai Bund Murders 1933   A Captain North adventure.

"GARDEN CITY, N.Y. 1933 PUBLISHED FOR/THE CRIME CLUB, INC./BY DOUBLEDAY,
DORAN & COMPANY, INC." on title page. Copyright page - 5th (of 5) line - "FIRST
EDITION". Full bound - yellow cloth with red top stain and map and write-up on
pastedowns. DJ price - $2.00.

	F/F	F/NF	NF/VG+	VG+/VG	VG/VG-	Good	w/o dj
1st ed	$500	$425	$350	$225	$175	$90	10%

The Sulu Sea Murders 1933   A Captain North adventure.

"GARDEN CITY, N.Y. 1933 PUBLISHED FOR/THE CRIME CLUB, INC./BY DOUBLEDAY,
DORAN & COMPANY, INC." on title page. Copyright page - 5th (of 5) line - "FIRST
EDITION". Full bound - black cloth with green top stain and white pastedowns. DJ price -
$2.00.

	F/F	F/NF	NF/VG+	VG+/VG	VG/VG-	Good	w/o dj
1st ed	$450	$375	$275	$200	$150	$80	10%

The Budapest Parade Murders 1935   A Captain North adventure.

"GARDEN CITY, N.Y. 1935 PUBLISHED FOR/THE CRIME CLUB, INC./BY DOUBLEDAY,
DORAN & COMPANY, INC." on title page. Copyright page - 5th (of 5) line - "FIRST
EDITION". Full bound - black cloth with burnt-orange top stain and white pastedowns.
DJ price - $2.00.

	F/F	F/NF	NF/VG+	VG+/VG	VG/VG-	Good	w/o dj
1st ed	$375	$300	$250	$175	$125	$60	10%

The Washington Legatoin Murders 1935   The ninth Captain North adventure.

"GARDEN CITY, N.Y. 1935 PUBLISHED FOR/THE CRIME CLUB, INC./BY DOUBLEDAY,
DORAN & COMPANY, INC." on title page. Copyright page - 5th (of 5) line - "FIRST
EDITION". Full bound - black cloth with green top stain and white pastedowns. DJ price -
$2.00.

	F/F	F/NF	NF/VG+	VG+/VG	VG/VG-	Good	w/o dj

1st ed		$375	$300	$250	$175	$125	$60	10%

The Seven Sea Murders   1936   A Captain North adventure.

"Published for/ THE CRIME CLUB, INC. Garden City, N.Y./BY DOUBLEDAY, DORAN & COMPANY, INC. 1936" on title page. Copyright page - 5th (of 5) line - "FIRST EDITION". Full bound - red cloth with red top stain and white pastedowns. DJ price - $2.00.

		F/F	F/NF	NF/VG +	VG + /VG	VG/VG -	Good	w/o dj
1st ed		$325	$275	$225	$150	$125	$60	10%

The Hong Kong Airbase Murders   1937   A Captain North adventure.

"GARDEN CITY, N.Y. Published for/THE CRIME CLUB, INC./By Doubleday, Doran & Company, Inc./1937" on title page. Copyright page - 5th (of 5) line - "FIRST EDITION". Full bound - black cloth with burnt-orange top stain and white pastedowns. DJ price - $2.00.

		F/F	F/NF	NF/VG +	VG + /VG	VG/VG -	Good	w/o dj
1st ed		$300	$250	$200	$125	$100	$50	10%

The Cairo Garter Murders   1938   A Captain North adventure.

"GARDEN CITY NEW YORK/PUBLISHED FOR THE CRIME CLUB, INC./BY DOUBLEDAY, DORAN & COMPANY, INC. 1938" on title page. Copyright page - 5th (of 5) line - "FIRST EDITION". Full bound - orange cloth with gray top stain and white pastedowns. DJ price - $2.00.

		F/F	F/NF	NF/VG +	VG + /VG	VG/VG -	Good	w/o dj
1st ed		$300	$250	$200	$125	$100	$50	10%

The Singapore Exile Murders   1939   A Captain North adventure.

		F/F	F/NF	NF/VG +	VG + /VG	VG/VG -	Good	w/o dj
1st ed		$300	$250	$200	$125	$100	$50	10%

The Bucherest Ballerina Murders   1940   A Major North adventure.

"FREDERICK A. STOKES COMPANY/NEW YORK   MCMXL" on title page. Copyright page - 5 lines with no mention of printing number. Last line - "Printed in the United States of America." Full bound - purple cloth with no top stain and maps on yellow background on pastedowns. DJ price - $2.00.

		F/F	F/NF	NF/VG +	VG + /VG	VG/VG -	Good	w/o dj
1st ed		$275	$225	$175	$125	$100	$50	20%

The Rio Casino Intrigue   1941   A Major North adventure.

"Reynal & Hitchcock New York" on title page. No date on title page. Copyright page - 6 lines with no mention of printing number. Last line - "BY THE CORNWELL PRESS, CORNWELL, N.Y." Full bound - blue cloth with blue-green top stain and maps on white background on pastedowns. DJ price - $2.00.

F/F	F/NF	NF/VG +	VG + /VG	VG/VG -	Good	w/o dj

1st ed		$225	$200	$150	$100	$75	$30	20%

Saigon Singer 1946   A Major North Story

"DOUBLEDAY & COMPANY, INC., Garden City, New York 1946" on title page.
Copyright page - 7th (of 7) line - "FIRST EDITION". DJ price -$2.50.
Full bound - maroon cloth with maroon top stain and white pastedowns.

		F/F	F/NF	NF/VG+	VG+/VG	VG/VG-	Good	w/o dj
1st ed		$60	$50	$35	$25	$20	$10	33%

Dardanelles Derelict 1949   A Major North Story

"Garden City, New York/ DOUBLEDAY & COMPANY, INC./1949" on title page. Copyright
page - 9th (of 9) line - "FIRST EDITION". DJ price -$2.75. Rear panel - 3/4 page portrait of
HUGH NORTH.   Full bound - tan cloth with no top stain and maps on pastedowns.

		F/F	F/NF	NF/VG+	VG+/VG	VG/VG-	Good	w/o dj
1st ed		$60	$50	$35	$25	$20	$10	33%

Himalayan Assignment 1952   A Colonel North Story

"DOUBLEDAY & COMPANY, INC./GARDEN CITY, NEW YORK, 1952" on title page.
Copyright page - 8th (of 9) line - "FIRST EDITION". DJ price - $3.00.
Full bound - light blue cloth with no top stain. Map of Nepal on pastedowns.

		F/F	F/NF	NF/VG+	VG+/VG	VG/VG-	Good	w/o dj
1st ed		$50	$40	$30	$20	$15	$10	50%

Two Tickets for Tangier 1955   A Colonel North Story

"DOUBLEDAY & COMPANY, INC., GARDEN CITY, NEW YORK 1957" on title page.
Copyright page - 9th (of 9) line - "FIRST EDITION". DJ price - $3.75.
Full bound - cream cloth with burnt orange top stain and white pastedowns.

		F/F	F/NF	NF/VG+	VG+/VG	VG/VG-	Good	w/o dj
1st ed		$50	$40	$30	$20	$15	$10	50%

The Gracious Lily Affair 1957   A Colonel North Story

"Doubleday & Company, Inc., Garden City, New York/1957" on title page.
Copyright page - 13th (of 13) line - "First Edition".
DJ price $3.75. Rear panel - 4/5 page portrait of Van Wyck Mason,
Full bound - green cloth with light orange top stain and white pastedowns.

		F/F	F/NF	NF/VG+	VG+/VG	VG/VG-	Good	w/o dj
1st ed		$40	$35	$25	$20	$15	$10	60%

Secret Mission to Bangkok 1960   A Colonel North Story

"1960/Doubleday & Company, Inc., Garden City, New York" on title page. Copyright page -
7th (of 7) line - "First Edition". DJ price - $3.95. Rear panel - 1/2 page portrait of Van Wyck
Mason with 7 line bio underneath. Full bound - blue cloth with red top stain and white
pastedowns.

123

	F/F	F/NF	NF/VG+	VG+/VG	VG/VG-	Good	w/o dj
1st ed	·	$35	$30	$25	$20	$15	$10	70%

Trouble in Burma 1962 A Colonel North Story

"1962/Doubleday & Company, Inc./GARDEN CITY, NEW YORK" on title page. Copyright page - 9th (of 9) line - "FIRST EDITION". DJ price $3.75. Rear panel - 2/3 page portrait of Van Wyck Mason. Quarter bound - green cloth with black sides and no top stain. White pastedowns.

	F/F	F/NF	NF/VG+	VG+/VG	VG/VG-	Good	w/o dj
1st ed		$40	$35	$25	$20	$15	$10	60%

Zanzibar Intrigue 1963 A Colonel North Story

"DOUBLEDAY & COMPANY, INC./GARDEN CITY, NEW YORK/1963" on title page.
Copyright page - 9th (of 9) line - "FIRST EDITION".
DJ price - $3.95. Rear panel - full page portrait of Van Wyck Mason with no bio.
Quarter bound - black cloth with light green sides and no top stain. White pastedowns.

	F/F	F/NF	NF/VG+	VG+/VG	VG/VG-	Good	w/o dj
1st ed		$35	$30	$25	$20	$15	$10	70%

Marcaibo Mission 1965 A Colonel North Story

"1965/DOUBLEDAY & COMPANY, INC./GARDEN CITY, NEW YORK" on title page.
Copyright page - 9th (of 9) line - "First Edition".
DJ price - $4.50. Rear panel - full page portrait of Van Wyck Mason with no bio.
Quarter bound - black cloth with green sides and no top stain. Green pastedowns.

	F/F	F/NF	NF/VG+	VG+/VG	VG/VG-	Good	w/o dj
1st ed		$35	$30	$25	$20	$15	$10	70%

The Deadly Orbit 1968 A Colonel North Story

"*Doubleday & Company, Inc./Garden City, New York/1968*" on title page.
Copyright page - 9th (of 9) line - "First Edition".
DJ price - $4.50. Rear panel - full page portrait of Van Wyck Mason with no bio.
Full bound - blue cloth with no top stain and red pastedowns.

	F/F	F/NF	NF/VG+	VG+/VG	VG/VG-	Good	w/o dj
1st ed		$35	$30	$25	$20	$15	$10	70%

Murder In The Senate 1935 Written as Geoffrey Coffin. A Blue Streak Mystery.

"DODGE PUBLISHING COMPANY/NEW YORK" on title page. No date on title page.
Copyright page - 6th (of 12) lines - "FIRST EDITION". DJ price $2.00.
Full bound - yellow with blue ink and blue top stain. White pastedowns.

	F/F	F/NF	NF/VG+	VG+/VG	VG/VG-	Good	w/o dj
1st ed		$600	$550	$400	$300	$200	$50	25%

The Forgotten Fleet 1936 Written as Geoffrey Coffin. A Blue Streak Mystery.

"DODGE PUBLISHING COMPANY, NEW YORK/1936" on title page. Copyright page - 6th (of 12) lines - "FIRST EDITION". DJ price $2.00.

Full bound - cream with blue ink and no top stain. White pastedowns.

		F/F	F/NF	NF/VG+	VG+/VG	VG/VG-	Good	w/o dj
1st ed		$600	$550	$400	$300	$200	$50	25%

Ed McBain

Evan Hunter, under the pseudonym of Ed McBain, wrote eight paperback 87th Precinct mystery novels between 1956 and 1958. These were all published as Perma Books paperback original first editions. First Printing of these is indicated on the copyright page. The values shown in the table below apply to each of these eight PBO's.

Cop Hater 1956   Perma Books #M3037 1st Paperback Original edition
The Con Man 1957   Perma Books #M3055 1st Paperback Original edition
The Mugger 1956   Perma Books #M3061 1st Paperback Original edition
The Pusher 1956   Perma Books #M3062 1st Paperback Original edition
Killer's Choice 1957   Perma Books #M3108 1st Paperback Original edition
Killer's Payoff 1958   Perma Books #M3113 1st Paperback Original edition
Lady Killer 1958   Perma Books #M3119 1st Paperback Original edition
Killer's Wedge 1958   Perma Books #M4150 1st Paperback Original edition

	Fine	NF	VG+	VG-
1st ed, PBO	$50	$35	$15	$7

The eight PBO's were printed in first hardbound editions in the following four volumes. The values shown in the table below apply to each of these four volumes.

Squad Room 1958   Simon & Schuster. Killer's Payoff and Lady Killer.
The 87th Precinct 1959   Simon & Schuster. Cop Hater, The Mugger and The Pusher. DJ price - $3.95
Killer's Wedge 1959   Simon & Schuster.
The 87th Squad 1960   Simon & Schuster. Killer's Choice and Con Man.

		F/F	F/NF	NF/VG+	VG+/VG	VG/VG-	Good	w/o dj
1st ed		$150	$125	$80	$50	$35	$15	15%

The following nine hardbound first editions were published by Simon & Schuster between 1959 and 1964. The copyright page of each of these contain the words "first printing". The values shown in the table below apply to each of these nine books.

Till Death 1959
Give The Boys a Big Hand 1960
The Hechler 1960
See Them Die 1960
Lady, Lady, I Did It 1961
Like Love 1962
The Empty Hours 1962
Ten Plus One 1963   DJ price - $3.50
Ax 1964

		F/F	F/NF	NF/VG+	VG+/VG	VG/VG-	Good	w/o dj
1st ed		$125	$110	$75	$50	$35	$15	20%

The following three hardbound first editions were published by Delacorte between 1965 and 1968. The values shown in the table below apply to each of these books.

Doll 1965
He Who Hesitates 1965   DJ price - $3.50
Eighty Million Eyes 1966   DJ price - $3.50

	F/F	F/NF	NF/VG+	VG+/VG	VG/VG-	Good	w/odj
1st ed		$125	$110	$75	$50	$35	$15	25%

The following six hardbound first editions were published by Doubleday between 1968 and 1972. The values shown in the table below apply to each of these books.

Fuzz 1968
Shotgun 1969
Jigsaw 1970   DJ price - $4.95
Hail, Hail, The Gang's All Here 1971
Sadie When She Died 1972   DJ Price - $5.95
Let's Hear It For The Deaf Man 1972

	F/F	F/NF	NF/VG+	VG+/VG	VG/VG-	Good	w/odj
1st ed		$50	$45	$30	$25	$20	$10	60%

The following seven hardbound first editions were published by Random House between 1973 and 1977. The values shown in the table below apply to each of these books.

Hail To The Chief 1973   DJ price - $5.95
Bread 1974   DJ price - $5.95
Where There's Smoke 1975
Blood Relatives 1976
Guns 1976   DJ price - $6.95
So Long As You Both Shall Live 1976
Long Time No See 1977

	F/F	F/NF	NF/VG+	VG+/VG	VG/VG-	Good	w/odj
1st ed		$45	$40	$30	$25	$20	$10	60%

The following seven hardbound first editions were published by Arbor House between 1976 and 1987. The values shown in the table below apply to each of these books.

Goldilocks 1976

	F/F	F/NF	NF/VG+	VG+/VG	VG/VG-	Good	w/odj
1st ed		$40	$35	$25	$20	$15	$6	70%

The McBain Brief 1982   DJ price - $14.95

	F/F	F/NF	NF/VG+	VG+/VG	VG/VG-	Good	w/odj
1st ed		$30	$25	$20	$15	$10	$6	70%

Ice 1983
Lightning 1984   DJ price - $15.95
Eight Black Horses 1985   DJ price - $15.95

Poison 1987 DJ price - $16.95
Tricks 1987 DJ price - $16.95

	F/F	F/NF	NF/VG+	VG+/VG	VG/VG-	Good	w/odj
1st ed	$20	$15	$10	$8	$6	$4	80%

The following four hardbound first editions were published by Viking between 1979 and 1981. The values shown in the table below apply to each of these books.

Calypso 1979 DJ price - $8.95
Ghosts 1980
Heat 1981
Rumpelstiltskin 1981 DJ price - $12.95

	F/F	F/NF	NF/VG+	VG+/VG	VG/VG-	Good	w/odj
1st ed	$20	$15	$10	$8	$6	$4	80%

The following five hardbound first editions were published by Henry Holt between 1984 and 1988. The values shown in the table below apply to each of these books.

Jack and the Bean-Stalk 1984 DJ price - $14.95
Snow White & Rose Red 1985 DJ price - $14.95
Cinderella 1986
Puss In Boots 1987 DJ price - $15.95
The House That Jack Built 1988 DJ price - $16.95

	F/F	F/NF	NF/VG+	VG+/VG	VG/VG-	Good	w/odj
1st ed	$20	$15	$10	$8	$6	$4	80%

The following two hardbound first editions were published by The Mysterious Press between 1986 and 1988. The values shown in the table below apply to each of these books.

Another Part of The City 1986 DJ price - $15.95.
Ed McBain's Ladies 1988 DJ price - $16.95.

	F/F	F/NF	NF/VG+	VG+/VG	VG/VG-	Good	w/odj
1st ed	$20	$15	$10	$8	$6	$4	80%

The 87th Precinct 1959

"SIMON AND SCHUSTER NEW YORK 1959" on title page. Copyright page - 12th (of 13) line *"First Printing"*. DJ price - $3.95. Full bound - yellow cloth with no top stain and white pastedowns.

	F/F	F/NF	NF/VG+	VG+/VG	VG/VG-	Good	w/odj
1st ed	$150	$125	$80	$50	$35	$15	15%

Till Death 1959

"SIMON AND SCHUSTER NEW YORK/1959" on title page. Copyright page - 8th (of 11) line *"FIRST PRINTING"*. Quarter bound - black cloth with blue green sides no top stain. White pastedowns.

	F/F	F/NF	NF/VG+	VG+/VG	VG/VG-	Good	w/odj
1st ed	$125	$110	$75	$50	$35	$15	20%

See Them Die 1960

"SIMON AND SCHUSTER NEW YORK/1960" on title page. Copyright page - 8th (of 11) line "FIRST PRINTING". DJ price - $2.95. Full bound - black cloth with no top stain and gray background pastedowns.

		F/F	F/NF	NF/VG+	VG+/VG	VG/VG-	Good	w/odj
1st ed		$125	$110	$75	$50	$35	$15	20%

Heckler 1960

"SIMON AND SCHUSTER/NEW YORK/1960" on title page. Copyright page - 8th (of 11) line "FIRST PRINTING". Quarter bound - gray cloth with red sides red top stain. White pastedowns.

		F/F	F/NF	NF/VG+	VG+/VG	VG/VG-	Good	w/odj
1st ed		$125	$110	$75	$50	$35	$15	20%

Lady I Did It 1961

"SIMON AND SCHUSTER NEW YORK/1961" on title page. Copyright page - 8th (of 11) line "FIRST PRINTING". Full bound - light gray cloth with violet top stain and black background with white reader and book symbols on pastedowns.

		F/F	F/NF	NF/VG+	VG+/VG	VG/VG-	Good	w/odj
1st ed		$125	$110	$75	$50	$35	$15	20%

Ten Plus One 1963

"Simon and Schuster New York 1963" on title page. Copyright page - 8th (of 11) line "FIRST PRINTING". DJ price - $3.50. Quarter bound - red cloth with black sides and black top stain. Black background pastedown.

		F/F	F/NF	NF/VG+	VG+/VG	VG/VG-	Good	w/odj
1st ed		$125	$110	$75	$50	$35	$15	20%

Ax 1964

"Simon and Schuster/New York 1964" on title page. Copyright page - 8th (of 11) line "FIRST PRINTING". Full bound - orange cloth with pink top stain. White pastedowns with violet "AN INNER SANCTUM MYSTERY"..

		F/F	F/NF	NF/VG+	VG+/VG	VG/VG-	Good	w/odj
1st ed		$125	$110	$75	$50	$35	$15	20%

He Who Hesitates 1965

"A DELACORTE PRESS BOOK" on title page. No date on title page. Copyright page - four lines with no mention of edition or printing number. DJ price - $3.50. Full bound - black cloth with lime green top stain and lime green pastedowns.

		F/F	F/NF	NF/VG+	VG+/VG	VG/VG-	Good	w/odj
1st ed		$125	$110	$75	$50	$35	$15	25%

Eighty Million Eyes 1966

"DELACORTE PRESS NEW YORK" on title page. No date on title page. Copyright page - 7th (of 7) line "FIRST PRINTING". DJ price - $3.50. Full bound - blue cloth with no top stain and white pastedowns.

		F/F	F/NF	NF/VG+	VG+/VG	VG/VG-	Good	w/o dj
1st ed		$125	$110	$75	$50	$35	$15	25%

Jigsaw 1970

"DOUBLEDAY & COMPANY, INC./*Garden City, New York*/ 1970" on title page. Copyright page - 5th (of 5) line "First Edition". DJ price - $4.95. Full bound - gray cloth with no top stain and black pastedowns.

		F/F	F/NF	NF/VG+	VG+/VG	VG/VG-	Good	w/o dj
1st ed		$50	$45	$30	$25	$20	$10	60%

Sadie When She Died 1972

"DOUBLEDAY & COMPANY, INC./GARDEN CITY, NEW YORK/ 1972" on title page. Copyright page - 5th (of 5) line "First Edition". DJ price - $5.95. Full bound - black cloth with no top stain and gold pastedowns.

		F/F	F/NF	NF/VG+	VG+/VG	VG/VG-	Good	w/o dj
1st ed		$50	$45	$30	$25	$20	$10	60%

Hail To The Chief 1973

"Random House New York" on title page. No date on title page. Copyright page - 11th and 12th (of 12) lines "9 8 7 6 5 4 3 2/First Edition". DJ price - $5.95. Quarter bound - blue cloth with light blue-green sides and no top stain. White pastedowns.

		F/F	F/NF	NF/VG+	VG+/VG	VG/VG-	Good	w/o dj
1st ed		$45	$40	$30	$25	$20	$10	60%

Calypso 1979

"The Viking Press New York" on title page. No date on title page. Copyright page - 3rd (of 15) line "First published in 1979 by the Viking Press". DJ price - $8.95. Quarter bound - Black cloth with brown sides and no top stain. White pastedowns.

		F/F	F/NF	NF/VG+	VG+/VG	VG/VG-	Good	w/o dj
1st ed		$20	$15	$10	$8	$6	$4	80%

Rumplestilskin 1981

"The Viking Press New York" on title page. No date on title page. Copyright page - 3rd (of 15) line "First published in 1981 by the Viking Press". DJ price - $12.95. Quarter bound - Black cloth with red sides and no top stain. White pastedowns.

		F/F	F/NF	NF/VG+	VG+/VG	VG/VG-	Good	w/o dj
1st ed		$20	$15	$10	$8	$6	$4	80%

The McBain Brief 1982

"ARBOR HOUSE/New York" on title page. No date on title page. Copyright page - 9th (of 13) line "10 9 8 7 6 5 4 3 2 1". DJ price - $14.95. Quarter bound - red cloth with white sides and no top stain. White pastedowns.

		F/F	F/NF	NF/VG+	VG+/VG	VG/VG-	Good	w/o dj
1st ed		$30	$25	$20	$15	$10	$6	70%

Lightning 1984

"ARBOR HOUSE New York" on title page. No date on title page. Copyright page - 12th (of 15) line "10 9 8 7 6 5 4 3 2 1". DJ price - $15.95. Quarter bound - black cloth with gray sides and no top stain. White pastedowns.

		F/F	F/NF	NF/VG+	VG+/VG	VG/VG-	Good	w/o dj
1st ed		$20	$15	$10	$8	$6	$4	80%

Jack and the Bean-Stalk 1984

"HOLT, RINEHART and WINSTON/NEW YORK" on title page. No date on title page. Copyright page - 18th and 20th (of 21) lines "First Edition/1 3 5 7 9 10 8 6 4 2". DJ price - $14.95. Quarter bound - black cloth with red sides and no top stain. White pastedowns.

		F/F	F/NF	NF/VG+	VG+/VG	VG/VG-	Good	w/o dj
1st ed		$20	$15	$10	$8	$6	$4	80%

Snow White & Rose Red 1985

"HOLT, RINEHART and WINSTON/NEW YORK" on title page. No date on title page. Copyright page - 18th and 20th (of 26) lines "First Edition/1 3 5 7 9 10 8 6 4 2". DJ price - $14.95. Quarter bound - black cloth with black sides and no top stain. White pastedowns.

		F/F	F/NF	NF/VG+	VG+/VG	VG/VG-	Good	w/o dj
1st ed		$20	$15	$10	$8	$6	$4	80%

Eight Black Horses 1985

"ARBOR HOUSE/New York" on title page. No date on title page. Copyright page - 10th (of 16) line "10 9 8 7 6 5 4 3 2 1". DJ price - $15.95.
Quarter bound - black cloth with gray sides and no top stain. Black pastedowns.
Note: A limited first edition of this book was published by The Mysterious Press.

		F/F	F/NF	NF/VG+	VG+/VG	VG/VG-	Good	w/o dj
1st ed		$20	$15	$10	$8	$6	$4	80%

Another Part of The City 1986

"THE MYSTERIOUS PRESS New York" on title page. No date on title page. Copyright page - 7th and 8th (of 14) lines "First Printing: April 1986/10 9 8 7 6 5 4 3 2 1". DJ price - $15.95. Quarter bound - black cloth with black sides and no top stain. Black pastedowns.

		F/F	F/NF	NF/VG+	VG+/VG	VG/VG-	Good	w/o dj
1st ed		$20	$15	$10	$8	$6	$4	80%

Tricks 1987

"ARBOR HOUSE/*New York*" on title page. No date on title page. Copyright page - 6th (of 12) line "10 9 8 7 6 5 4 3 2 1". DJ price - $16.95. Quarter bound - red cloth with black sides and no top stain. Red pastedowns.

		F/F	F/NF	NF/VG+	VG+/VG	VG/VG-	Good	w/o dj
1st ed		$20	$15	$10	$8	$6	$4	80%

Poison 1987

"Arbor House/New York" on title page. No date on title page. Copyright page - 6th (of 12) line "10 9 8 7 6 5 4 3 2 1". DJ price - $16.95.
Quarter bound - black cloth with red sides and no top stain. black pastedowns.

		F/F	F/NF	NF/VG+	VG+/VG	VG/VG-	Good	w/o dj
1st ed		$20	$15	$10	$8	$6	$4	80%

Ed McBain's Ladies 1988

"THE MYSTERIOUS PRESS/New York London Tokyo" on title page. No date on title page. Copyright page - 31st and 32nd (of 38) lines "First Mysterious Press Printing: May 1988/10 9 8 7 6 5 4 3 2 1". DJ price - $16.95.
Quarter bound - black cloth with black sides and no top stain. Black pastedowns.

		F/F	F/NF	NF/VG+	VG+/VG	VG/VG-	Good	w/o dj
1st ed		$20	$15	$10	$8	$6	$4	80%

The House That Jack Built 1988

"HENRY HOLT and COMPLANY/NEW YORK" on title page. No date on title page. Copyright page - 16th and 18th (of 19) lines "First Edition/1 3 5 7 9 10 8 6 4 2". DJ price - $16.95. Quarter bound - black cloth with black sides and no top stain. White pastedowns.

		F/F	F/NF	NF/VG+	VG+/VG	VG/VG-	Good	w/o dj
1st ed		$20	$15	$10	$8	$6	$4	80%

Ralph McInerny

Her Death of Cold 1977 A Father Dowling Mystery.

"THE VANGUARD PRESS/NEW YORK" on title page. No date on title page. Copyright page - 16 lines with no mention of printing number. DJ price - $7.95. Full bound - black cloth with no top stain and violet pastedowns.

		F/F	F/NF	NF/VG+	VG+/VG	VG/VG-	Good	w/o dj
1st ed		$85	$75	$50	$35	$25	$10	70%

The Seventh Station 1977 A Father Dowling Mystery.

"THE VANGUARD PRESS" on title page. No date on title page. Copyright page - 16 lines with no mention of printing number. DJ price - $7.95. Full bound - black cloth with no top stain and red pastedowns.

		F/F	F/NF	NF/VG+	VG+/VG	VG/VG-	Good	w/o dj
1st ed		$60	$50	$35	$20	$15	$8	70%

Bishop as Pawn   1978   A Father Dowling Mystery.

"THE VANGUARD PRESS/NEW YORK" on title page. No date on title page.
Copyright page - 16 lines with no mention of printing number. DJ price - $7.95.
Full bound - black cloth with no top stain and white pastedowns.

		F/F	F/NF	NF/VG+	VG+/VG	VG/VG-	Good	w/o dj
1st ed		$50	$40	$30	$20	$15	$8	70%

Lying Three   1979   A Father Dowling Mystery.

"THE VANGUARD PRESS/NEW YORK" on title page. No date on title page.
Copyright page - 16 lines with no mention of printing number. DJ price - $8.95.
Full bound - black cloth with no top stain and lime green pastedowns.

		F/F	F/NF	NF/VG+	VG+/VG	VG/VG-	Good	w/o dj
1st ed		$50	$40	$30	$20	$15	$8	70%

Second Vespers   1980   A Father Dowling Mystery.

"THE VANGUARD PRESS/NEW YORK" on title page. No date on title page.
Copyright page - 15th (of 15) line - "1 2 3 4 5 6 7 8 9 0". No price on DJ; no reference to book
club. Full bound - black cloth with no top stain and white pastedowns.

		F/F	F/NF	NF/VG+	VG+/VG	VG/VG-	Good	w/o dj
1st ed		$35	$30	$20	$15	$10	$6	70%

Thicker Than Water   1981   A Father Dowling Mystery.

		F/F	F/NF	NF/VG+	VG+/VG	VG/VG-	Good	w/o dj
1st ed		$35	$30	$20	$15	$10	$6	70%

Loss of Patients   1982   A Father Dowling Mystery.

"THE VANGUARD PRESS/NEW YORK" on title page. No date on title page.
Copyright page - 13th (of 19) line - "1 2 3 4 5 6 7 8 9 0". No price on DJ; no reference to book
club. Full bound - black cloth with no top stain and red pastedowns.

		F/F	F/NF	NF/VG+	VG+/VG	VG/VG-	Good	w/o dj
1st ed		$35	$30	$20	$15	$10	$6	70%

The Grass Widow   1983   A Father Dowling Mystery.

"THE VANGUARD PRESS/NEW YORK" on title page. No date on title page.
Copyright page - 20th (of 20) line - "1 2 3 4 5 6 7 8 9 0". No price on DJ; no reference to book
club. Quarter bound - black cloth with black sides and no top stain. Lime green pastedowns.

		F/F	F/NF	NF/VG+	VG+/VG	VG/VG-	Good	w/o dj
1st ed		$35	$30	$20	$15	$10	$6	70%

Getting a Way with Murder   1984   A Father Dowling Mystery.

"THE VANGUARD PRESS/NEW YORK" on title page. No date on title page.
Copyright page - 20th (of 20) line - "1 2 3 4 5 6 7 8 9 0". No price on DJ; no reference to book
club. Quarter bound - black cloth with black sides and no top stain. Red pastedowns.

		F/F	F/NF	NF/VG+	VG+/VG	VG/VG-	Good	w/o dj
1st ed		$20	$15	$12	$10	$8	$5	80%

Rest in Pieces 1985   A Father Dowling Mystery.

"THE VANGUARD PRESS/NEW YORK" on title page. No date on title page.
Copyright page - 20 lines with no mention of printing number. No price on DJ; no reference
to book club. Quarter bound - black cloth with black sides and no top stain. White
pastedowns.

		F/F	F/NF	NF/VG+	VG+/VG	VG/VG-	Good	w/o dj
1st ed		$20	$15	$12	$10	$8	$5	80%

James Michener (1907-)

Tales of the South Pacific 1947

		F/F	F/NF	NF/VG+	VG+/VG	VG/VG-	Good	w/o dj
1st ed		$800	$650	$500	$400	$325	$150	20%

The Fires of Spring 1949

		F/F	F/NF	NF/VG+	VG+/VG	VG/VG-	Good	w/o dj
1st ed		$350	$300	$250	$175	$125	$75	20%

Return to Paradise 1951

"RANDOM HOUSE   NEW YORK" on title page. No date on title page,   Copyright page -
10th (of 10) line - "FIRST PRINTING".   No printing exists below this line on true first
editions.   "BOOK-OF-THE-MONTH CLUB SELECTION" on top of inside front flap of DJ. DJ
price - $3.50. Full bound - tan cloth with blue-green top stain. White pastedowns.
Note: A Book Club edition with "FIRST PRINTING" was also produced and is very common. This book is
distinguished by no top stain, a small dark green circle on the bottom of the rear board, near the spine, and lines
such as "PRINTED IN THE UNITED STATES OF AMERICA BY/KINGSPORT PRESS, INC., KINGSPORT,
TENNESSEE" at the bottom of the Copyright page on the title page. DJ on the Book Club edition has no price.
This is not a true First Edition.

		F/F	F/NF	NF/VG+	VG+/VG	VG/VG-	Good	w/o dj
1st ed		$200	$175	$150	$100	$75	$40	33%

The Voice of Asia 1951

"*Random House   New York*" on title page. No date on title page.   Copyright page - 1st (of
7) line - "FIRST PRINTING".   DJ price - $3.50. Matte finish, inside front flap quote by author
(no different for later issues).
Full bound - tan cloth with gray top stain. Maps on pastedowns.

		F/F	F/NF	NF/VG+	VG+/VG	VG/VG-	Good	w/o dj
1st ed		$250	$175	$125	$95	$75	$50	80%

The Bridge at Toko-Ri 1953

"Random House" on title page. No date on title page. Copyright page - seven lines with no mention of printing number. DJ price - $2.50. Full bound - top half, light blue cloth; bottom half, dark blue cloth with light blue top stain and blue pastedowns.

		F/F	F/NF	NF/VG+	VG+/VG	VG/VG-	Good	w/o dj
1st ed		$150	$125	$110	$75	$65	$40	20%

Sayonara 1954

No publisher's information or date on the title page. Copyright page - 1st (of 11) line - "First Printing". DJ price -$2.50 First issue dj is distinguished by price on the upper right of the rear flap. This makes price clipping unusually rare. Also the first issue dj is covered with a light laminate which tends to pull loose or bubble in areas.
Half bound - Black cloth spine and edge with brown paper sides and gray top stain.

		F/F	F/NF	NF/VG+	VG+/VG	VG/VG-	Good	w/o dj
1st ed		$150	$100	$75	$65	$50	$25	33%

The Floating World 1954

"RANDOM HOUSE NEW YORK" on title page. No date on title page.
Copyright page -1st (of 26) line - "FIRST PRINTING". DJ price - $8.75. Quarter bound - black cloth with wavy white and blue sides and black top stain. White pastedowns.

		F/F	F/NF	NF/VG+	VG+/VG	VG/VG-	Good	w/o dj
1st ed		$250	$200	$150	$125	$100	$50	30%

The Bridge at Andau 1957

"RANDOM HOUSE   NEW YORK" on title page. No date on title page.
Copyright page - 1st (of 8) line - "FIRST PRINTING".
DJ price - $3.50. Full bound - cream cloth with red top stain and white pastedowns.

		F/F	F/NF	NF/VG+	VG+/VG	VG/VG-	Good	w/o dj
1st ed		$100	$85	$70	$50	$40	$20	50%

Rascals in Paradise 1957 Written with A. Grove Day

"Random House   New York" on title page. No date on title page.
Copyright page - 1st (of 8) line - "FIRST EDITION".
DJ price - $4.75. Date 6/57 at bottom of inside front flap.
Full bound - cream cloth with brown top stain and maps on pastedowns.

		F/F	F/NF	NF/VG+	VG+/VG	VG/VG-	Good	w/o dj
1st ed		$100	$85	$70	$50	$40	$20	33%

Hawaii 1959

"RANDOM HOUSE   NEW YORK" on title page. No date on title page.
Copyright page - 1st (of 8) line - "FIRST PRINTING".
DJ price - $6.95. Full bound - cream cloth with light blue top stain and map on pastedowns.

		F/F	F/NF	NF/VG+	VG+/VG	VG/VG-	Good	w/o dj
1st ed		$90	$75	$60	$50	$40	$25	33%

Report of the County Chairman 1961

"Random House New York"on title page.   No date on title page.
Copyright page - 1st (of 8) line - "First Printing". Last line - "by H. Wolff, New York".
DJ price - $3.95.   Full bound - blue cloth with red top stain and white pastedowns.

		F/F	F/NF	NF/VG+	VG+/VG	VG/VG-	Good	w/o dj
1st ed		$75	$60	$45	$35	$30	$20	50%

Caravans 1963

"RANDOM HOUSE NEW YORK" opposite title page.   No date. Copyright page - 3rd (of 9)
line - "FIRST PRINTING".   Last line "MANUFACTURED IN THE UNITED STATES OF
AMERICA". DJ price - $5.95. Full page portrait of author on rear panel.
Full bound - black cloth with orange top stain. Maps on pastedown. Variation exist with
front pastedown map upside down.
Note: A Book Club edition with "First Edition" was also produced. This book is distinguished by small square
indentation on the bottom of the rear board, near the spine. DJ on the Book Club edition has no price. This is not a
true First Edition.

		F/F	F/NF	NF/VG+	VG+/VG	VG/VG-	Good	w/o dj
1st ed		$65	$50	$40	$30	$25	$15	33%

The Source 1965

"*Random House   New York*" on title page. No date on title page. Copyright page - 1st (of
11) line - "FIRST PRINTING".   DJ price - $7.95.   Full bound - light blue cloth with royal blue
waves and orange top stain. Maps on pastedowns.

		F/F	F/NF	NF/VG+	VG+/VG	VG/VG-	Good	w/o dj
1st ed		$60	$45	$35	$25	$20	$12	50%

Iberia 1968

"RANDOM HOUSE NEW YORK"on page opposite title page. No date on title page.
Copyright page - 1st (of 9) line - "*First Printing*". DJ price $10.00. Full bound - gold cloth
with red top stain and map of Iberia on front pastedown and The Rulers of Spain on rear
pastedowns.

		F/F	F/NF	NF/VG+	VG+/VG	VG/VG-	Good	w/o dj
1st ed		$75	$60	$45	$35	$30	$20	50%

Presidential Lottery 1969

"Random House New York" opposite the title page.   No date on either page.
Copyright page - 1st (of 18) line - "First Printing". Last line - "by H. Wolff, New York".
DJ price - $5.95. Full bound - black cloth with blue top stain. White pastedowns.

		F/F	F/NF	NF/VG+	VG+/VG	VG/VG-	Good	w/o dj
1st ed		$60	$55	$45	$35	$30	$20	50%

The Quality of Life   1970   Sent as a companion piece to the bank's 1969 annual report to
shareholders. Contains nine color plates by painter James Wyeth. Issued in slipcover.

"Written for and published by Girard Bank   February 1970" on title page.
Copyright page - 21 lines with no mention of printing number.
Full bound - olive green cloth with no top stain and green pastedowns. Olive green slipcase.

		F/F	F/NF	NF/VG+	VG+/VG	VG/VG-	Good	w/o slip
1st ed	Slipcase	$75	$60	$50	$35	$30	$20	67%

The Drifters 1971

"Random House New York" on title page. No date on title page. Copyright page - 13th
and 14th (of 15) line - "98765432/First Edition". DJ price - $10.00 (no different for later
issues). Quarter bound - black cloth with red cloth front side (back is continuation of black
cloth spine) and blue-gray top stain. Maps on pastedowns.

		F/F	F/NF	NF/VG+	VG+/VG	VG/VG-	Good	w/o dj
1st ed		$50	$40	$30	$25	$20	$10	80%

Kent State: What Happened and Why 1971

"Random House New York/A Reader's Digest Press Book" opposite title page. No date on
either page. Copyright page - 12 (of 12) line - "First Edition". DJ price - $10.00 (no different
for later issues). Full bound - dark blue cloth with gray top stain. Campus pastedowns.

		F/F	F/NF	NF/VG+	VG+/VG	VG/VG-	Good	w/o dj
1st ed		$50	$40	$30	$25	$20	$10	80%

A Michener Miscellany 1950-1970 1973

"Random House New York" on title page. "A Reader's Digest Press Book" opposite title
page. No date on either page. Copyright page - 16th (of 34) line - "Manufactured in the
United States of America/First Edition".   DJ price - $8.95 (no different for later issues)
Full bound - black cloth with gray top stain. White pastedowns.

		F/F	F/NF	NF/VG+	VG+/VG	VG/VG-	Good	w/o dj
1st ed		$60	$50	$40	$25	$20	$8	75%

Centennial 1974

"Random House New York" on title page. No date on title page. Copyright page - 21st (of
21) line - "First Edition". DJ price - $10.95. ($12.50 on dj for 2nd and later printings)
Full bound - maroon cloth with light blue top stain. Maps on pastedowns.

		F/F	F/NF	NF/VG+	VG+/VG	VG/VG-	Good	w/o dj
1st ed		$50	$40	$30	$25	$20	$10	33%

About Centennial 1974 The publisher's note states that this book "has been especially
produced for the librarians and booksellers of the United States. Only 3200 copies of this
book have been made and no more will be printed. No copies are for sale."

"RANDOM HOUSE NEW YORK" on title page. No date on title page. Copyright page -
14 lines - no reference to edition or printing number. DJ without price and solid black rear
panel and rear flap. Full bound -cream cloth with blue top stain. Maps on pastedowns.

	F/F	F/NF	NF/VG+	VG+/VG	VG/VG-	Good	w/o dj

		F/F	F/NF	NF/VG+	VG+/VG	VG/VG-	Good	w/o dj
1st ed		$100	$85	$65	$55	$40	$25	25%

Sports in America 1976.

"Random House New York" on title page. No date on title page. Copyright page - 13th and 14th (of 28) line - "Manufactured in the United States of America/98765432/First Edition". Quarter bound - black cloth with blue paper and no top stain. White pastedowns.

		F/F	F/NF	NF/VG+	VG+/VG	VG/VG-	Good	w/o dj
1st ed		$30	$25	$20	$15	$12	$8	75%

Chesapeake 1978

"Random House New York" on title page. No date on title page. Copyright page - 15th and 16th (of 17) line - "2 4 6 8 9 7 5 3/First Edition". DJ price - $12.95. (no different for later issues). Full bound - green cloth with no top stain. Maps on pastedowns.

		F/F	F/NF	NF/VG+	VG+/VG	VG/VG-	Good	w/o dj
1st ed		$30	$24	$19	$13	$10	$8	80%

The Covenant 1980

"Random House New York" on title page. No date on title page. Copyright page - 10th and 20th (of 22) line - "2 4 6 8 9 7 5 3/FIRST TRADE EDITION". DJ price -$15.95 (no different for later issues). Full bound - gold cloth with no top stain. Maps on pastedowns.

		F/F	F/NF	NF/VG+	VG+/VG	VG/VG-	Good	w/o dj
1st ed		$15	$12	$10	$8	$6	$4	80%

Space 1982

"Random House/New York" on title page. No date on title page. Copyright page - 14th and 15th (of 17) lines - "2 4 6 8 9 7 5 3/FIRST EDITION". DJ price - $17.95 (no different for later issues). Full bound - blue cloth with no top stain. Maps on pastedowns.
Note: There are books with "FIRST EDITION" on the 14th line and not the entire 15th line (for example the "2" missing) present. These are not true first editions.

		F/F	F/NF	NF/VG+	VG+/VG	VG/VG-	Good	w/o dj
1st ed		$15	$12	$10	$8	$6	$4	80%

Poland 1983

"Random House New York" on title page. No date on title page.
Copyright page - 15th and 16th (of 17) line - "2 4 6 8 9 7 5 3/FIRST EDITION".
DJ price - $17.95 (no different for later issues).
Full bound - red cloth with no top stain. Maps on pastedowns.

		F/F	F/NF	NF/VG+	VG+/VG	VG/VG-	Good	w/o dj
1st ed		$15	$12	$10	$8	$6	$4	80%

Texas 1985

"Random House New York" on title page. No date on title page.
Copyright page - 14th and 15th (of 16) line - "2 4 6 8 9 7 5 3/FIRST EDITION".

DJ price - $21.95 (no different for later issues).
Full bound - blue cloth with no top stain. Maps on pastedowns.

		F/F	F/NF	NF/VG +	VG + /VG	VG/VG -	Good	w/o dj
1st ed		$15	$12	$10	$8	$6	$4	80%

Legacy 1987

"Random House New York" on title page. No date on title page. Copyright page - 12th and 13th (of 14) line - "98765432/FIRST EDITION". DJ price - $16.95 (no different for later issues). Full bound - red cloth with no top stain. Declaration of Independence on pastedowns.

		F/F	F/NF	NF/VG +	VG + /VG	VG/VG -	Good	w/o dj
1st ed		$15	$12	$10	$8	$6	$4	80%

Alaska 1988

"Random House New York" on title page. No date on title page. Copyright page - 15th and 16th (of 18) line - "2 4 6 8 9 7 5 3/FIRST EDITION". DJ price - $22.50 (no different for later issues). Full bound - gold cloth with no top stain. Maps on pastedowns.

		F/F	F/NF	NF/VG +	VG + /VG	VG/VG -	Good	w/o dj
1st ed		$15	$12	$10	$8	$6	$4	80%

Journey 1988 Canada 1989 U.S.

"Random House New York" on title page. No date on title page. Copyright page - 16th and 17th (of 18) line - "2 4 6 8 9 7 5 3/FIRST AMERICAN EDITION". DJ price - $16.95 (no different for later issues). Full bound - navy blue cloth with no top stain and maps on pastedowns.

		F/F	F/NF	NF/VG +	VG + /VG	VG/VG -	Good	w/o dj
1st ed	Can	$40	$35	$27	$20	$15	$10	50%
1st ed	U.S.	$25	$20	$15	$12	$10	$6	50%

Caribbean 1989

"Random House New York" on title page. No date on title page. Copyright page - 17th and 18th (of 19) line - "2 4 6 8 9 7 5 3/FIRST EDITION". DJ price - $22.95 (no different for later issues). Full bound - orange cloth with no top stain. Maps on pastedowns.

		F/F	F/NF	NF/VG +	VG + /VG	VG/VG -	Good	w/o dj
1st ed		$15	$12	$10	$8	$6	$4	80%

The Eagle and the Raven 1990   4,650 copies

"State House Press/Austin, Texas" on title page. No date on title page.
Copyright page - 3rd (of 19) line "First edition". DJ price - $19.95.
First edition is distinguished by lack of accent on second A of "YUCATAN" on front pastedown map. First issue dj contains bar code box beneath author's picture on rear panel. Full bound - burnt orange cloth with no top stain. Maps on pastedowns.
Note: Later versions have dj with no price and the number 17720 in a white box instead of the bar code box.

		F/F	F/NF	NF/VG +	VG + /VG	VG/VG -	Good	w/o dj
1st ed		$40	$30	$25	$20	$15	$10	50%

138

Pilgrimage 1990

"Rodale Press, Emmanus, Pennsylvania" on title page.   No date on title page.
Copyright page - 25th (of 25) line - "2 4 6 8 10 9 7 5 3 1 hardcover".
DJ price - $14.95. Full bound - cream cloth with no top stain and tan speckled pastedowns.

	F/F	F/NF	NF/VG+	VG+/VG	VG/VG-	Good	w/o dj
1st ed	$15	$12	$10	$7	$5	$3	80%

The Novel 1991

"RANDOM HOUSE   NEW YORK" on title page.   No date on title page.
Copyright page - 20th and 21st (of 22) line - "2 4 6 8 9 7 5 3/FIRST EDITION".
DJ price - U.S.A. $23.00/Canada $30.00 (no different for later issues).
Quarter bound - black cloth with white paper and no top stain. Maps on pastedowns.

	F/F	F/NF	NF/VG+	VG+/VG	VG/VG-	Good	w/o dj
1st ed	$14	$11	$9	$6	$4	$2	75%

The World is My Home: A Memoir 1992

"RANDOM HOUSE/NEW YORK" on title page.   No date on title page.
Copyright page - 31st and 32nd (of 34) line - "2 4 6 8 9 7 5 3/FIRST EDITION".
DJ price - U.S.A. $25.00/Canada $30.00 (no different for later issues).
Quarter bound - blue cloth with white paper and no top stain. Maps on pastedowns.

	F/F	F/NF	NF/VG+	VG+/VG	VG/VG-	Good	w/o dj
1st ed	$15	$12	$10	$7	$5	$3	75%

Mexico 1992

"RANDOM HOUSE/NEW YORK" on title page.   No date on title page.
Copyright page - 21st and 22nd (of 23) line - "2 4 6 8 9 7 5 3/FIRST EDITION".
DJ price - U.S.A. $25.00/Canada $31.50 (no different for later issues).
Quarter bound - maroon cloth with gold paper and no top stain. Maps on pastedowns.

	F/F	F/NF	NF/VG+	VG+/VG	VG/VG-	Good	w/o dj
1st ed	$15	$12	$10	$6	$4	$2	75%

My Lost Mexico 1992   Author's own photographs illustrate the events leading to the
publication of his novel _Mexico_ thirty years after it was begun.
State House Press   Austin, Texas

	F/F	F/NF	NF/VG+	VG+/VG	VG/VG-	Good	w/o dj
1st ed	$20	$15	$12	$10	$8	$5	80%

John O'Hara

Appointment in Samarra 1934

"HARCOURT, BRACE AND COMPANY/NEW YORK" on title page. No date on title page.
Copyright page - "first edition".   Erratum slip pasted to dedication page.

Advance copies in pictorial wrapps exist.

		F/F	F/NF	NF/VG+	VG+/VG	VG/VG-	Good	w/o dj
1st ed		$600	$500	$400	$300	$250	$100	25%

The Doctor's Son and Other Stories 1935   37 short stories.

"HARCOURT, BRACE AND COMPANY/NEW YORK" on title page. No date on title page.
Copyright page - *"first edition"*.

		F/F	F/NF	NF/VG+	VG+/VG	VG/VG-	Good	w/o dj
1st ed		$300	$250	$200	$150	$125	$50	25%

Butterfield 8 1935

"HARCOURT, BRACE AND COMPANY/NEW YORK" on title page. No date on title page.
Copyright page - *"first edition"*. DJ price - $2.50.

		F/F	F/NF	NF/VG+	VG+/VG	VG/VG-	Good	w/o dj
1st ed		$400	$350	$275	$200	$150	$75	25%

Hope of Heaven 1938

"Harcourt, Brace and Company New York" on title page. No date on title page. Copyright
page - 6th (of 9) line - *"first edition"*. DJ price - $2.00.
Full bound - dark blue cloth with no top stain and white pastedowns.

		F/F	F/NF	NF/VG+	VG+/VG	VG/VG-	Good	w/o dj
1st ed		$150	$125	$110	$75	$60	$30	25%

Files on Parade 1939   35 short stories.

"Harcourt, Brace and Company New York" on title page. No date on title page.
Copyright page - *"first edition"*.

		F/F	F/NF	NF/VG+	VG+/VG	VG/VG-	Good	w/o dj
1st ed		$350	$250	$175	$125	$100	$50	25%

Pal Joey 1940   14 short stories

"Duell, Sloan and Pearce New York" on title page. No date on title page. Copyright page -
6th (of 6) line - *"first edition"*. DJ price - $2.00.
Full bound - black cloth with no top stain and white pastedowns.
Advance copies in printed wrappers exist.

		F/F	F/NF	NF/VG+	VG+/VG	VG/VG-	Good	w/o dj
1st ed		$350	$250	$175	$125	$100	$50	25%

Pipe Night 1945   31 short stories.

"DUELL, SLOAN AND PEARCE/NEW YORK" on title page. No date on title page. DJ price
- $2.50. Second printing stated on 2nd issue dj.

		F/F	F/NF	NF/VG+	VG+/VG	VG/VG-	Good	w/o dj
1st ed		$100	$85	$70	$50	$40	$20	40%

<u>Hellbox</u> 1947   26 short stories.

"Random House New York" on title page. No date on title page. Copyright page - 1st (of 11) line - "FIRST PRINTING". DJ price - $2.50.   Front panel and spine - red background. Full bound - black cloth with blue top stain and white pastedowns.

		F/F	F/NF	NF/VG+	VG+/VG	VG/VG-	Good	w/o dj
1st ed		$100	$85	$70	$50	$40	$20	40%

A Rage To Live 1949

"RANDOM HOUSE NEW YORK" on title page.   No date on title page. Copyright page - 1st (of 8) line   "FIRST EDITION".   Full bound - black cloth with purple top stain and white pastedowns. 750 copies were gold stamped *"PRESENTATION EDITION"* on the front cover.

		F/F	F/NF	NF/VG+	VG+/VG	VG/VG-	Good	w/o dj
1st ed		$75	$65	$50	$40	$30	$15	50%

The Farmers Hotel 1951

"RANDON HOUSE NEW YORK" on title page. No date on title page. Copyright page - 1st (of 6) line - "FIRST PRINTING".   DJ price - $2.00. Full bound - blue cloth with dark blue top stain and white pastedowns.

		F/F	F/NF	NF/VG+	VG+/VG	VG/VG-	Good	w/o dj
1st ed		$70	$60	$50	$40	$30	$15	60%

The Libretto and Lyrics: Pal Joey 1952

"RANDON HOUSE NEW YORK" on title page. No date on title page. Only one printing.

		F/F	F/NF	NF/VG+	VG+/VG	VG/VG-	Good	w/o dj
1st ed		$125	$100	$75	$50	$40	$20	50%

Sweet and Sour 1954

"RANDOM HOUSE NEW YORK" on title page. No date on title page. Copyright page - 1st (of 11) line - "First Printing".   DJ price - $3.00.   One printing only.   Quarter bound - brown cloth with brown leatherette sides and black top stain. White pastedowns

		F/F	F/NF	NF/VG+	VG+/VG	VG/VG-	Good	w/o dj
1st ed		$60	$50	$40	$30	$25	$10	60%

Ten North Frederick 1955

"RANDON HOUSE NEW YORK" in gold box on title page. No date on title page. Copyright page - 1st (of 8) line - "FIRST PRINTING".   DJ price - $3.95. Full bound - blue cloth with yellow top stain and blue-gray pastedowns.   Advance copies in wrapps exist.

		F/F	F/NF	NF/VG+	VG+/VG	VG/VG-	Good	w/o dj
1st ed		$60	$50	$40	$30	$25	$10	60%

A Family Party 1956

"*RANDOM HOUSE NEW YORK*" on title page. No date on title page.
Copyright page - 1st (of 7) line - "First Printing". DJ price - $1.95.
Quarter bound - light gray cloth with wavy blue sides and gray top stain. White pastedowns.

		F/F	F/NF	NF/VG+	VG+/VG	VG/VG-	Good	w/o dj
1st ed		$50	$45	$35	$25	$20	$10	60%

From the Terrace 1958

"RANDON HOUSE NEW YORK" on title page. No date on title page.
Copyright page - 1st (of 10) line - "FIRST PRINTING".   DJ price - $6.95.
Full bound - dark blue cloth with blue top stain and beige pastedowns.

		F/F	F/NF	NF/VG+	VG+/VG	VG/VG-	Good	w/o dj
1st ed		$40	$35	$25	$20	$15	$8	70%

Ourselves To Know 1960

"RANDON HOUSE NEW YORK" on title page. No date on title page.
Copyright page - 1st (of 8) line - "First Printing".   DJ price - $4.95.
Full bound - maroon cloth with maroon top stain and tan pastedowns.

		F/F	F/NF	NF/VG+	VG+/VG	VG/VG-	Good	w/o dj
1st ed		$25	$20	$15	$10	$8	$6	80%

Sermons and Soda Water 3 volumes in slipcase   1960

"RANDON HOUSE NEW YORK" on title page of each volume. No date on title page.
Copyright page - 1st (of 9) line -"*First Printing*".   No price on slipcase.
Slipcase - blue paper front and rear; black spine, top, and bottom. Each volume has yellow
front, black spine, dark blue top stain, and white pastedowns. Volume one has gray back;
volume two has white back; and volume three has blue back.

		F/F	F/NF	NF/VG+	VG+/VG	VG/VG-	Good	w/o dj
1st ed		$60	$50	$40	$30	$25	$10	50%

Assembly 1961   26 short stories.

"RANDON HOUSE NEW YORK" on title page. No date on title page.
Copyright page - 1st (of 11) line - "FIRST PRINTING".   DJ price - $5.95.
Full bound - cream cloth with tan top stain and light gray pastedowns.

		F/F	F/NF	NF/VG+	VG+/VG	VG/VG-	Good	w/o dj
1st ed		$25	$20	$15	$10	$8	$6	80%

Five Plays 1961

"*Random House New York*" on title page. No date on title page.
Copyright page - "First Printing". One printing only.

		F/F	F/NF	NF/VG+	VG+/VG	VG/VG-	Good	w/o dj
1st ed		$50	$40	$30	$20	$15	$8	70%

The Cape Cod Lighter 1962   23 short stories.

"RANDOM HOUSE NEW YORK" on title page. No date on title page.
Copyright page - 1st (of 11) line - "FIRST PRINTING". Full bound - red cloth with gold top stain and gold pastedowns.

	F/F	F/NF	NF/VG+	VG+/VG	VG/VG-	Good	w/o dj
1st ed	$15	$12	$10	$8	$7	$4	80%

The Big Laugh 1962

"RANDON HOUSE NEW YORK" on title page. No date on title page.
Copyright page - 1st (of 8) line - "FIRST PRINTING". DJ price - $4.95. One printing only.
Full bound - black cloth with red top stain and red pastedowns.

	F/F	F/NF	NF/VG+	VG+/VG	VG/VG-	Good	w/o dj
1st ed	$15	$12	$10	$8	$7	$4	80%

Elizabeth Appleton 1963

"RANDOM HOUSE NEW YORK" on title page. No date on title page.
Copyright page - 1st (of 10) line - "FIRST PRINTING". DJ price - $4.95.
Full bound - blue cloth with yellow top stain and light blue-green pastedowns.

	F/F	F/NF	NF/VG+	VG+/VG	VG/VG-	Good	w/o dj
1st ed	$15	$12	$10	$8	$7	$4	80%

The Hat on the Bed 1963   24 short stories.

"RANDOM HOUSE NEW YORK" on title page. No date on title page.
Copyright page - 1st (of 11) line - "FIRST PRINTING". DJ price - $5.95.
Full bound - green cloth with blue-green top stain and lime green pastedowns.

	F/F	F/NF	NF/VG+	VG+/VG	VG/VG-	Good	w/o dj
1st ed	$15	$12	$10	$8	$7	$4	80%

The Horse Knows the Way 1964   28 short stories.

"RANDOM HOUSE NEW YORK" on title page. No date on title page. Copyright page - 1st (of 11) line - "FIRST PRINTING". DJ price - $5.95. Full bound - light blue cloth with dark blue top stain and red pastedowns. A limited printing of 250 numbered and signed copies on laid paper. Value is six times amount shown for first edition.

	F/F	F/NF	NF/VG+	VG+/VG	VG/VG-	Good	w/o dj
1st ed	$15	$12	$10	$8	$7	$4	80%

The Lockwood Concern 1965

"RANDOM HOUSE NEW YORK" on title page. No date on title page. Copyright page - 1st (of 9) line - *"First Printing"*. DJ price - $5.95. Full bound - green cloth with red top stain and light blue pastedowns. A limited printing of 300 numbered and signed copies on laid paper, boxed. Value is five times amount shown for first edition.

	F/F	F/NF	NF/VG+	VG+/VG	VG/VG-	Good	w/o dj
1st ed	$15	$12	$10	$8	$7	$4	80%

My Turn 1966

"RANDON HOUSE NEW YORK" on title page. No date on title page.
Copyright page - 1st (of 10) line - *"First Printing"*. 10th line - *"by H. Wolff, New York"*.
Full bound - navy cloth with purple top stain and purple pastedowns. One printing only.

		F/F	F/NF	NF/VG+	VG+/VG	VG/VG-	Good	w/o dj
1st ed		$25	$20	$15	$10	$8	$6	70%

Waiting for Winter 1966   21 short stories.

"RANDON HOUSE NEW YORK" on title page. No date on title page. Copyright page - 1st
(of 10) line - *"First Printing"*. DJ price - $5.95. Full bound - maroon cloth with maroon top
stain and gold pastedowns. One trade printing only. A limited printing of 300 numbered
and signed copies on laid paper, boxed. Value is five times amount shown for first edition.

		F/F	F/NF	NF/VG+	VG+/VG	VG/VG-	Good	w/o dj
1st ed		$15	$12	$10	$8	$7	$4	80%

The Instrument 1967

"RANDON HOUSE/NEW YORK" on title page. No date on title page. Copyright page - 1st
(of 10) line - *"First Printing"*. DJ price - $5.95. Full bound - gray-green cloth with blue top
stain and tan pastedowns. A limited printing of 300 numbered and signed copies on laid
paper, boxed. Value is five times amount shown for first edition.

		F/F	F/NF	NF/VG+	VG+/VG	VG/VG-	Good	w/o dj
1st ed		$15	$12	$10	$8	$7	$4	80%

And Other Stories 1968   12 short stories.

"RANDON HOUSE NEW YORK" on title page. No date on title page. Copyright page - 1st
(of 11) line - *"First Printing"*. DJ price - $5.95. Full bound - kelly green cloth with kelly
green top stain and dark blue-green pastedowns. A limited printing of 300 numbered and
signed copies on laid paper, boxed. Value is five times amount shown for first edition.

		F/F	F/NF	NF/VG+	VG+/VG	VG/VG-	Good	w/o dj
1st ed		$15	$12	$10	$8	$7	$4	80%

Lovey Childs: A Philadelphian's Story 1969

"RANDON HOUSE NEW YORK" on title page. No date on title page. Copyright page - 1st
(of 13) line - "FIRST PRINTING". DJ price - $5.95. Full bound - tan cloth with brown top
stain and green pastedowns. One printing only. A limited printing of 200 numbered and
signed copies on laid paper, boxed. Value is five times amount shown for first edition.

		F/F	F/NF	NF/VG+	VG+/VG	VG/VG-	Good	w/o dj
1st ed		$15	$12	$10	$8	$7	$4	80%

The Ewings 1972

"Random House New York" on title page. No date on title page. Copyright page - 10th and
11th (of 11) lines - "9 8 7 6 5 4 3 2/First Edition". First state has error on pg 231 lines 16-17. DJ

price - $6.95. Full bound - gold cloth with lime-green top stain and olive pastedowns.

	F/F	F/NF	NF/VG+	VG+/VG	VG/VG-	Good	w/o dj
1st ed	$15	$12	$10	$8	$7	$4	80%

The Time Element 1972 34 short stories.

"RANDON HOUSE NEW YORK" on title page. No date on title page.
Copyright page - 17th and 18th (of 18) lines - "9 8 7 6 5 4 3 2/First Edition". DJ price - $6.95.
Full bound - green cloth with pea-green top stain and pea-green pastedowns.

	F/F	F/NF	NF/VG+	VG+/VG	VG/VG-	Good	w/o dj
1st ed	$15	$12	$10	$8	$7	$4	80%

Sara Paretsky

Indemnity Only 1982

"The Dial Press New York" on title page. No date on title page. Copyright page - 8th (of 15)
line - "First printing". DJ price - $14.95. "0182" on bottom of rear DJ flap.

	F/F	F/NF	NF/VG+	VG+/VG	VG/VG-	Good	w/o dj
1st ed	$600	$500	$350	$225	$125	$40	60%

Deadlock 1984

"The Dial Press/DOUBLEDAY & COMPANY, INC./GARDEN CITY, NEW YORK 1984" on
title page. Copyright page - 5th (of 11) line - "First Printing". DJ price - $14.95. Quarter
bound - black cloth and blue sides with no top stain. White pastedowns.

	F/F	F/NF	NF/VG+	VG+/VG	VG/VG-	Good	w/o dj
1st ed	$400	$350	$250	$175	$100	$35	60%

Killing Orders 1985

"WILLIAM MORROW AND COMPANY, INC./NEW YORK" on title page. No date on title
page. Copyright page - 15th and 16th (of 17) lines - "First Edition/1 2 3 4 5 6 7 8 9 10". DJ price
- $15.95. Quarter bound - blue cloth and white sides with no top stain. Blue pastedowns.

	F/F	F/NF	NF/VG+	VG+/VG	VG/VG-	Good	w/o dj
1st ed	$125	$100	$75	$50	$35	$15	70%

Bitter Medicine 1987

"WILLIAM MORROW AND COMPANY, INC./New York" on title page. No date on title
page. Copyright page - 15th and 16th (of 17) lines - "First Edition/1 2 3 4 5 6 7 8 9 10". DJ price
- $17.95. Quarter bound - blue cloth and white sides with no top stain. Red pastedowns.

	F/F	F/NF	NF/VG+	VG+/VG	VG/VG-	Good	w/o dj
1st ed	$100	$80	$60	$40	$25	$10	70%

Blood Shot 1988

"Delacorte/Press" on title page. No date on title page. Copyright page - 23rd and 24th (of 24) lines - "10 9 8 7 6 5 4 3 2 1/BG". DJ price - $17.95. Quarter bound - purple cloth and blue sides with no top stain. Maroon pastedowns.

	F/F	F/NF	NF/VG+	VG+/VG	VG/VG-	Good	w/o dj
1st ed	$35	$30	$25	$20	$15	$10	80%

Burn Marks 1990

"Delacorte/Press" on title page. No date on title page. Copyright page - 26th and 27th (of 27) lines - "10 9 8 7 6 5 4 3 2 1/BVG". DJ price - $17.95 U.S./$22.95 Can. Quarter bound - gold cloth and red sides with no top stain. Red pastedowns.

	F/F	F/NF	NF/VG+	VG+/VG	VG/VG-	Good	w/o dj
1st ed	.	$25	$20	$15	$12	$8	$6	90%

Robert B. Parker

The Godwulf Manuscript 1974

"Houghton Mifflin Company Boston/1974" on title page. Copyright page - 3rd (of 19) line - "First Printing C". DJ price - $5.95. Full bound - brown cloth with pink top stain and tan pastedowns.

	F/F	F/NF	NF/VG+	VG+/VG	VG/VG-	Good	w/o dj
1st ed	$300	$275	$200	$125	$75	$30	70%

God Save the Child 1974

"Houghton Mifflin Company Boston/1974" on title page. Copyright page - 1st (of 16) line - "FIRST PRINTING C". DJ price - $5.95. Full bound - black cloth with gray top stain and gray pastedowns.

	F/F	F/NF	NF/VG+	VG+/VG	VG/VG-	Good	w/o dj
1st ed	$250	$225	$150	$75	$50	$20	70%

Mortal Stakes 1974

"Houghton Mifflin Company Boston/1975" on title page. Copyright page - 15th (of 22) line - "C 10 9 8 7 6 5 4 3 2 1"". DJ price - $6.95. Full bound - black cloth with no top stain and gold pastedowns.

	F/F	F/NF	NF/VG+	VG+/VG	VG/VG-	Good	w/o dj
1st ed	$250	$225	$150	$75	$50	$20	70%

Promised Land 1976 Boston: Houghton Mifflin

	F/F	F/NF	NF/VG+	VG+/VG	VG/VG-	Good	w/o dj
1st ed	$100	$80	$60	$40	$30	$15	70%

The Judas Goat 1978

"Houghton Mifflin Company Boston/1978" on title page. Copyright page - 13th (of 13) line - "S 10 9 8 7 6 5 4 3 2 1". DJ price - $7.95.

	F/F	F/NF	NF/VG+	VG+/VG	VG/VG-	Good	w/o dj

1st ed		$75	$65	$45	$35	$25	$10	70%

Wilderness 1979 Delacorte Press

		F/F	F/NF	NF/VG+	VG+/VG	VG/VG-	Good	w/o dj
1st ed		$60	$50	$35	$25	$18	$8	70%

Looking for Rachel Walker 1980

"DELACORTE PRESS/SEYMOUR LAWRENCE" on title page. No date on title page. Copyright page - 15th (of 22) line - "First Printing". DJ price - $8.95. Quarter bound - black cloth with gray sides and no top stain. Red pastedowns.

		F/F	F/NF	NF/VG+	VG+/VG	VG/VG-	Good	w/o dj
1st ed		$45	$35	$25	$20	$15	$7	70%

Early Autumn 1981

"DELACORTE PRESS/SEYMOUR LAWRENCE" on title page. No date on title page. Copyright page - 13th (of 20) line - "First printing". DJ price - $10.95. Quarter bound - black cloth with pumpkin sides and no top stain. White pastedowns.

		F/F	F/NF	NF/VG+	VG+/VG	VG/VG-	Good	w/o dj
1st ed		$40	$35	$25	$20	$15	$7	70%

A Savage Place 1981

"DELACORTE PRESS/SEYMOUR LAWRENCE" on title page. No date on title page. Copyright page - 16th (of 23) line - "First printing". DJ price - $10.95. Quarter bound - black cloth with gray sides and no top stain. White pastedowns.

		F/F	F/NF	NF/VG+	VG+/VG	VG/VG-	Good	w/o dj
1st ed		$40	$35	$25	$20	$15	$7	70%

Ceremony 1982

"Delacorte Press/Seymour Lawrence" on title page. No date on title page. Copyright page - 12th (of 19) line - "First printing". DJ price - $12.95. Quarter bound - black cloth with gray sides and no top stain. White pastedowns.

		F/F	F/NF	NF/VG+	VG+/VG	VG/VG-	Good	w/o dj
1st ed		$35	$30	$25	$20	$15	$7	70%

The Widening Gyre 1983

"Delacorte Press/Seymour Lawrence" on title page. No date on title page. Copyright page - 18th (of 24) line - "First printing". DJ price - $12.95. Quarter bound - black cloth with blue-gray sides and no top stain. White pastedowns.

		F/F	F/NF	NF/VG+	VG+/VG	VG/VG-	Good	w/o dj
1st ed		$35	$30	$25	$18	$12	$7	80%

Love and Glory 1983

"Delacorte Press/Seymour Lawrence" on title page. No date on title page. Copyright page - 15th (of 21) line - "FIRST PRINTING". DJ price - $13.95. Quarter bound - red cloth with dark green sides and no top stain. White pastedowns.

		F/F	F/NF	NF/VG+	VG+/VG	VG/VG-	Good	w/o dj
1st ed		$30	$25	$20	$15	$12	$7	80%

Valediction 1984

"Delacorte Press/Seymour Lawrence" on title page. No date on title page. Copyright page - 14th (of 20) line - "First printing". DJ price - $12.95. Quarter bound - black cloth with black sides and no top stain. White pastedowns.

		F/F	F/NF	NF/VG+	VG+/VG	VG/VG-	Good	w/o dj
1st ed		$30	$25	$20	$15	$12	$7	80%

A Catskill Eagle 1985

"Delacorte Press/Seymour Lawrence" on title page. No date on title page. Copyright page - 19th (of 25) line - "First printing". DJ price - $14.95. Quarter bound - brown cloth with blue-green sides and no top stain. White pastedowns.

		F/F	F/NF	NF/VG+	VG+/VG	VG/VG-	Good	w/o dj
1st ed		$25	$20	$17	$13	$10	$6	80%

Taming a Sea Horse 1986

"Delacorte Press/Seymour Lawrence" on title page. No date on title page. Copyright page - 20th (of 20) line - "FIRST PRINTING". DJ price - $15.95. Quarter bound - Green cloth with gold sides and no top stain. Green pastedowns.

		F/F	F/NF	NF/VG+	VG+/VG	VG/VG-	Good	w/o dj
1st ed		$20	$15	$10	$8	$6	$4	80%

Pale Kings and Princes 1987

"Delacorte Press/New York" on title page. No date on title page. Copyright page - 11th (of 19) line - "FIRST PRINTING". DJ price - $15.95. Quarter bound - Blue cloth with gray sides and no top stain. Light blue pastedowns.

		F/F	F/NF	NF/VG+	VG+/VG	VG/VG-	Good	w/o dj
1st ed		$20	$15	$10	$8	$6	$4	80%

The Early Spenser 1989

"DELACORTE PRESS/SEYMOUR LAWRENCE" on title page. No date on title page. Copyright page - last four (of 43) lines - "First Delacorte edition/June 1989/10 9 8 7 6 5 4 3 2 1/BG". DJ price - $13.95 U.S./$17.95 Can. Quarter bound - black cloth with black sides and no top stain. Gray pastedowns.

		F/F	F/NF	NF/VG+	VG+/VG	VG/VG-	Good	w/o dj
1st ed		$25	$22	$18	$15	$10	$6	80%

C. Northcote Parkinson

The Life and Times of Horatio Hornblower 1973

"Little, Brown and Company Boston Toronto" on tilte page. No date on title page.
Copyright page - 9th (of 10) line - "FIRST AMERICAN EDITION". DJ price - $6.95. Full
bound - light blue-green cloth with no top stain and blue-green pastedowns.

	F/F	F/NF	NF/VG+	VG+/VG	VG/VG-	Good	w/o dj
1st ed	$75	$60	$50	$35	$20	$10	75%

James Patterson

The Thomas Berryman Number 1976   Edgar Award winner

	F/F	F/NF	NF/VG+	VG+/VG	VG/VG-	Good	w/o dj
1st ed	$125	$100	$80	$60	$45	$20	50%

The Jericho Commandment 1979

"CROWN PUBLISHERS, INC. NEW YORK" on title page. No date on title page. Copyright
page - 19 lines with no mention of printing or edition number. DJ price $10.00.
Full bound - black cloth with no top stain and white pastedowns.

	F/F	F/NF	NF/VG+	VG+/VG	VG/VG-	Good	w/o dj
1st ed	$75	$60	$45	$30	$20	$10	60%

Virgin 1980

	F/F	F/NF	NF/VG+	VG+/VG	VG/VG-	Good	w/o dj
1st ed	$65	$55	$45	$30	$20	$10	60%

Black Market 1986

"SIMON AND SCHUSTER NEW YORK" on title page. No date on title page. Copyright
page - 18th (of 27) line - "1 3 5 7 9 10 8 6 4 2". DJ price - $17.95. Quarter bound - tan cloth with
gray sides and no top stain. White pastedowns.

	F/F	F/NF	NF/VG+	VG+/VG	VG/VG-	Good	w/o dj
1st ed	$45	$40	$30	$25	$20	$10	70%

The Midnight Club 1989

"Little, Brown and Company/Boston Toronto London" on title page. No date on title page.
Copyright page - 11th (of 27) line - "FIRST EDITION" and 24th line - "10 9 8 7 6 5 4 3 2 1".
DJ price - $17.95/$24.95 in Canada. Quarter bound - black cloth with gray sides and no top
stain. White pastedowns.

	F/F	F/NF	NF/VG+	VG+/VG	VG/VG-	Good	w/o dj
1st ed	$40	$35	$25	$20	$15	$7	70%

Along Came a Spider 1993

"Little, Brown and Company/Boston Toronto London" on title page. No date on title page. Copyright page - 18th (of 22) line - "10 9 8 7 6 5 4 3 2 1"; 6th line - "First Edition". DJ price $21.95/$27.95 in Canada.
Quarter bound - purple cloth with gray sides and no top stain. Gray pastedowns.

		F/F	F/NF	NF/VG+	VG+/VG	VG/VG-	Good	w/o dj
1st ed		$25	$20	$15	$10	$8	$5	90%

Kiss The Girls 1995

"Little, Brown and Company/BOSTON NEW YORK TORONTO LONDON" on title page. No date on title page. Copyright page - 20th (of 24) line - "10 9 8 7 6 5 4 3 2 1"; 7th line - "First Edition". DJ price $22.95/$29.95 in Canada.
Quarter bound - red cloth with maroon sides and no top stain. White pastedowns.

		F/F	F/NF	NF/VG+	VG+/VG	VG/VG-	Good	w/o dj
1st ed		$15	$12	$10	$8	$6	$3	90%

Hide & Seek 1996

"LITTLE, BROWN AND COMPANY/BOSTON NEW YORK TORONTO LONDON" on title page. No date on title page. Copyright page - 20th (of 24) line - "10 9 8 7 6 5 4 3 2 1"; 7th line - "First Edition". DJ price $23.95/$31.95 in Canada. Issued in one of two different DJs. One with a blue background, the other with a violet background. Full bound - black cloth with no top stain and white pastedowns.

		F/F	F/NF	NF/VG+	VG+/VG	VG/VG-	Good	w/o dj
1st ed		$15	$12	$10	$8	$6	$3	90%

Anne Rice

Interview with the Vampire 1976

"ALFRED A. KNOPF NEW YORK 1976" on title page.
Copyright page - 12th (of 12) line - "FIRST EDITION". Gold dj with price - $8.95.
Quarter bound - black cloth with black sides and red top stain. White pastedowns.

		F/F	F/NF	NF/VG+	VG+/VG	VG/VG-	Good	w/o dj
1st ed		$500	$350	$250	$175	$150	$100	75%

The Feast of All Saints 1979

"SIMON & SCHUSTER NEW YORK" on title page. No date on title page.
Copyright page - 13th (of 19) line - "1 2 3 4 5 6 7 8 9 10". DJ price - $14.95.
Quarter bound - red cloth with speckled tan sides and no top stain. Red pastedowns.

		F/F	F/NF	NF/VG+	VG+/VG	VG/VG-	Good	w/o dj
1st ed		$60	$50	$40	$30	$20	$10	75%

Cry to Heaven 1982

"ALFRED A. KNOPF *New York* 1982" on title page.   Copyright page - 14th (of 14) line - "FIRST EDITION". DJ price - $15.95.

		F/F	F/NF	NF/VG +	VG+/VG	VG/VG-	Good	w/o dj
1st ed		$60	$50	$40	$30	$20	$10	75%

The Vampire Lastat 1985

"ALFRED A. KNOPF/New York/1985" on title page.   Copyright page - 16th (of 16) line - "FIRST EDITION". DJ price - $17.95.
Quarter bound - cream cloth with cream sides and no top stain. White pastedowns.

		F/F	F/NF	NF/VG	VG /VG	VG/VG-	Good	w/o dj
1st ed		$150	$120	$90	$75	$50	$25	80%

The Queen of the Damned 1988

"ALFRED A. KNOPF/New York/1988" on title page.   Copyright page - 25th (of 25) line - "FIRST EDITION". DJ price - $18.95.
Quarter bound - cream cloth with cream sides and no top stain. White pastedowns.

		F/F	F/NF	NF/VG +	VG+/VG	VG/VG-	Good	w/o dj
1st ed		$35	$30	$25	$20	$15	$10	75%

The Witching Hour 1990

"ALFRED A. KNOPF/NEW YORK/1990" on title page. Copyright page - 19th (of 19) line - "FIRST EDITION". DJ price - U.S.A. $22.95/Canada $30.50.
Quarter bound - black cloth with black sides and no top stain. White pastedowns.

		F/F	F/NF	NF/VG +	VG+/VG	VG/VG-	Good	w/o dj
1st ed		$35	$30	$25	$20	$15	$10	75%

The Tale of the Body Thief 1992

"ALFRED A. KNOPF/New York/1992" on title page. Copyright page - 11th (of 11) line - "FIRST EDITION". DJ price - $24.00.
Quarter bound - light gray cloth with light gray sides and no top stain. White pastedowns.

		F/F	F/NF	NF/VG +	VG+/VG	VG/VG-	Good	w/o dj
1st ed		$25	$20	$15	$12	$10	$8	75%

Lasher 1993

"ALFRED A. KNOPF/NEW YORK/1993" on title page. Copyright page - 21st (of 21) line - "First Edition". DJ price - $25.00.
Quarter bound - black cloth with black sides and no top stain. White pastedowns.

		F/F	F/NF	NF/VG +	VG+/VG	VG/VG-	Good	w/o dj
1st ed		$20	$17	$12	$10	$8	$6	75%

The Claiming of Sleeping Beauty 1983 Written as A.N. Roquelaure

	F/F	F/NF	NF/VG+	VG+/VG	VG/VG-	Good	w/o dj
1st ed	$200	$175	$150	$125	$100	$40	50%

Beauty's Punishment 1984 Written as A.N. Roquelaure

	F/F	F/NF	NF/VG+	VG+/VG	VG/VG-	Good	w/o dj
1st ed	$175	$150	$125	$100	$75	$25	50%

Beauty's Release 1985 Written as A.N. Roquelaure

"E.P. DUTTON NEW YORK" on title page. No date on title page.
Copyright page - 25th and 26th (of 26) lines -"10 9 8 7 6 5 4 3 2 1/First Edition".
DJ price - $15.95. Full bound - violet cloth with no top stain white pastedowns.

	F/F	F/NF	NF/VG+	VG+/VG	VG/VG-	Good	w/o dj
1st ed	$175	$150	$125	$100	$75	$25	50%

Exit to Eden 1985 Written as Anne Rampling.

"A Belvedere Book/ARBOR HOUSE/NEW YORK" on title page. No date on title page.
Copyright page - 6th (of 17) line - "10 9 8 7 6 5 4 3 2 1". DJ price - $17.95.
Quarter bound - black cloth with violet sides and no top stain. Violet pastedowns.

	F/F	F/NF	NF/VG+	VG+/VG	VG/VG-	Good	w/o dj
1st ed	$50	$35	$25	$17	$15	$10	80%

Belinda 1986 Written as Anne Rampling.

"A Belvedere Book /ARBOR HOUSE NEW YORK" on title page. No date on title page.
Copyright page - 7th (of 22) line - "10 9 8 7 6 5 4 3 2 1". DJ price - $17.95.
Quarter bound - maroon cloth with white sides and no top stain. White pastedowns.

	F/F	F/NF	NF/VG+	VG+/VG	VG/VG-	Good	w/o dj
1st ed	$45	$35	$30	$20	$15	$10	70%

Harold Robbins

Never Love A Stranger 1948

	F/F	F/NF	NF/VG+	VG+/VG	VG/VG-	Good	w/o dj
1st ed	$200	$150	$100	$75	$50	$25	50%

The Dream Merchants 1949

"ALFRED A KNOPF/New York/1949" on title page. Copyright page - 10th (of 10) line -
"FIRST EDITION". DJ price - $3.50. Matte finish.
Full bound - blue cloth with gold print on spine and purple top stain. White pastedowns.

	F/F	F/NF	NF/VG+	VG+/VG	VG/VG-	Good	w/o dj
1st ed	$50	$40	$30	$20	$15	$10	60%

A Stone For Danny Fisher 1952

"ALFRED A KNOPF/New York/1952" on title page. Copyright page - 11th (of 11) line - "FIRST EDITION". DJ price - $3.95. View of brownstones on front and back panels and one spine. Matte finish.
Full bound - green cloth with gold print on spine and maroon top stain. White pastedowns.

		F/F	F/NF	NF/VG+	VG+/VG	VG/VG-	Good	w/o dj
1st ed		$75	$65	$50	$35	$25	$10	60%

79 Park Avenue 1955

"ALFRED A KNOPF/New York/ 1955" on title page. Copyright page - 12th (of 12) line - "FIRST EDITION". Quarter bound - orange cloth with gold print on spine and gray top stain with gray sides. White pastedowns.

		F/F	F/NF	NF/VG+	VG+/VG	VG/VG-	Good	w/o dj
1st ed		$50	$40	$30	$20	$15	$10	60%

The Carpetbaggers 1961

		F/F	F/NF	NF/VG+	VG+/VG	VG/VG-	Good	w/o dj
1st ed		$200	$150	$100	$75	$50	$25	50%

Robert Ruark

Something of Value 1955

"DOUBLEDAY & COMPANY., Garden City, N.Y., 1955" on title page. Copyright page - 5th (of 5) line "First Edition". DJ price - $5.00. Quarter bound - black cloth with maroon cloth sides and light orange top stain. White pastedowns.

		F/F	F/NF	NF/VG+	VG+/VG	VG/VG-	Good	w/o dj
1st ed		$45	$35	$30	$25	$20	$10	60%

Poor No More 1959

"HENRY HOLT AND COMPANY   NEW YORK" on title page. No date on title page.
Copyright page - 5th (of 8) line - "First Edition". DJ price - $5.95.
Quarter bound - red cloth with black sides and no top stain. White pastedowns.

		F/F	F/NF	NF/VG+	VG+/VG	VG/VG-	Good	w/o dj
1st ed		$45	$35	$30	$25	$20	$10	60%

The Old Man and the Boy 1957

"Henry Holt and Company New York" on title page. No date on title page. Copyright page - 5th (of 9) line - "First Edition". DJ price - $4.95.
Full bound - brown cloth with no top stain and white pastedowns.

		F/F	F/NF	NF/VG+	VG+/VG	VG/VG-	Good	w/o dj
1st ed		$90	$70	$50	$35	$25	$15	70%

The Old Man's Boy Grows Older   1961

"*Holt, Rinehart and Winston New York*" on title page. No date on title page.
Copyright page - 6th (of 9) line - "First Edition". Wrap around DJ with zebras on savannah.
Full bound - brown with no top stain and white pastedowns.

		F/F	F/NF	NF/VG +	VG + /VG	VG/VG -	Good	w/o dj
1st ed		$80	$65	$45	$30	$20	$10	70%

The Honey Badger   1965

"McGraw-Hill Book Company/New York Toronto London/1965" on title page. Copyright
page - 13th and 14th (of 14) lines - "FIRST EDITION/54182". DJ price - $6.95.
Quarter bound - black cloth with gold sides and no top stain. Gold pastedowns.

		F/F	F/NF	NF/VG +	VG + /VG	VG/VG -	Good	w/o dj
1st ed		$30	$25	$20	$15	$12	$7	80%

John Steinbeck (1902-68)

U.S. novelist, born in Salinas, CA who gained critical notice in 1935 with his fourth novel <u>Tortilla Flat</u>. His
works are characterized by realistic dialogue and concern for the downtrodden. Among his novels are <u>Of Mice and</u>
<u>Men</u> (1937), <u>The Grapes of Wrath</u> (1939; Pulitzer Prize 1940), <u>Cannery Row</u> (1945), <u>East of Eden</u> (1952), and <u>The</u>
<u>Winter of Our Discontent</u> (1961). He was awarded the Nobel Prize for Literature in 1962.
The authoritative reference for Steinbeck's works is *John Steinbeck A Bibliographical*
Catalog of the Adrian H. Goldstone Collection by Adrian Goldstone and John R. Payne;
Humanities Research Center, The University of Texas at Austin (1974).

<u>Cup of Gold</u> 1929   A Life of Henry Morgan, Buccaneer.
First issued in 1929 by McBride Publishing, NY. Top edge of pages is stained blue.
Approximately 1,500 copies.
Reissued in 1936 by Corvici Friole, NY in two versions - maroon cloth (2nd issue, 1st
printing) (approximately 900 copies) and blue cloth (2nd issue, 2nd printing). Limited
edition issued in 1937with blue cloth binding and spine stamped in gilt.

		F/F	F/NF	NF/VG +	VG + /VG	VG/VG -	Good	w/o dj
1st ed	1st st	$4,000	$3,500	$3,000	$2,200	$1,600	$1,000	
1936 ed	Maroon	$450	$400	$350	$250	$180	$100	
1936 ed	Blue	$125	$100	$80	$60	$45	$30	
Ltd ed	L,'37	$1,400	$1,200	$1,000	$800	$600	$300	

<u>The Pastures of Heaven</u> 1932   All first editions were assembled from the same set of
2,500 sheets, originally printed in 1932 by Brewer. All issued with dj.
First issue (1932) (approximately 600 copies) has green cloth boards with top edges stained
black and front board stamped in gilt. "Brewer, Warren & Putnam" listed as publishers.
Second issue (1932) (approximately 1,000 copies) with "Robert O. Ballou" imprinted on cloth
spine but with Brewer still on the dj.
Third issue (1932) with "Robert O. Ballou" imprinted on cloth spine and on the dj.
Fourth issue (1935) has "Covici-Friede" as publishers.

First UK ed (1933) with "Phillip Allan" as publisher. Green cloth, spine printed in black.

	F/F	F/NF	NF/VG +	VG + /VG	VG/VG -	Good	w/o dj

		F/F	F/NF	NF/VG+	VG+/VG	VG/VG-	Good	w/o dj
1st ed	1st iss	$1,800	$1,600	$1,200	$900	$750	$500	10%
1st ed	2nd iss	$600	$500	$400	$300	$250	$200	10%
1st ed	3rd iss	$200	$160	$120	$100	$80	$60	20%
1st ed	4th iss	$125	$100	$80	$60	$45	$30	33%
1st ed	U.K.	$500	$400	$300	$225	$175	$125	25%

A God Unknown 1933 1st issue. 598 copies in green cloth, stamped in gilt , with black top stain. Ballou publisher.
2nd issue - Covici Friede (1935) 900 copies in beige, green print, with green top stain.
Copyright page "First published 1933"

First UK edition - blue cloth spine stamped in gilt. Heinemann publisher.

		F/F	F/NF	NF/VG+	VG+/VG	VG/VG-	Good	w/o dj
1st ed	1st iss	$1,000	$900	$750	$550	$400	$300	20%
1st ed	2nd iss	$400	$350	$300	$275	$225	$125	20%
1st ed	U.K.	$400	$350	$300	$275	$225	$125	20%

Tortilla Flat 1935

4,000 copies issued in dw. Covici Friede publisher. Full bound - tan cloth printed in blue with blue stained top edges.

		F/F	F/NF	NF/VG+	VG+/VG	VG/VG-	Good	w/o dj
1st ed	U.S.	$1,000	$750	$600	$500	$400	$250	20%
1st ed	U.K.	$1,100	$825	$650	$550	$425	$275	20%

In Dubious Battle 1936 1st issue 99 signed copies in tissue dj in black case with orange paper label printed in black. 2nd issue - yellow cloth with red top stain.

		F/F	F/NF	NF/VG+	VG+/VG	VG/VG-	Good	w/o dj
1st ed	1st iss	$2,500	$2,200	$1,900	$1,500	$1,100	$600	50%
1st ed	2nd iss	$400	$350	$300	$275	$225	$125	50%
1st ed	U.K.	$500	$400	$350	$300	$250	$150	50%

Saint Katy the Virgin 1936 199 copies of signed 1st edition printed. Decorated boards, gilt cloth spine printed in red with glassine dj. Some copies in slipcase with laid-in for *Of Mice and Men.*

		F/F	F/NF	NF/VG+	VG+/VG	VG/VG-	Good	w/o dj
1st ed		$2,000	$1,700	$1,300	$1,000	$800	$400	80%

Nothing So Monstrous 1936 Limited edition of 375 copies. Printed for use as Christmas gifts.

		F/F	F/NF	NF/VG+	VG+/VG	VG/VG-	Good	w/o dj
1st ed		$800	$700	$600	$500	$400	$250	

Of Mice and Men 1937 2,500 copies. 1st edition, 1st issue has the following phrase on the 20th and 21st lines of page 9 - "and only moved because the hands were pendula." First issue also has bullet between the 8's on page 88. Issued in dw. 2nd state has phrase corrected to read "but hung loosely" and the bullet removed.

"NEW YORK COVICI-FRIEDE PUBLISHERS" on title page. No date on title page. Copyright page - nine lines, no mention of printing number. Last three lines - "PRINTED AND BOUND IN THE UNITED STATES OF AMERICA/BY THE HADDON CRAFTSMEN, INC., CAMDEN, N.J./DESIGNED BY ROBERT JOSEPHY" Later printings are labelled as such in the space between the sixth line and the bottom three lines discussed above. DJ price $2.50 Spine contains continuation of drawing on front panel. Bottom of inside front flap lists printing number for later printings. Rear panel "OTHER BOOKS BY/JOHN . . . FRIEDE - *Publishers*" Full bound in tan cloth with no top stain.

Heinemann Publisher. Blue cloth with spine stamped in gilt and top edges stained blue. Blue dj.

		F/F	F/NF	NF/VG+	VG+/VG	VG/VG-	Good	w/o dj
1st ed	1st iss	$800	$625	$500	$400	$350	$250	20%
1st ed	2nd iss	$175	$125	$100	$90	$80	$60	20%
1st ed	U.K.	$800	$650	$550	$425	$375	$250	20%

The Red Pony 1937   699 signed copies.   Covici Friede. Flexible beige cloth with clear cellophane dj, in tan slipcase with limitation number on spine.

		F/F	F/NF	NF/VG+	VG+/VG	VG/VG-	Good	w/o dj
1st ed		$900	$800	$700	$550	$475	$350	50%

Their Blood is Strong   1938   Simon J. Lubin Society, San Francisco. Later printings stated. Title page is cover.

		F/F	F/NF	NF/VG+	VG+/VG	VG/VG-	Good	w/o dj
1st ed		$1,000	$900	$750	$625	$550	$400	--

The Long Valley 1938   8,000 copies

"THE VIKING PRESS/NEW YORK/1938" on title page.
Copyright page - 2nd (of 9) line "FIRST PUBLISHED IN SEPTEMBER 1938". No other mention of printings. Last line "BY J. J. LITTLE AND IVES COMPANY, NEW YORK".
DJ price - $2.50. No mention of printing on dj.
Quarter bound - beige buckram spine and terra cotta cloth, printed in red, with red top stain.

First U.K. Edition - Heinemann Publisher.   1939

		F/F	F/NF	NF/VG+	VG+/VG	VG/VG-	Good	w/o dj
1st ed	U.S.	$500	$400	$325	$250	$225	$150	20%
1st ed	U.K.	$600	$450	$350	$275	$225	$150	20%

The Grapes of Wrath 1939   50,000 copies

"THE VIKING PRESS   NEW YORK" on title page. No date on title page.
Copyright page - last (of 5) line "FIRST PUBLISHED IN APRIL 1939". No other mention of printings. Issued in pictorial dj with "FIRST/EDITION" slug - the triangle at the bottom right of the inside flap of the dj. On later editions, this slug describes the number of volumes in print, e.g. "480th Thousand".   When the slug has been clipped, the dj must be assumed to be other than a first edition. DJ price - $2.75. Full bound - tan cloth with tan top

stain.

		F/F	F/NF	NF/VG+	VG+/VG	VG/VG-	Good	w/o dj
1st ed	U.S.	$1,500	$1,050	$900	$700	$600	$400	20%
1st ed	U.K.	$500	$425	$350	$275	$225	$150	20%

The Forgotten Village 1941   15,000 copies. Oversized (7 1/8" by 10 1/4") pictorial book

illustrated with 136 photos from movie of the same name.

"NEW YORK 1941 THE VIKING PRESS" on title page. Copyright page - 13th (of 17) line -
"FIRST PUBLISHED IN MAY 1941". B&W photo of Mexican village framed in green cactus.
Full bound - speckled tan cloth with gray-green top stain and white pastedowns.

	F/F	F/NF	NF/VG+	VG+/VG	VG/VG-	Good	w/o dj
1st ed	$250	$175	$125	$100	$90	$75	33%

Sea of Cortez (with Ricketts) 1941 7,500 copies.

Green cloth with top edges stained orange.

	F/F	F/NF	NF/VG+	VG+/VG	VG/VG-	Good	w/o dj
1st ed	$550	$475	$400	$300	$225	$150	33%

The Moon is Down 1942   The story of a small town's resistance to Nazi occupation at the beginning of

WWII. Steinbeck was violently critized when the book first appeared because he chose to portray a policy of
passive resistance, contrary to an extreme position which many in this country advocated at the time.

1st state has tiny printer's mark, slightly larger than a period, on line 11 of page 112 between
"talk" and "this". 65,000 copies.   "NEW YORK: THE VIKING PRESS: MCMXLII" on title
page. Copyright page - seven lines:
"COPYRIGHT 1942 BY JOHN STENBECK
SET IN BULMER AND CALEDONIA TYPES
PRINTED IN U.S.A.
PUBLISHED ON THE SAME DAY IN THE
DOMINION OF CANADA BY THE MACMILLAN
COMPANY OF CANADA LIMITED
FIRST PUBLISHED IN MARCH 1942"
DJ price $2.00 (No difference for later editions). Full bound - blue cloth with gray top stain.

Second state has printer's mark removed and printer's name (Haddon of Kingsport) added
to copyright page page. Most books are full bound in blue cloth. Some are full bound in red
cloth.

First U.K. edition: Full bound terra cotta cloth.

		F/F	F/NF	NF/VG+	VG+/VG	VG/VG-	Good	w/o dj
1st ed	1st st	$150	$110	$90	$75	$60	$40	75%
1st ed	2nd st	$50	$40	$35	$30	$25	$20	75%
1st ed	U.K.	$100	$80	$70	$65	$50	$35	75%

Bombs Away 1942 20,000 copies. With 60 photographs by John Swope.

"NEW YORK THE VIKING PRESS 1942" on title page.
DJ - bottom of front flap has box with "Send this book to a boy in the armed forces anywhere
for only 6c." Full bound - blue cloth with light blue top stain and white pastedowns.

	F/F	F/NF	NF/VG+	VG+/VG	VG/VG-	Good	w/o dj

1st ed		$200	$150	$125	$100	$80	$60	50%

The Viking Portable Library Steinbeck 1943 26,000 copies. Stories selected by Pascal Covici. Reissued in 1946 with title changed to *The Portable Steinbeck* and with introduction by Lewis Gannett.

Issue in UK in 1950 as The Steinbeck Omnibus. Heinemann publisher and edited by Covici.

		F/F	F/NF	NF/VG+	VG+/VG	VG/VG-	Good	w/o dj
1st ed	U.S.	$100	$80	$60	$45	$35	$25	50%
1st ed	U.K.	$175	$125	$100	$75	$60	$45	50%

How Edith McGillguddy met R.L.S. 1943

152 copies produced for The Rowfant Club, Cleveland. Plain green dj.

		F/F	F/NF	NF/VG+	VG+/VG	VG/VG-	Good	w/o dj
1st ed		$3,000	$2,000	$1,500	$1,000	$800	$400	33%

The Red Pony (illustrated) 1945

"*NEW YORK VIKING PRESS 1945*" on title page. Copyright page - 6th (of 15) line - "ILLUSTRATED EDITION FIRST PUBLISHED IN 1945". Slipcase gray paper over cardboard with color label showing water color drawing of pony.
Full bound - tan cloth with blue top stain and water color drawing of horses on pastedowns.

		F/F	F/NF	NF/VG+	VG+/VG	VG/VG-	Good	w/o dj
1st ed	slipcase	$75	$50	$40	$35	$30	$15	33%

Cannery Row 1945 78,000 copies.
First State: Full bound - light buff cloth with blue top stain.

Second State: "*1945*/THE VIKING PRESS NEW YORK" on title page.
Copyright page - 4th (of 7) line "FIRST PUBLISHED BY THE VIKING PRESS IN JANUARY 1945." Last line "PRINTED IN U.S.A. BY THE HADDON CRAFTSMEN."
DJ price - $2.00. Viking Press symbol on bottom of inside front flap.
Full bound - yellow cloth with light blue top stain.

First U.K. edition - full bound - bright orange-yellow cloth.

		F/F	F/NF	NF/VG+	VG+/VG	VG/VG-	Good	w/o dj
1st ed	1st st	$225	$180	$150	$120	$100	$60	67%
1st ed	2nd st	$150	$125	$100	$80	$70	$40	50%
1st ed	U.K.	$300	$250	$200	$150	$125	$75	50%

The Wayward Bus 1947

"THE VIKING PRESS NEW YORK 1947" on title page.
Copyright page - six lines "COPYRIGHT 1947 BY JOHN STEINBECK
PUBLISHED BY THE VIKING PRESS IN FEBRUARY 1947
PUBLISHED ON THE SAME DAY IN THE DOMINION OF CANADA
BY THE MACMILLAN COMPANY OF CANADA LIMITED

PRINTED IN U.S.A.

BY HADDON CRAFTSMEN"
100,000 copies. DJ price $2.75 Pictorial dj with view of rutted road from inside bus. Rear
panel "The Wayward Bus/ By John . . . . A Book-of-the-Month Club Selection" (no different
for early later editions)
First state is full bound in dark reddish-orange cloth with light blue-green top stain and
white pastedowns. First state has the blind-stamped impression of bus on bottom of front
cover board showing up lighter than the rest of the binding. Second state has two versions:
one with blown cloth and the bus darker and the other is a pinkish-brown with the bus the
same shade.

		F/F	F/NF	NF/VG+	VG+/VG	VG/VG-	Good	w/o dj
1st ed	1st st	$200	$175	$150	$100	$80	$50	80%
1st ed	2nd st	$80	$65	$50	$40	$35	$25	50%
1st ed	U.K.	$175	$150	$125	$90	$70	$50	50%

The Pearl 1947

40,000 copies. First state dj has photo of author looking to his left, toward spine. Second
state dj has photo of author looking to his right.

		F/F	F/NF	NF/VG+	VG+/VG	VG/VG-	Good	w/o dj
1st ed	1st st	$150	$125	$90	$60	$45	$20	40%
1st ed	2nd st	$75	$65	$50	$35	$25	$12	80%
1st ed	U.K.	$60	$55	$45	$30	$22	$10	40%

A Russian Journal 1948 Oversized (6 7/8" x 9 3/4") pictorial book illustrated with photos by Robert Capa.

"1948/The Viking Press NEW YORK" on title page. Copyright page - 2nd (of 11) line -
"PUBLISHED BY THE VIKING PRESS IN APRIL 1948". DJ - price 3.75.
Four variations on the binding exist. All are quarter bounded. Rarest - light gray-yellow-
brown cloth with gray-green cloth sides and gray top stain. White pastedowns.
Most common - moderately yellow cloth with light blue-green cloth sides and gray top stain.
White pastedowns.

First U.K. edition - Heinemann publisher 1949.

		F/F	F/NF	NF/VG+	VG+/VG	VG/VG-	Good	w/o dj
1st ed	rarest	$150	$125	$90	$60	$45	$20	80%
1st ed	common	$75	$65	$50	$35	$25	$12	40%
1st ed	U.K.	$250	$200	$150	$100	$80	$40	40%

Burning Bright 1950   15,000 copies.

"THE VIKING PRESS   NEW YORK   1950" on title page. Copyright page -
"COPYRIGHT 1950 BY JOHN STEINBECK
FIRST PUBLISHED BY THE VIKING PRESS IN NOVEMBER 1950
PUBLISHED ON THE SAME DAY IN THE DOMINION OF CANADA
BY THE MACMILLAN COMPANY OF CANADA LIMITED"
then 15 lines about use of the book as a play and the viking ship symbol. Last two lines -
"PRINTED IN THE U.S.A.
BY H. WOLFF BOOK MANUFACTURING COMPANY"
Full bound - gray-tan cloth with orange top stain and white pastedowns. DJ price - $2.50.
Front and rear panel of dj are the same, with yellow/gray/orange horizontal bands and
"JOHN STEINBECK" across the top and "BURNING/BRIGHT" on two lines in the middle.

First U.K. edition - Heinemann publisher.

		F/F	F/NF	NF/VG+	VG+/VG	VG/VG-	Good	w/o dj
1st ed	U.S.	$150	$110	$90	$75	$65	$45	33%
1st ed	U.K.	$125	$100	$80	$70	$60	$40	33%

The Log from the Sea of Cortez 1950   7,500 copies.

"New York /THE VIKING PRESS 1951" on title page. Copyright page - 3rd (of 6) line - "PUBLISHED BY THE VIKING PRESS IN SEPTEMBER 1951". DJ price - $4.00.
Full bound - maroon cloth with no top stain and maps on red background on pastedowns. Reissue of 1941 book with new title and with narrative portion only. New "About Ed Ricketts" by Steinbeck added.

First U.K. edition 1958 - Heinemann publisher.

		F/F	F/NF	NF/VG+	VG+/VG	VG/VG-	Good	w/o dj
1st ed	U.S.	$250	$175	$140	$110	$95	$60	33%
1st ed	U.K.	$150	$110	$90	$75	$65	$45	33%

East of Eden 1952

110,000 copies. 1,500 special signed copies were produced. These were in glassine dj and slipcase. Value of these is four times the value of the normal first edition listed below.
"1952/THE VIKING PRESS NEW YORK" on title page. DJ price - $4.50.
Copyright page - 2nd (of 5) line - "First published by The Viking Press in September 1952".
Last line - "Printed in the U.S.A. by H. Wolff Book Manufacturing Co."
Full bound - lime green cloth with no top stain and white pastedowns.
First issue has "bite" instead of "bight" on line 38, page 281. Second issue has "bight".

First U.K. edition - Heinemann publisher.

		F/F	F/NF	NF/VG+	VG+/VG	VG/VG-	Good	w/o dj
1st ed	1st iss	$300	$250	$150	$100	$85	$60	60%
1st ed	2nd iss	$200	$175	$110	$75	$65	$40	50%
1st ed	U.K.	$150	$100	$80	$70	$60	$30	50%

The Short Novels of John Steinbeck 1953

15,000 copies. Brick red cloth printed in black with yellow top stain. Front edge untrimmed.

First U.K. edition 1954 - Heinemann publisher.

		F/F	F/NF	NF/VG+	VG+/VG	VG/VG-	Good	w/o dj
1st ed	U.S.	$75	$60	$50	$40	$35	$20	60%
1st ed	U.K.	$100	$90	$75	$60	$50	$30	60%

Sweet Thursday 1954 Steinbeck returns to Monterey, scene of Cannery Row, for this amusing sequel to
that novel. Doc is back from WWII and the down-and-outs of the Palace set off on match-making adventures between Doc and the newly arrived Suzy.

"1954/THE VIKING PRESS NEW YORK" on title page. *Sweet Thursday* and the seven horizontal lines on title page printed in red. Copyright page - six lines:

"Copyright 1954 by John Steinbeck
First published by The Viking Press in June 1954
Published on the same day in the Dominion of Canada
by The Macmillan Company of Canada Limited

Library of Congress catalog card number: 54-7983
(viking ship symbol)
PRINTED IN THE U.S.A. BY THE COLONIAL PRESS INC."
Note: Later printings are indicated as such by an extra line (inserted after the 4th line) on the copyright page -
such as "Second Printing June 1954". A book club edition exists without the red ink on the title page.
DJ price $3.50. Full bound - biege cloth with red top stain and white pastedowns.

		F/F	F/NF	NF/VG+	VG+/VG	VG/VG-	Good	w/o dj
1st ed		$90	$65	$50	$40	$35	$30	60%

The Short Reign of Pippin IV 1957 40,000 copies.

"NEW YORK THE VIKING PRESS 1957" on title page. Copyright page - 2nd (of 9) line -
"FIRST PUBLISHED IN 1957". Last line "BY AMERICAN BOOK-STRATFORD PRESS, INC.,
NEW YORK". DJ price - $3.00. Quarter bound - green-yellow cloth with burnt-orange sides
and burnt-orange top stain. White pastedowns.

"HEINEMANN/MELBOURNE LONDON TORONTO" on title page. Copyright page - 5th
(of 8) line - "First published 1957". DJ price - 12s 6d. Full bound - blue cloth with no top
stain and white pastedowns.

		F/F	F/NF	NF/VG+	VG+/VG	VG/VG-	Good	w/o dj
1st ed	U.S.	$60	$40	$30	$25	$20	$15	60%
1st ed	U.K.	$60	$40	$30	$25	$20	$15	60%

Once There Was a War 1958 10,000 copies.

"THE VIKING PRESS/NEW YORK/1958" on title page. Copyright page - nine lines with no
mention of printing number. DJ price - $3.95.
Quarter bound - yellow cloth with brown sides and red top stain. White pastedowns.

First U.K. edition 1959 - Heinemann publisher.

		F/F	F/NF	NF/VG+	VG+/VG	VG/VG-	Good	w/o dj
1st ed	U.S.	$125	$90	$75	$60	$50	$40	50%
1st ed	U.K.	$100	$75	$60	$50	$45	$30	50%

The Winter of Our Discontent 1961

"*The Viking Press New York 1961*" on title page. Copyright page - 3rd (of 9) line - "First
published in 1961 by The Viking Press, Inc." DJ price - $4.50. Full bound - blue cloth with
light blue top stain and white pastedowns. Spine stamped in silver.

First U.K. edition 1961 - Heinemann publisher.

		F/F	F/NF	NF/VG+	VG+/VG	VG/VG-	Good	w/o dj
1st ed	U.S.	$60	$50	$40	$30	$25	$15	80%
1st ed	U.K.	$75	$65	$50	$40	$35	$25	80%

Travels with Charley in Search of America 1962 30,000 copies

First U.S. edition 1962 - Viking publisher.

First U.K. edition 1962 - Heinemann publisher.

		F/F	F/NF	NF/VG+	VG+/VG	VG/VG-	Good	w/o dj
1st ed	U.S.	$75	$65	$50	$40	$35	$20	40%
1st ed	U.K.	$75	$65	$50	$40	$35	$20	40%

America and Americans 1966

"The Viking Press New York" on title page. No date on title page. Copyright page - 6th (of 13) line - "First published in 1966 by the Viking Press, Inc." DJ price - $12.50. 1st state binding - half blue and half green cloth with spine reading from top to bottom. 2nd state binding - spine reading bottom to top. No top stain and map of U.S.A. on pastedown.

First U.K. edition 1966 - Heinemann publisher.

		F/F	F/NF	NF/VG+	VG+/VG	VG/VG-	Good	w/o dj
1st ed	1st st	$85	$75	$60	$45	$35	$20	75%
1st ed	2nd st	$40	$35	$25	$20	$15	$10	50%
1st ed	U.K.	$75	$65	$50	$40	$30	$20	75%

Journal of a Novel: East of Eden 1969 20,000 copies.

"The Viking Press NEW YORK" on title page. No date on title page.
Copyright page - ten lines with no mention of printing number. DJ price - $6.50.
Quarter bound - dark blue cloth with blue-green paper sides and light blue top stain.
Pastedowns - gray copy of manuscript.
A limited edition of 600 copies with "This first edition is limited to 600 copies." was issued in glassine dj and slipcase.

First U.K. edition 1970 - Heinemann publisher.

		F/F	F/NF	NF/VG+	VG+/VG	VG/VG-	Good	w/o dj
1st ed	Ltd. ed	$225	$175	$125	$85	$65	$40	33%
1st ed	U.S.	$50	$45	$35	$25	$20	$10	70%
1st ed	U.K.	$45	$40	$30	$20	$17	$10	70%

The Acts of King Arthur and His Noble Knights 1976

"EDITED BY CHASE/HORTON FARRAR, STRAUS/AND GIROUX NEW YORK" on title page. No date on title page. Copyright page - 7th (of 22) line "First printing 1976".
DJ price - $10.00. Full bound - maroon cloth with light orange top stain and dark green pastedowns.

First U.K. edition 1976 - Heinemann publisher.

		F/F	F/NF	NF/VG+	VG+/VG	VG/VG-	Good	w/o dj
1st ed	U.S.	$40	$35	$30	$20	$15	$8	70%
1st ed	U.K.	$40	$35	$30	$20	$15	$8	70%

Clifford Stoll

The Cuckoo's Egg 1989   An astronomer by training, Mr. Stoll became a leading computer security expert almost by accident. This griping account of his pursuit of the "Hannover Hacker" details his back and forth adventure over the research and military computer networks.

"Doubleday - New York, London, Toronto, Sydney, Auckland" on title page.   No date on title page.   Copyright page - bottom 4 (of 27) lines   "October 1989/FIRST EDITION/DH/O O O O O O O O O".   DJ price - U.S. $19.95/Canada $24.95.   Quarter bound - black cloth with black sides and no top stain.   Computer flow diagrams on pastedowns.

		F/F	F/NF	NF/VG+	VG+/VG	VG/VG-	Good	w/o dj
1st ed		$30	$25	$20	$15	$10	$5	-$3

Jacqueline Susann

Valley of the Dolls 1966

"Published by Bernard Geis Associates/*Distributed by* Random House" opposite title page. No date on title page.   Copyright page - 8th (of 11) line - "*First Edition*". DJ price - $5.95 (no different for later printings).

		F/F	F/NF	NF/VG+	VG+/VG	VG/VG-	Good	w/o dj
1st ed		$30	$25	$20	$15	$10	$5	80%

Booth Tarkington

The Gentleman from Indiana 1899

"*New York/Doubleday & McClure Co./1899*" on title page.
Copyright page - four lines "COPYRIGHT, 1899, BY/DOUBLEDAY & MCCLURE CO./Press of J.J. Little & Co./Astor Place, New York".   No specific reference to first edition or first printing is made.   Issued without dj.   First state has several errors which were corrected in later issues.   First issue has "eye" on line 12, pg 245 (245:12); "so pretty" on 245:16; "brainy bumps" on 291:7; and "brain of zeus" on 342:23.
Full bound - dark green decorative boards with green top stain and uncut page edges.   Plain white pastedowns.   Upside down ear of corn on spine.

		Fine	NF	VG+	VG	VG-	Good
1st ed	1st st	$100	$75	$50	$40	$25	$10
1st ed	2nd st	$40	$30	$20	$15	$10	$6
1st ed	3rd st	$15	$12	$10	$8	$6	$4

Monsieur Beaucaire   1900

Illustrated.   First issue has the publisher's logo opposite the last page of text and measuring only 1/2 inch in diameter.   Full bound in crimson cloth with uncut page edges.   Issued without dj.

		Fine	NF	VG+	VG	VG-	Good
1st ed	1st iss	$80	$65	$45	$35	$25	$10

Beasley's Christmas Party   1909

"HARPER & BROTHERS/NEW YORK AND LONDON/M - C - M - I - X" on title page.
Copyright page - "Copyright, 1909, by HARPER & BROTHERS./All rights reserved/
Published October, 1909." in box at bottom of page. Full bound - red cloth with no top stain
and white pastedowns. Issued without dj.

		Fine	NF	VG+	VG	VG-	Good
1st ed		$75	$60	$40	$30	$20	$10

The Flirt   1913

		Fine	NF	VG+	VG	VG-	Good
1st ed		$75	$60	$40	$30	$20	$10

Penrod   1914

First issue, in blue mesh-cloth binding, measures 1 1/4 inches across top of boards. First
issue has "sence" instead of "sense" on page 19, line 23. Doubleday, Page publishers on
bottom of spine. Issue without dj.

		Fine	NF	VG+	VG	VG-	Good
1st ed	1st iss	$150	$125	$90	$60	$40	$20

Spring Concert   1916

		Fine	NF	VG+	VG	VG-	Good
1st ed	1st iss	$150	$125	$90	$60	$40	$20

Penrod and Sam   1916

First issue, in light green-cloth binding has perfect type on pages 86, 141, 144, 149, 210.
Doubleday, Page publishers on bottom of spine. Issued without dj.

		Fine	NF	VG+	VG	VG-	Good
1st ed	1st iss	$125	$100	$75	$50	$35	$15

Seventeen   1916

First edition has "B-Q" under the copyright notice. Doubleday, Page publishers on bottom of
spine. Issue without dj.

		Fine	NF	VG+	VG	VG-	Good
1st ed		$75	$60	$40	$30	$20	$10

Alice Adams   1921   Pulitzer Prive novel of 1921.

"GARDEN CITY, N.Y., AND TORONTO/DOUBLEDAY, PAGE & COMPANY/1921" on title
page. Copyright page - "COPYRIGHT , 1921, BY/DOUBLEDAY, PAGE & COMPANY/ ALL
RIGHTS RESERVED INCLUDING THAT FROM TRANSLATION/INTO FOREIGN
LANGUAGES INCLUDING THE SCANDINAVIAN/COPYRIGHT, 1921, BY THE
PICTORIAL REVIEW COMPANY".   "PRINTED AT GARDEN CITY, N.Y., U.S.A." added as
bottom line on later editions.
Full bound - burnt orange cloth with no top stain and white pastedowns. Issued without dj.

First issue contains error in line 14 of page 419. Second issue correct to read "Disregarding this, Mrs. Adams looked her over".

		Fine	NF	VG+	VG	VG-	Good
1st ed	1st iss	$75	$60	$40	$30	$20	$10
1st ed	2nd iss	$30	$25	$20	$15	$10	$5

The Plutocrat   1927

"GARDEN CITY   NEW YORK/DOUBLEDAY, PAGE & COMPANY/1927" on title page. Copyright page - "COPYRIGHT , 1927, BY DOUBLEDAY, PAGE &/COMPANY. COPYRIGHT, 1926, BY THE CUR-/TIS PUBLISHING COMPANY. ALL RIGHTS RE- /SERVED. PRINTED IN THE UNITED STATES AT/ THE COUNTRY LIFE PRESS, GARDEN CITY, N.Y/FIRST EDITION"
DJ price - $2.00. Wrap around drawing in green, orange, white and black of two men and a woman on deck of ocean liner.   Full bound - black cloth with orange and black pasted on labels. Light orange top stain with black webbed pastedowns.

	F/F	F/NF	NF/VG+	VG+/VG	VG/VG-	Good	w/odj
1st ed	$65	$50	$40	$30	$20	$10	33%

Claire Ambler   1928

"GARDEN CITY   NEW YORK/DOUBLEDAY, DORAN & COMPANY., INC./1928" on title page. Copyright page - "COPYRIGHT, 1928, BY DOUBLEDAY, DORAN &/COMPANY, INC. COPYRIGHT, 1927, BY THE CURTIS/PUBLISHING COMPANY. ALL RIGHTS RESERVED./PRINTED IN THE UNITED STATES AT THE/COUNTRY LIFE PRESS, GARDEN CITY, N.Y./FIRST EDITION"
DJ price - $2.50. Wrap around scenes in check drawn in yellow, gray, white and black.   Full bound - blue cloth with yellow and black pasted on labels. Yellow top stain with blue and yellow checkerboard pastedowns. Women dressed in 20's style in blue squares.

	F/F	F/NF	NF/VG+	VG+/VG	VG/VG-	Good	w/odj
1st ed	$65	$50	$40	$30	$20	$10	33%

Penrod and Jashber   1929

"1929/Garden City, New York/Doubleday, Doran & Company, Inc," on title page. Copyright page - 1st (of 9) line "COPYRIGHT 1929". Last line - "FIRST EDITION". DJ price - $2.00. Full bound - dark blue cloth with no top stain and white pastedowns.

	F/F	F/NF	NF/VG+	VG+/VG	VG/VG-	Good	w/odj
1st ed	$90	$75	$60	$50	$40	$20	33%

Mary's Neck   1932

"MCMXXXII/DOUBLEDAY, DORAN/& Company., Inc./Garden, City,/N.Y." on title page. Copyright page - top of page - one line "PRINTED AT THE Country Life Press, GARDEN CITY, N.Y., U.S.A." Bottom of page - four lines "COPYRIGHT, 1929, 1932/BY BOOTH TAKINGTON/ALL RIGHTS RESERVED/FIRST EDITION"
DJ price - $2.50. Front panel - color painting of scene on front porch.   Rear panel - photo of The Floats and description of Portrait Gallery of America.   Full bound - red cloth with printed on labels. Red top stain and white pastedowns.

	F/F	F/NF	NF/VG+	VG+/VG	VG/VG-	Good	w/odj

1st ed		$50	$40	$30	$20	$15	$6	33%

Rumbin Galleries 1937

"DOUBLEDAY, DORAN & CO., INC./ Garden City 1937 New York" on title page.
Copyright page - Top of page - one line "PRINTED AT THE *Country Life Press*, GARDEN CITY, N.Y., U.S.A." Bottom of page - four lines "COPYRIGHT, 1936, 1937/BY BOOTH TAKINGTON/ALL RIGHTS RESERVED/FIRST EDITION"
DJ price - $2.50. Front panel - pencil painting of Georgie. Rear panel - advertisement for One-by-One Editions of the works of Booth Tarkington. Gold background on spine of dj.
Full bound - cream cloth with gray top stain and white pastedowns.

		F/F	F/NF	NF/VG+	VG+/VG	VG/VG-	Good	w/o dj
1st ed		$50	$40	$30	$20	$15	$6	33%

Image of Josephine 1945

"DOUBLEDAY, DORAN & COMPANY, INC./ *Garden City, New York*/1945" on title page.
Copyright page - Bottom of page - seven lines "COPYRIGHT, 1945/BY BOOTH TAKINGTON/ALL RIGHTS RESERVED/PRINTED IN THE UNITED STATES/AT/THE COUNTRY LIFE PRESS, GARDEN CITY, N.Y./FIRST EDITION"
Top of inside front flap - notice about wartime regulations on printing books.. Rear panel - advertisement for Booth Tarkington His Classic Contributions to American Literature.
Full bound - red cloth with light yellow top stain and white pastedowns.

		F/F	F/NF	NF/VG+	VG+/VG	VG/VG-	Good	w/o dj
1st ed		$30	$25	$20	$15	$10	$5	33%

The Show Piece 1947

"1947/DOUBLEDAY & COMPANY, INC./ GARDEN CITY, NEW YORK" on title page.
Copyright page - Bottom of page - six lines "COPYRIGHT, 1946, 1947, BY SUSANAH TAKINGTON/ALL RIGHTS RESERVED/PRINTED IN THE UNITED STATES/AT/THE COUNTRY LIFE PRESS, GARDEN CITY, N.Y./FIRST EDITION"
DJ price - $2.00. Rear panel - advertisement for Booth Tarkington His Classic Contributions to American Literature.
Full bound - green cloth with light brown top stain and white pastedowns.

		F/F	F/NF	NF/VG+	VG+/VG	VG/VG-	Good	w/o dj
1st ed		$25	$20	$17	$13	$9	$5	33%

Your Amiable Uncle 1949

"THE BOBBS-MERRILL COMPANY, INC./*Publishers*/INDIANAPOLIS NEW YORK" on title page. Copyright page - FOUR lines "COPYRIGHT, 1949, BY JOHN T. JAMESON, DONALD JAMESON/AND BOOTH T. JAMESON/PRINTED IN THE UNITED STATES OF AMERICA/*First Edition*".
DJ price - $2.75. Wrap around with Tarkington sketches on light blue background.
Full bound - blue cloth with no top stain and blue pastedowns with white sketches.

		F/F	F/NF	NF/VG+	VG+/VG	VG/VG-	Good	w/o dj
1st ed		$25	$20	$17	$13	$9	$5	33%

Leon Uris

Battle Cry 1953

G.P. Putnam's Sons/New York" on title page. No date on title page. Copyright page - 9th and 10th (of 10) lines - "MANUFACTURED IN THE UNITED STATES OF AMERICA/Van Rees Press New York". No specific reference to first edition or first printing is made. Later printings are indicated both on the dj (e.g. "SECOND PRINTING" across top of inside front dj flap next to price) and on the copyright page (extra line added so that 9th (of 11) line reads "Second Impression". DJ price - $3.75. Rear panel, "Sure, it's got guts.......".
Full bound - dark blue cloth with no top stain. White pastedowns.

		F/F	F/NF	NF/VG+	VG+/VG	VG/VG-	Good	w/o dj
1st ed		$150	$125	$100	$80	$60	$40	33%

The Angry Hills

"Random House New York" on title page. No date on title page.
Copyright page - 2nd (of 9) line - "First Printing". DJ price $3.00
Full bound - maroon cloth with no top stain and white pastedowns.

		F/F	F/NF	NF/VG+	VG+/VG	VG/VG-	Good	w/o dj
1st ed		$80	$70	$60	$50	$40	$20	40%

Exodus 1958

Copyright page - last (of 18) line "First Edition". DJ price $4.50
Quarter bound - blue cloth with gray sides and blue top stain. Map on pastedowns.

		F/F	F/NF	NF/VG+	VG+/VG	VG/VG-	Good	w/o dj
1st ed		$100	$85	$70	$55	$45	$30	70%

Mila 18 1961

"Doubleday & Company, Inc., Garden City, New York 1961" on title page.
Copyright page - last (of 8) line - "All Rights Reserved. Printed in the United States of America. First Edition". DJ price $4.95 (no different for later editions).
Quarter bound - gray cloth with black paper and no top stain. White pastedowns.

"HEINEMANN/LONDON MELBOURNE TORONTO ". No date on title page.
Copyright page - 5th (of 10) line "First published in Great Britain 1961". DJ price - 21s.
Full bound -maroon cloth with no top stain. White pastedowns.

		F/F	F/NF	NF/VG+	VG+/VG	VG/VG-	Good	w/o dj
1st ed		$50	$35	$30	$25	$20	$15	80%

Armageddon 1964

"DOUBLEDAY & COMPANY, INC./GARDEN CITY, NEW YORK/1964" on title page.
Copyright page - last line (of 19) - " FIRST EDITION". DJ price - $6.95 (no different for later editions). Full bound - black cloth with no top stain. Navy blue pastedowns.

		F/F	F/NF	NF/VG+	VG+/VG	VG/VG-	Good	w/o dj
1st ed		$50	$35	$30	$25	$20	$15	80%

Topaz 1967

"McGraw-Hill Book Company - New York - Toronto - London - Sydney" on title page. No date on title page. Copyright page - 9th (of 9) line - "First Edition 66102". DJ price - $5.95 (no different for later editions). Full bound - black cloth with no top stain. Red pastedowns.

		F/F	F/NF	NF/VG+	VG+/VG	VG/VG-	Good	w/o dj
1st ed		$12	$10	$9	$8	$6	$5	80%

QB VII 1970

"DOUBLEDAY & COMPANY, INC./*Garden City, New York 1970* " on title page. Copyright page - last (of 5) line - "First Edition". DJ price - $7.95 (no different for later editions). Full bound - black cloth with no top stain. Pea green pastedowns.

		F/F	F/NF	NF/VG+	VG+/VG	VG/VG-	Good	w/o dj
1st ed		$30	$25	$20	$15	$12	$8	80%

Trinity 1976

"DOUBLEDAY & COMPANY, INC./GARDEN CITY, NEW YORK/1976" on title page. Copyright page - last (of 8) line - "FIRST EDITION". DJ price - $10.95 (no different for later editions). Full bound - green cloth with no top stain and maps on pastedowns.

		F/F	F/NF	NF/VG+	VG+/VG	VG/VG-	Good	w/o dj
1st ed		$30	$25	$20	$15	$12	$8	80%

The Haj 1984

"Doubleday & Company, Inc./GARDEN CITY, NEW YORK/1984" on title page. Copyright page - 12th (of 14) line - "FIRST EDITION". DJ price - $17.95 (no different for later editions). Full bound - black cloth with no top stain. Pastedowns map of the middle east.

		F/F	F/NF	NF/VG+	VG+/VG	VG/VG-	Good	w/o dj
1st ed		$15	$12	$10	$8	$6	$5	80%

Mitla Pass 1988

"Doubleday   New York   London   Toronto   Sydney   Auckland" on title page. No date on title page. Copyright page - 34th and 35th (of 35) lines - "First Edition/BG". DJ price - $19.95 (no different for later editions). Quarter bound - blue cloth with blue paper and no top stain. Red pastedown.

		F/F	F/NF	NF/VG+	VG+/VG	VG/VG-	Good	w/o dj
1st ed		$10	$9	$7	$6	$5	$3	80%

Mika Waltari

The Egyptian 1949

		F/F	F/NF	NF/VG+	VG+/VG	VG/VG-	Good	w/o dj
1st ed		$60	$50	$40	$30	$20	$10	50%

The Adventurer 1950

"G.P. Putnam's Sons   New York" on title page. No date on title page.
Copyright page - five lines, no reference to edition or printing number. Last line
"MANUFACTURED IN THE UNITED STATES OF AMERICA".
DJ price - $3.50. No reference to printing number on dj.
Full bound - burnt orange with no top stain and white pastedowns.

		F/F	F/NF	NF/VG+	VG+/VG	VG/VG-	Good	w/o dj
1st ed		$45	$35	$25	$20	$15	$8	50%

The Wanderer 1951

"G.P. Putnam's Sons   New York" on title page. No date on title page. Copyright page - five
lines, no reference to edition or printing number. Last line "MANUFACTURED IN THE
UNITED STATES OF AMERICA". No reference to printing number on dj. Later issues
contain words such as "Second Printing" on front flap of dj. Full bound - light green with
no top stain and white pastedowns.

		F/F	F/NF	NF/VG+	VG+/VG	VG/VG-	Good	w/o dj
1st ed		$45	$35	$25	$20	$15	$8	50%

Dark Angel 1953

"G.P. PUTNAM'S SONS   NEW YORK" on title page. No date on title page.
Copyright page - eight lines, no reference to edition or printing number. Last two lines
"MANUFACTURED IN THE UNITED STATES OF AMERICA/CORNWALL PRESS, INC.,
NEW YORK". Later printings have a ninth line, inserted in the middle of the page, such as
"Second Impression". No price or reference to printing number on 1st issue dj. Later
issues contain words such as "Second Printing" on front flap of dj.
Full bound - light blue green with no top stain and sketch of Constaninople on pastedowns.

		F/F	F/NF	NF/VG+	VG+/VG	VG/VG-	Good	w/o dj
1st ed		$50	$40	$30	$25	$20	$10	50%

The Etruscan 1956

"G.P. Putnam's Sons/New York" on title page. No date on title page.
Copyright page - eight lines, no reference to edition or printing number. Last two lines
"MANUFACTURED IN THE UNITED STATES OF AMERICA/VAN REES PRESS NEW
YORK".   DJ price - $4.50. No reference to printing number on dj.
Quarter bound - red cloth with gray cloth sides no top stain. Red map on white pastedowns.

		F/F	F/NF	NF/VG+	VG+/VG	VG/VG-	Good	w/o dj
1st ed		$40	$30	$22	$15	$10	$6	50%

A Stranger Came To The Farm 1952

"G.P. PUTNAM'S SONS/NEW YORK" on title page. No date on title page. Copyright page -
seven lines, no reference to edition or printing number. Last line "Manufactured in the
United States of America". DJ price - $3.00. No reference to printing number on dj.
Quarter bound - dark blue cloth with no top stain gray-green pastedowns.

	F/F	F/NF	NF/VG+	VG+/VG	VG/VG-	Good	w/o dj

1st ed		$30	$25	$17	$12	$8	$5	50%

Moonscape 1954

"G.P. PUTNAM'S SONS/NEW YORK" on title page. No date on title page. Copyright page - ten lines, no reference to edition or printing number. Last line - "Manufactured in the United States of America". DJ price - $3.50. No reference to printing number on dj. Full bound - green cloth with no top stain and white pastedowns.

		F/F	F/NF	NF/VG+	VG+/VG	VG/VG-	Good	w/o dj
1st ed		$30	$25	$17	$12	$8	$5	50%

The Secret of the Kingdom 1961

"G.P. *Putnam's Sons New York*" on title page. No date on title page.
Copyright page - nine lines, no reference to edition or printing number. Last two lines "MANUFACTURED IN THE UNITED STATES OF AMERICA/VAN REES PRESS NEW YORK". DJ price - $4.95. No reference to printing number on dj.
Quarter bound - off-white cloth with maroon sides and no top stain. White pastedowns.

		F/F	F/NF	NF/VG+	VG+/VG	VG/VG-	Good	w/o dj
1st ed		$30	$25	$17	$12	$8	$5	50%

The Roman 1966

"G.P. PUTNAM'S SONS/NEW YORK" on title page. No date on title page. Copyright page - nine lines, no reference to edition or printing number. Last line "PRINTED IN THE UNITED STATES OF AMERICA". DJ price - $6.95. No reference to printing number on dj. Full bound - dark blue cloth with no top stain. Red map on white pastedowns.

		F/F	F/NF	NF/VG+	VG+/VG	VG/VG-	Good	w/o dj
1st ed		$30	$25	$17	$12	$8	$5	50%

Joseph Wambaugh

The Choirboys 1975

"DELACORTE PRESS/NEW YORK" on title page. No date on title page.
Copyright page - 14th (of 22) line "*First printing*". DJ price - $8.95.
Full bound - blue cloth with light orange top stain and burnt orange pastedowns.

		F/F	F/NF	NF/VG+	VG+/VG	VG/VG-	Good	w/o dj
1st ed		$25	$20	$15	$12	$10	$7	80%

The Glitter Dome 1981

"APERIGORD PRESS BOOK/WILLIAM MORROW AND COMPANY, INC./*New York 1981*" on title page. Copyright page - 30th and 31st (of 31) lines - "First Edition/1 2 3 4 5 6 7 8 9 10". DJ price - $12.95. Quarter bound - cream cloth with light blue sides and no top stain. Dark blue pastedowns.

		F/F	F/NF	NF/VG+	VG+/VG	VG/VG-	Good	w/o dj
1st ed		$25	$20	$15	$10	$7	$4	70%

Mary Jane Ward

The Snake Pit 1946

"RANDOM HOUSE NEW YORK" on title page. No date on title page.
DJ price - $2.50. Top of inside front flap "A BOOK-OF-THE-MONTH CLUB SELECTION".
Top of inside rear flap - photo of author with bio beneath.
Copyright page - 1st (of 7) line "FIRST PRINTING"
Full bound - green cloth with light gray top stain and white pastedowns

	F/F	F/NF	NF/VG +	VG + /VG	VG/VG -	Good	w/o dj
1st ed	$125	$100	$90	$75	$70	$40	33%

Herman Wouk (1915 -)

Wouk's first work to be printed was _The Man in The Trench Coat_, published in 1941 by the Jewish Welfare Board. This 20-page pamphlet contained the dialog for a playlet about a Jewish refugee girl unhappy in a New York family that had given her room and board and still haunted by her experiences in Nazi Germany. The JWB distributed the work to amateur companies as a way to spread the message of sympathy for Jewish refugees. Wouk estimates that 1,000 copies were distributed.

Aurora Dawn 1947 25,000 copies

"A Venture Press Book/Published by Simon and Schuster, New York, 1947".
Copyright page, in total - "ALL RIGHTS RESERVED/INCLUDING THE RIGHT OF REPRODUCTION/IN WHOLE OR IN PART IN ANY FORM/COPYRIGHT, 1947, BY HERMAN WOUK/PUBLISHED BY SIMON AND SCHUSTER, INC./ROCKEFELLER CENTER, 1230 SIXTH AVENUE/NEW YORK 20, N.Y.//MANUFACTURED IN THE UNITED STATES OF AMERICA/BY AMERICAN BOOK-STRATFORD PRESS, INC., NEW YORK". DJ price - $2.75 shown on bottom inside front flap. Rear dj flap contains a clip off triangle at the bottom with "Aurora Dawn/by Herman Wouk/Simon and Schuster". Full bound - blue cloth with pink top stain.
First editions are quite rare. Many Book Club edition exist. DJ's for these have no price. Book Club books are printed by either Kingsport Press, The Haddon Craftsmen, or H. Wolf. Book Club books all have asmall dot or depression on the bottom of the outside of the rear board.

	F/F	F/NF	NF/VG +	VG + /VG	VG/VG -	Good	w/o dj
1st ed	$80	$70	$60	$50	$40	$20	33%

The City Boy 1948 10,000 copies

"Simon and Schuster, New York/1948" on title page. Copyright page contains no mention of printing number. DJ price - $2.95. Gray dust jacket with boy holding books watching other boys playing. Bound in red boards with blue top stain. All edges trimmed.

	F/F	F/NF	NF/VG +	VG + /VG	VG/VG -	Good	w/o dj
1st ed	$200	$175	$140	$100	$75	$30	33%

The Caine Mutiny 1951 22,500 copies

"1951 DOUBLEDAY & COMPANY, INC., GARDEN CITY, N.Y." Copyright page - last (of 26) line "First Edition". DJ - price $3.95 . Full bound - blue cloth with no top stain. Rear dj panel refers to "The City Boy". All later issues refer only to "City Boy, omitting "The". No mention is made of the Pulitzer Prize.

Note: The page tops on most later printings have a dark top stain.

	F/F	F/NF	NF/VG+	VG+/VG	VG/VG-	Good	w/o dj
1st ed	$135	$110	$85	$65	$50	$25	50%

The City Boy - Illustrated 1952

"Doubleday & Company, Inc., Garden City, New York 1952" on title page.
Copyright page, in total - "LIBRARY OF CONGRESS CATALOG CARD NUMBER: 52-6369/COPYRIGHT, 1948, 1952, BY HERMAN WOUK/ALL RIGHTS RESERVED/PRINTED IN THE UNITED STATES/AT THE COUNTRY LIFE PRESS, GARDEN CITY, N.Y."
DJ price - $3.50. Marquand quote and line drawing on rear panel.
Quarter bound - light blue cloth with black paper and no top stain.

	F/F	F/NF	NF/VG+	VG+/VG	VG/VG-	Good	w/o dj
1st ed	$80	$70	$60	$50	$40	$20	33%

The Caine Munity - Illustrated 1952

"DOUBLEDAY & COMPANY, INC., GARDEN CITY, NEW YORK, 1952" on title page.
Copyright page - last (of 27) line "FIRST ILLUSTRATED EDITION".
Full bound - blue cloth with no top stain and map on pastedown. DJ wrap around view of sea rescue with "DELUXE EDITION ILLUSTRATED IN FULL COLOR/by LAWRENCE BEALL SMITH" on bottom of front panel.

	F/F	F/NF	NF/VG+	VG+/VG	VG/VG-	Good	w/o dj
1st ed	$300	$250	$175	$150	$100	$50	33%

Slattery's Hurricane 1956   Issued only in paperback.

Perma Books M-4050 35c Copyright page - 5th (of 13) line "1st Printing ......March, 1956"

	Fine	VG+	VG-	Good
1st ed wrapps	$25	$15	$9	$3j

The Caine Mutiny Court Martial 1954   30,000 copies

"1954/Doubleday & Company, Inc., Garden City, New York" on title page. Copyright page - "First Edition" after printer's name and address. DJ price - $2.75. Blue dj printed in white and orange (yellow on later issues). Rear panel shows National Tour reviews (reviews of New York opening on later issues) and rear flap lists 1953 as publication year. Black boards with blue-green top stain and blue pastedowns. A later variant contains photos after pages (iii), 30, 64, and 96.

	F/F	F/NF	NF/VG+	VG+/VG	VG/VG-	Good	w/o dj
1st ed	$80	$70	$60	$50	$40	$20	50%

Marjorie Morningstar 1955

"Doubleday & Company, Inc., Garden City, New York 1955" on title page. Copyright page - bottom (15th) line - "First Edition". DJ - price $4.95 Full page photo of Wouk on rear panel. Quarter bound - black cloth with blue sides and no top stain. White pastedowns.

		F/F	F/NF	NF/VG+	VG+/VG	VG/VG-	Good	w/o dj
1st ed		$90	$70	$55	$45	$35	$15	50%

This is My God 1959

"Doubleday & Company, Inc., Garden City, New York 1959" on title page.
Copyright page - bottom (5th) line - "First Edition". DJ price - $3.95
Full bound - blue cloth with no top stain and white pastedowns.

		F/F	F/NF	NF/VG+	VG+/VG	VG/VG-	Good	w/o dj
1st ed		$35	$30	$25	$20	$15	$10	50%

Youngblood Hawke 1962

"1962/DOUBLEDAY & COMPANY, INC., GARDEN CITY, NEW YORK" on title page.
Copyright page - 5th (of 20) line *"First Edition"* . DJ price - $7.95.
Full bound - gray cloth with no top stain and white pastedowns.
Note: A Book Club edition with "First Edition" was also produced. This book is distinguished by small square indentation on the bottom of the rear board, near the spine. DJ on the Book Club edition has no price. This is not a true First Edition.

		F/F	F/NF	NF/VG+	VG+/VG	VG/VG-	Good	w/o dj
1st ed		$75	$60	$50	$40	$35	$25	60%

Don't Stop The Carnival 1965

"Doubleday & Company, Inc./Garden City, New York/1965" on title page. Copyright page - bottom line "First Edition". Three different dust jackets were issued for the first edition. All show a DJ price - $4.95. The first issue has the credit over the rear panel photo as "Photo by Gunter Hett" and no reference to BOMC on the rear dj flap. The second issue adds "A BOOK-OF-THE-MONTH CLUB SELECTION" to the bottom of the front dj flap. The third issue corrects the photo credit to "Photo by Gunter Hasse". DJs for later editions are identical to the third issue. Prices for 2nd and 3rd issue DJs would be slightly less than shown.
Note: A Book Club edition with "First Edition" was also produced. This book is distinguished by small square indentation on the bottom of the rear board, near the spine. DJ on the Book Club edition has no price. This is not a true First Edition.

		F/F	F/NF	NF/VG+	VG+/VG	VG/VG-	Good	w/o dj
1st ed	1st iss dj	$30	$25	$20	$15	$12	$8	80%

The Winds of War 1971

"BOSTON TORONTO/Little, Brown and Company" on title page. No date on title page.
Copyright page - 8th and 9th (of 12) lines - "FIRST EDITION/T11/71". DJ price - $10.00.
Quarter bound - black cloth with red sides and no top stain. Black pastedowns.

		F/F	F/NF	NF/VG+	VG+/VG	VG/VG-	Good	w/o dj
1st ed		$30	$25	$15	$10	$7	$5	80%

War and Remembrance 1978

"Little, Brown and Company/BOSTON TORONTO" on title page. No date on title page.
Copyright page - 7th and 8th (of 38) lines - "FIRST TRADE EDITION/T10/78".
DJ price - $15.00. Full page photo of Wouk on rear panel. Quarter bound - red cloth with black sides and no top stain. Red pastedowns.

		F/F	F/NF	NF/VG+	VG+/VG	VG/VG-	Good	w/o dj
1st ed		$25	$20	$12	$8	$6	$4	80%

176

177